The I
in
*history*

<>

C000181528

MANCHESTER
1824

Manchester University Press

# The kiss
# in
# history

EDITED BY

Karen Harvey

MANCHESTER
UNIVERSITY PRESS
MANCHESTER AND NEW YORK

*distributed exclusively in the USA by Palgrave*

Copyright © Manchester University Press 2005

While copyright in the volume as a whole is vested in Manchester University Press,
copyright in individual chapters belongs to their respective authors,
and no chapter may be reproduced wholly or in part
without the express permission in writing of both author and publisher.

*Published by* Manchester University Press
Oxford Road, Manchester M13 9NR, UK
*and* Room 400, 175 Fifth Avenue, New York, NY 10010, USA
www.manchesteruniversitypress.co.uk

*Distributed exclusively in the USA by*
Palgrave, 175 Fifth Avenue, New York, NY 10010, USA

*Distributed exclusively in Canada by*
UBC Press, University of British Columbia, 2029 West Mall,
Vancouver, BC, Canada V6T 1Z2

*British Library Cataloguing-in-Publication Data*
A catalogue record for this book is available from the British Library

*Library of Congress Cataloging-in-Publication Data applied for*

ISBN 0 7190 6594 1 *hardback*
EAN 978 0 7190 6594 1
ISBN 0 7190 6595 X *paperback*
EAN 978 0 7190 6595 8

First published 2005

13 12 11 10 09 08 07 06 05    10 9 8 7 6 5 4 3 2 1

Typeset in 10.5/12.5 Minion
by Graphicraft Limited, Hong Kong
Printed in Great Britain CPI, Bath

DEDICATED TO
THE MEMORY OF

ALAN BRAY

1948 TO 2001

# Contents

<>

# Illustrations

<>

# Contributors

<>

Helen Berry is Senior Lecturer in History at the University of Newcastle. Her publications include *Gender, Society and Print Culture in Later-Stuart England: The Cultural World of the Athenian Mercury* (2003) and numerous articles on print culture, consumption and politeness in eighteenth-century Britain. Her next book is a cultural history of the English coffee house.

Elaine Chalus is a Senior Lecturer in History at Bath Spa University College. She is fascinated by the political culture of eighteenth-century England and specifically by the paradoxical relationship of women to the polity. She has just completed a monograph on women's involvement in eighteenth-century English political life for Oxford University Press.

Santanu Das is a Research Fellow at St John's College, Cambridge. He is completing a monograph titled *Touch, Testimony and First World War Literature*. His work has appeared in journals such as *Modernism/modernity* and *The American Scholar*, and he is now working on Commonwealth responses to the First World War.

Luke Davidson has published articles on the history of ophthalmology, drowning, resuscitation and the psychological character of contemporary scientism. His PhD dissertation, 'Raising up Humanity: A Cultural History of Resuscitation and the Royal Humane Society of London, 1774–1808', was completed in 2001.

Jonathan Durrant is currently a Postdoctoral Fellow in the history department at King's College, London. He did his doctoral research on the witch persecutions in Germany, and is now looking at the masculinity of the soldier in the Thirty Years' War (1618–48).

Karen Harvey is Lecturer in Cultural History at the University of Sheffield. She has published articles on masculinity, the body, space and women's work, and her forthcoming book *Reading Sex in the Eighteenth Century: Bodies and Gender in Erotic Culture* will be published by Cambridge University Press in 2005. Her current project explores the nature of men's engagement with the home and household in the eighteenth century.

Craig Koslofsky received his PhD in history from the University of Michigan in 1994. His monograph *The Reformation of the Dead: Death and Ritual in Early Modern Germany, 1450–1700* (2000) presents a cultural history of death in early modern Lutheran Germany. It examines the end of belief in purgatory in Lutheranism, and therewith the separation of the dead from the world of the living. His current project is a study of darkness and the night in early modern Europe.

Keith Thomas is a Fellow of All Souls College, Oxford. He was formerly President of Corpus Christi College, Oxford, and is a past President of the British Academy. He has written extensively on the social and cultural history of early modern England. His books include *Religion and the Decline of Magic* (1971) and *Man and the Natural World* (1983). He is currently preparing for publication his Ford Lectures on 'The Ends of Life: Roads to Fulfilment in Early Modern England' and his Menahem Stern Jerusalem Lectures on 'Civility and its Discontents: The Meaning of Manners in Early Modern England'.

David M. Turner is Senior Lecturer in Gender History at the University of Wales, Swansea. He has written widely on the history of the family, marriage, gender and sexuality in early modern England. His publications include *Fashioning Adultery: Gender, Sex and Civility in England, 1660–1740* (Cambridge, 2002). His present research is concerned with the history of multiple marriages in early modern Britain.

Carole Williams is currently finishing her PhD dissertation, 'Ideology and Identity: Married Women's Experience *c.*1800–1900', at Essex University. Her recent work has explored attitudes towards women's suffrage in Colchester between 1880 and 1895, and the involvement of women in the economy of late nineteenth-century Essex and Suffolk towns. Carole was awarded the Pop Ronson Memorial Prize for Local History for her research on dame schools.

# Acknowledgements

<>

THIS BOOK arose from a conference, supported by the Royal Historical Society, which took place at the Institute of Historical Research, University of London. The event was held under the auspices of the Bedford Centre for the History of Women, Royal Holloway, University of London. I would like to thank Amanda Vickery and Lyndal Roper in their capacity as directors of the Centre for facilitating the event, and to Katie Price (Royal Holloway), Debra Birch (Institute of Historical Research) and particularly Suzette Starmer (Bedford Centre) for ensuring the event was a success. I would also like to thank all the speakers and delegates at the conference, and to express my gratitude to Tim Hitchcock, Colin Jones and Penelope J. Corfield for the part they played on the day. Finally, I am indebted to the vital role of Helen Berry, with whom the conference was conceived during a number of exciting conversations over the summer of 1999.

I have worked on the project during posts in the Department of History at the University of Manchester and at the AHRB Centre for the Study of the Domestic Interior (based at the Royal College of Art, the Victoria and Albert Museum, and Royal Holloway). I am very appreciative of the support from Hannah Barker at Manchester and from Jeremy Aynsley, John Styles and Amanda Vickery at the Centre for the Study of the Domestic Interior. The finishing touches to the book were made during a British Academy Exchange Fellowship at the Huntington Library, California, where the staff were unfailingly helpful. I am also grateful to Keith Thomas, who read a draft of the entire book, and to the staff at Manchester University Press for all their efforts.

Lastly, I want to give heartfelt thanks to Mike Braddick for supporting me throughout the project, and particularly for enabling me to run the home-stretch so soon after the birth of our daughter Cora.

The book is dedicated to the memory of Alan Bray, to mark his intellectual generosity, the advice he gave me personally in preparation for the conference, and the characteristic enthusiasm with which he launched the event in July 2000.

Chapter 8 by Santanu Das was originally published as ' "Kiss me, Hardy": Intimacy, gender, and gesture in First World War trench literature', *Modernism/modernity*, 9:1 (2002), 51–74. © The Johns Hopkins University Press. Reprinted with permission of the Johns Hopkins University.

# Introduction

<>

Karen Harvey

For the sheer range of kisses in the past, the student of kissing should look no further than C. C. Bombaugh's *The Literature of Kissing, Gleaned from History, Poetry, Fiction and Anecdote* (1876). From 'Kissing Hands in Austria' to 'Arabian Salutation', from 'Wedding-Ceremony in Turkey' to 'New Year's Day in Amsterdam', Bombaugh's book is a disorienting mellay of kisses. Christopher Nyrop's later *The Kiss and its History* (1901) attempted to bring order to the study of the kiss, placing kisses into five categories: kisses of love, affection, peace, respect and friendship. These were contrived and overlapping groups, he admitted; they struggled to accommodate an act of which the French language defined twenty different kinds and the German language counted thirty.[1] These works by Bombaugh and Nyrop sought to show their readers the variety of kisses in the past. The focus of this collection is somewhat different: rather than seeking to assemble a mass of kisses or to marshal examples of types of kiss, the chapters of this book each take a single kind of kiss as an index to the past. The chapters are united by this approach. But how and why has the history of the kiss moved from an antiquarian interest in instances and types of kiss to an academic interest in meaning and exemplarity? Central to this shift is the emergence of cultural history. The shared intellectual heritage of this field serves as an important context for this book. In this introduction, I want to sketch just some of the key historiographical developments that have fed into this field, in order to show why this book is about the kiss in history, and not the history of the kiss.

One of the most distinctive features of cultural history is its use of an exceptionally wide range of evidence. The contributors to this book reflect this, exploring the kiss through sources as divergent as canonical religious texts, popular prints, court depositions, periodicals, diaries and poetry. In casting the net so wide, these authors demonstrate how cultural history has been shaped by a broad concept of culture, encompassing more than simply the canons of art and literature, and integrating apparently 'historical' and 'non-historical' sources. Cultural historians have been much influenced by anthropology, and it is from this discipline that they have gleaned the 'coherent conception of culture' so important to their field.[2] Perhaps the most influential definition is that of Clifford Geertz, for whom culture was 'an historically transmitted pattern of meanings embodied in symbols'.[3] This rigorous definition is broad enough to allow historians to consider texts, images and objects outside traditional canons, opening the way for an analysis of meaning in a more general field of representation. Cultural history's broad vision of culture also has its roots in the early twentieth-century French Annales school, and in particular in the approach of historians of mentalities. The history of mentalities shifted the focus of intellectual history away from decontextualised, formal bodies of thought or canons of ideas, and towards the ordinary and the everyday, modes of collective thought and their unspoken assumptions. This move from high culture to 'the culture of the common man' helped prepare the ground for cultural history.[4] At the same time, new questions were being asked about the genesis and diffusion of ideas, giving rise to a 'social history of ideas' which considered the production and consumption of both great and marginal literature.[5] From these developments – the use of a wide range of sources and a focus on the creation and use of ordinary ideas – cultural history has derived considerable breadth.

Cultural *history* is also informed by the idea that culture changes over time and space. According to Peter Burke, this idea – that '[w]hat had previously been considered as unchanging is now viewed as a "cultural construction", subject to variation over time as well as in space' – transformed history as a discipline and placed cultural history at the centre of a newly drafted historical map.[6] The notions of cultural relativism and cultural construction imply that culture is generative and that it plays a part in explaining change. The focus on this potential of culture to induce change has taken a number of forms. In part it is rooted in social history, for example in the 'culturalist perspective' of the Marxist social historian E. P. Thompson, for whom language and culture were integrated into analyses of cause and change.[7] Though some see Thompson as placing material relations of production at the heart of change and the foundation of culture, Thompson's brand of social history can also be seen as 'presag[ing] the deconstructionist perspective on the determinative force of discourse'.[8] But the interest in how culture might determine experience predominantly took the form of analysing patterns and structures in culture. This derived both from the anthropological method of 'interpreting culture' by locating 'patterns of meaning', and from the Annales interest in structures or 'the forms which regularise mental activity, whether these be aesthetic images, linguistic codes, expressive gestures, religious rituals, or social customs.'[9] The same interest in these defining structures can be seen in Michel de Certeau's interest in the everyday as 'modes of operation or schemata of action'.[10] In all these approaches, structures shape both the content of ideas and their form of expression. The generative potential of these shaping structures of culture has enabled us to see the economic and social realms as 'themselves fields of cultural practice and cultural production'.[11] Indeed, material practices and social experiences can be explained by culture: '[a]ll practices, whether economic or cultural, depend on the representations individuals use to make sense of their world.'[12] Studying culture has become a serious objective for historians, because the structures and meanings in culture not only shape experience, but are constitutive of experience.

Cultural historians' insistence on the primacy of meaning aligns them with literary scholars, but the impact of literary studies on the field of cultural history is a remarkably recent phenomenon. In a review of 1972, E. P. Thompson bemoaned the fact that in his then new book – *Religion and the Decline of Magic* (1971) – Keith Thomas had not been as much influenced by literary criticism as he had by anthropology. Thompson suggested that literary criticism was as valuable to historians using literary texts as numeracy was when dealing with quantities; but 'it is not in fashion to mention this', he remarked.[13] Thomas later married the study of history and literature in *Man and the Natural World* (1983), despite the use of certain literary sources still being considered 'not currently fashionable among historians'.[14] By 1989, Lynn Hunt declared that the two fields having most impact on cultural history were anthropology and literary theory, although even at that stage Hunt regarded the former as holding greater sway.[15] The belated meeting of history and literary studies is exemplified by 'new historicism'. New historicism, as described by Stephen Greenblatt – who coined the term – is not a doctrine but a practice, and one that shares many key assumptions with cultural history.[16] The integration of both literary and non-literary texts by new historicists, for example, parallels the expansive interests of cultural historians.[17] Key to new historicist practice is the analysis of how material is 'transferred from one discursive sphere to another and becomes aesthetic property'.[18] The interest is in 'the work of art [as] the product of a negotiation between a creator or class of creators, equipped with a complex, communally shared repertoire of conventions, and the institutions and practices of society'.[19] In other words, art is not a given, but is the product of a specific configuration of power relations and related practices. New historicists are therefore very much concerned with the context of literary texts.

There is much sympathy between cultural history and new historicism, not least this interest in context. Practitioners in both fields would agree with Darnton that 'symbols work not merely because of their metaphorical power but also by virtue of their position within a cultural frame'.[20] But the nature of this cultural frame differs. While new historicists and literary historians are interested in the literary, canonical context of their evidence – context for new historicists is usually other texts – cultural historians are interested in the context of ideas, practices and behaviours which might be studied through non-literary texts. Related to this, we can also distinguish the objectives of scholars in these fields. The aim for new historicists is an understanding of poetic, cultural and aesthetic objects through the social functions they perform. Cultural historians, by contrast, try to understand the social and cultural partly through an analysis of art or literature.[21]

It is a focus on context in the broadest terms that makes cultural history historical. As Thompson wrote, '[t]he discipline of history is, above all, the discipline of context; each fact can be given meaning only within an ensemble of other meanings'.[22] Too liberal a use of anthropological methods by historians threatened history's distinctiveness, leading them to explore meanings without situating them in place *and* time. It was for this reason that Thompson complimented the work of Keith Thomas, in which insights 'derived from anthropology are subdued to the historical discipline'.[23] In accordance with this, the inflection of cultural historians towards anthropology or literary studies remains restrained, ensuring that cultural history remains firmly ensconced within Thompson's 'discipline of context'. This interest in context is often expressed through a focus on experience – an important concept for all historians, indicating their concern for the non-textual world. Indeed, conventional characterisations of cultural historians as being interested less in what actually happened than in 'what a happening actually meant', or pronouncements that 'Social history gives priority to describing practices, while cultural history records meanings', threaten to underestimate just how much cultural historians share with others in the wider discipline.[24] As Victoria Bonnell and Lynn Hunt have pointed out, cultural historians do emphasise practice, precisely in order to resist too great an emphasis on language and discourse.[25] And certainly in French scholarship, any division between happenings and meanings is less pronounced: Roger Chartier, for example, denies any gap between 'the objectivity of structures' and 'the subjectivity of representation'.[26]

The integration of both meaning and practice in their work means that cultural historians grapple with standard historical questions about their sources, and in particular about the relationship between representations and the world they purport to represent. In responding to such questions, cultural historians tend to reject dichotomies such as representation and reality or prescription and practice. Ideas, meanings, and representations have a 'reality', whether in material forms as objects or as agents which cause and effect. Prescription conventionally suggests guidelines, instructions and rules, against which practice or application is then measured. Not only does this reify these realms as wholly separate, denying (for example) the extent to which representations are also practices; it also implies that we can read in a text a clear meaning which may or may not be followed. The use of the term 'representation' by cultural historians is significant here. Representation signals the interest of historians in language and meaning. It enables historians to regard their sources as being akin to art and literature, sharing modes of expression, for example, or narrative structures. But it also signals the active role of culture, because representation is regarded as a creative element, not simply reflecting reality, but transforming it.[27] The linguistic nature of representation is largely where its constructive capacity is located: language constitutes and facilitates meaning and thus shapes people's experience of the world.[28] But representation does not simply mean language; integral to the concept of representation are both the material processes of representation, and the specific historical contexts in which representations are produced. The concept of representation therefore also invites an analysis of the physical object together with the study of its use and appropriation.[29] As Roger Chartier has claimed, cultural history is both the analysis of how social structures are produced by the practice or 'process of representation', and 'the study of the processes by which meaning is constructed', taking account of the potential for plural and contradictory meanings.[30] Representation is thus rooted in the experiential realm. It renders cultural history a search for meanings, their production, exchange, consumption and uses. The chapters that follow can therefore be placed in the context of a form of cultural history which is interested not simply in meaning, but in practice and the social workings of language. Conceiving culture as comprising systems of meaning *and* sets of practices is part of achieving a delicate balance between the social and the cultural, between what happened and what things meant.

The history of gesture – one area into which many of the following chapters can be positioned – is a very good example of how these historiographical strands converge in cultural history. Most of the kisses explored in this book were gestures – they were generally fleeting and not formalised, but none the less loaded with meaning. As Keith Thomas has said of the potential of the history of gesture, 'To interpret and account for a gesture is to unlock the whole social and cultural system of which it is a part'.[31] Such a study aims not simply to chart the nature of and changes in the practice itself, but to consider the changing meanings of that practice, by examining the social and cultural context in which those meanings were generated and consumed. In this way, the act itself is not quite the central point of focus. The interest here is not in how people kissed, then, but in what representations of the kiss were 'about' and what they enabled contemporaries to articulate. In these chapters, the kiss was an exemplary gesture and a marker of something else: of ideas of shame in Durrant, of the nature of intimacy in Turner, of the limits of platonic relationships in Berry, of the 'master fiction' of the male polity in Chalus, of an intimate relationship borne of ill health and the complex workings of household power in Williams. Each contributor has taken a relatively simple, often fleeting act and used it to reveal some of the deeply embedded values and anxieties of a particular time and place. Not all the kisses in this book were gestures, most notably the 'kiss of life' in late eighteenth-century England. Yet the aim remains the same: to explore the embeddedness of the kiss in a range of social contexts and symbolic codes.

Unified by an approach which regards the kiss as an index to a time and place, several of the chapters discuss a number of related themes. The kiss has evidently been a potent marker of boundaries: between clean and impure in early seventeenth-century Germany, for example, and between proper and improper sociability in early modern narratives of marital infidelity. In several chapters, these boundaries were mapped onto hierarchies of rank and social status. In Eichstätt – a prince-bishopric in south-eastern Germany – the female defendants in witch trials tried to shore up their honour by refusing to admit to the shameful act of kissing the Devil's anus during the sabbath. Restrictions on intimacy with one's social inferiors rendered the 'kiss of life' difficult for the gentlemen advocating mouth-to-mouth ventilation in the eighteenth century. Certainly, in the late eighteenth-century kisses-for-votes scandal, the Duchess of Devonshire compromised her public reputation by allegedly kissing a man below her rank. The establishment of and conformity to such boundaries thus led to the accretion or loss of status. Indeed, in early modern accounts of adultery and in reports of eighteenth-century election campaigns, crossing the line between appropriate and inappropriate kissing signalled a rupture in normal power relations – between those of different ranks, the married and unmarried, and between men and women.

In several chapters, boundaries were expressed through the erotic kiss. Indeed, despite a breadth of meaning, the kiss seems to have held an ineradicable erotic potential. It is this potential, as Keith Thomas points out in his Afterword, that lends the kiss an ambiguity that sets it apart from other gestures. Anxieties regarding the treacherous and erotic nature of the kiss informed Reformation debates about the kiss of peace, while similar worries pervaded debates about resuscitation in eighteenth-century England. The line between the sexual and platonic was explicitly discussed in periodicals and miscellanies of late seventeenth- and early eighteenth-century England, but this theme exercised writers from the Reformation to the First World War. Historians of sexuality have recently been exhorted to think about sex in the broadest of terms, to 'start the definition at the kiss rather than at the point of mutual genital contact'.[32] By starting with the kiss, these chapters raise the possibility of a history of sexuality that explores the subtle shades of human emotion and intimacy. Narrow accounts of sexual practice fail to do justice to the range of activities through which past men and women experienced pleasure and closeness; as the contributions by Williams and Das caution, we should not reduce all acts of intimacy to sex.

During the period covered by this book (*c*.1500–1918), the potency of the kiss has endured. Yet the practices and meanings of the kiss have changed. Bonnell and Hunt have pointed out that, 'The cultural turn might be viewed as either the cause or the effect of the collapse of explanatory paradigms'.[33] Certainly, cultural history is weak in its approach to change, tending towards the 'analysis of structures' rather than a 'narrative of events'.[34] Cultural history draws on a number of ways of approaching change, however. One is to integrate change and persistence. This was the approach of historians who adopted the structural techniques typified by the Annales school – such as Philippe Ariès, Norbert Elias and Michel Foucault – who were all interested in the role played by mental structures in the civilising process. 'Together', Hutton claims, 'they converge upon a theory of civilisation which emphasises man's ongoing effort to establish an equilibrium between his need to give new forms of meaning to his experience and his desire to cling to the existing forms in which conventional wisdom lies'.[35] Thus, 'new structures may be superimposed upon old ones'.[36] In his chapter on resuscitation, for example, Davidson makes the point that while disgust is universal among humans, it was patterned by ideals of decorum in the eighteenth century. Change does not occur in spite of continuity; rather the persistence of traditions integrates transformation as each generation alters its cultural inheritance.[37] Another way of casting the problem of change is in terms of the transmission of ideas or cultural reproduction. Cultural historians are at pains to expose contradictions in and conflict over meanings; a focus on conflict exposes dynamism, because conflict can generate new positions. This process was at work in Reformation debates on the kiss of peace, periodical treatments of platonic friendship and scientific discussions of the treatment of the apparently dead. These chapters thus insist on the contestation surrounding meanings of the kiss and the resulting processes of change.

As Thomas shows in his Afterword, kisses can be usefully compared across space; the collective burden of these chapters, however, is to focus on comparisons across time. While each contributor limits himself or herself to a particular time and place, these essays have more than synchronic value, raising questions about long-term change. Part I considers two instances of early debates over kisses, Part II charts attempts to establish norms in kissing practice in the seventeenth and eighteenth centuries, and Part III explores three types of kiss which previous developments had apparently rendered out of place. The chosen chronology of this book allows it to engage with models of emerging modernity and corresponding developments in standards of civility. Discussed most famously by Elias, one aspect of this process was the emergence of more rigid codes of social behaviour, intimacy and emotion, inducing a rising threshold of shame, in the context of a process of state formation and associated structural change. Elias regarded the sixteenth, seventeenth and eighteenth centuries as the period of 'relatively rapid movement and change'; after this, change was slow.[38] Certainly, this collection adheres to the contours of this 'civilising process'. For example, the early modern chapters act as the pivot of this book; it does seem that the period c.1660–1800 produced the most intense and broad debate around kissing. The later essays therefore allow us to observe historical discontinuity. In Chapter 1, Koslofsky claims the 'shift of the kiss from the social to the erotic, and from the communal to the private'. The later contributions by Chalus, Williams and Das appear to confirm that the kiss had been privatised and that early modern taxonomies of gesture had made certain kisses sites of cultural anxiety.

In his Afterword, Thomas questions this alleged sexualisation of the kiss. He also suggests that Elias's model of change is not wholly confirmed by the history of the kiss. These chapters certainly invite a revision of the story of civilisation in a number of ways. First, discussions of decorum may be seen as freeing rather than containing desires. For example, Berry argues that didactic discussions of morality expressed the very desires these authors claimed to be policing. 'Talking about kisses was', she argues, '. . . an eroticised metaphor for the articulation of sexual desire, which also licensed multiple readings and fantasies'. A second way in which these chapters undermine a civilising narrative is by presenting a plurality of discourses, not all of them civilising. For Turner, Elias's model is inadequate because while the work of moralists suggested a process of civilisation, adulterous lovers developed their own 'lexicon of kissing' that challenged the codes of good conduct developed elsewhere. Similarly, Das describes how writers resisted the saturation of the male-to-male kiss with sexuality. The writers of memoirs and fiction he examines contrasted with writers of sexology, and invite a reconceptualisation of 'masculinity, conventional gender roles and notions of same-sex intimacy in postwar England'. These chapters suggest that there have been a variety of 'emotional communities', each with its own culture of emotion.[39] Third, these chapters do not confirm Elias's claim that there are continuities in social modes of behaviour, and that 'the essential basis of what is required and what is forbidden in society' remained consistent.[40] They locate continuity elsewhere, not in the standards of civility and specific codes of behaviour (which most assuredly do change), but in the ways in which civilising practices have been used to establish and demarcate social relations of power.

Finally, these chapters conduct history on a different scale. Elias saw that the movement of civilisation was not smooth: there were 'regressive moments', and change displayed 'manifold fluctuations, following smaller and larger curves'. In this context, he argued, 'It clearly does not suffice to consider in isolation each single stage'; rather, Elias stood well back in order to assemble a series of historical moments, in order to see the process 'as a whole, as if speeded up'.[41] Each chapter in this collection take the approach shunned by Elias, and explores a stage in isolation. Just as Elias's methodology was designed to bring a process and its gradual transformation into view, so the case studies collected here bring the fluctuations and curves of the past into relief. The book does not tell one story, and it does not intend to give an account of the civilising process 'overall'.[42] Yet it is organised both chronologically and thematically, with sections on 'Worship and ritual', 'Ambiguity and transgression' and 'Power and intimacy'. As the book charts one possible route through over 400 years of the anxieties and emotions of human relationships by focusing on eight kisses, chronological progress does emerge. These chapters lightly sketch a narrative in which early modern public debates about kissing were superseded by nineteenth- and twentieth-century private worries. They question the extent to which the modern state entered people's lives and obliged them to restrain themselves. The intention of the book, however, is less ambitious: it is an exercise in cultural history and a demonstration of the potential of histories of gesture.

## WORSHIP AND RITUAL

The chapters by Koslofsky and Durrant explore ritual forms of worship. Chapter 1 charts the changing role of the kiss of peace in religious worship. The kiss of peace was that point in the mass when the priest took the peace of God from the body of Christ on the altar, and then passed it among those present, who each received the peace from his neighbour. This practice was part of late medieval liturgy, but the Reformation ultimately excised the kiss of peace from Protestant liturgy.[43] Koslofsky places this change in the context of new understandings of gesture and the body. As he demonstrates in his chapter on central and southern Germany during the Reformation, the worshipper's body was pushed out of Christian worship during this period. Indeed, there was a 'devaluation of the body and its gestures' in a rejection of the medieval understanding of gesture in which the outer body was connected to the inner spirit in acts of public worship. Chapter 2 considers a vivid perversion of the kiss of peace: the placing of a kiss on the anus of the Devil by witches, as an expression of their unity as a group and loyalty to the Devil. Elite and popular renditions of the witches' sabbath presented the kiss as polluting, sinful and shameful. Despite the use of torture, however, Eichstätt witch-suspects strived to resist the claims of the prosecutors and asserted their standing as honourable women. Durrant demonstrates that while stereotypes of the witches' sabbath were well developed, they were not all-consuming. Witch-suspects did not simply reproduce a standard demonological version of the sabbath under duress; rather, 'as far as was humanly possible under torture and psychological duress, [they] attempted to present themselves as honourable women'.

## AMBIGUITY AND TRANSGRESSION

The themes of transgression and ambiguity are central to a history of the kiss. In the early modern period, confusion arose over kissing in social situations, and a taxonomy of kissing developed which was part of a wider attempt to codify practices of civility and politeness. Focusing on the periodical press, Chapter 3 argues that the ambiguity of kissing was taken as an opportunity to toy with the range and limits of intimate relationships, in particular the shady ground between platonic friendship and erotic love. This was, Berry writes, part of a process of 'opening up the realm of personal and affective relationships to general scrutiny'. In the process, platonic relationships between men and women were sexualised, thereby becoming comprehensible in a heterosexual culture in which 'friendship without desire between the sexes' was difficult to imagine. Chapter 4 also considers the blurred line between social and sexual kisses, arguing that the kiss served as a locus of anxieties surrounding politeness and manners. Indeed, 'The contested interpretation of the gesture', Turner argues, 'provided an occasion for debating and defining the limits of licit and illicit behaviour, friendship and betrayal, virtue and deceit'. Exploring a broad range of sources which deal with the question of adultery, Turner shows not simply how the social practice of kissing played a critical role in the initiation of adulterous relationships, but also that it was around kissing that 'notions of proper and improper sociability were formed'. Chapter 5 concludes this section with an exploration of a medical practice in the light of the solidification of polite conventions. Mouth-to-mouth ventilation was first found to be an efficient method of resuscitation in the late eighteenth century. However, despite its efficacy, the 'kiss of life' was not established as a respected medical practice until the 1950s. Davidson demonstrates that it was the reluctance of people to perform the procedure that meant that the kiss of life failed as a popular form of resuscitation. Powerful contemporary notions of propriety and purity worked against its adoption. Masculine behaviour in particular was constrained by polite ideals of gentlemanly behaviour. As Davidson points out, the 'kiss of life' is not supposed to be meaningful, yet its adoption was in part determined by the ambiguous status of its kiss-like nature.

## POWER AND INTIMACY

The intimacy of the kiss has rendered it problematic in relationships of power. Chapter 6 considers the symbolic role of the kiss in characterising power itself. In late eighteenth-century England, politically active women risked stepping out of an acceptable familial realm, threatening what was perceived to be a masculine political order. Such concerns about women's independent political involvement were expressed through the kisses-for-votes scandal of 1784. Indeed, Chalus demonstrates how this scandal articulated worries about sex, class and political corruption more generally. In contemporary depictions of the incident – in which an aristocratic lady allegedly kissed a butcher – and in the related debates about kissing for votes, corruption was gendered as female. The disintegration of gender and class boundaries, therefore, was seen to undermine the British polity. The kisses exchanged between the Victorian mistress Lady Frederica Loraine and her governess Miss Freestone also reveal a complex relationship between power and intimacy. Intense physical displays of affection between women had long been acceptable, but the encounters between these women disrupted class and status boundaries. As Williams demonstrates in Chapter 7, these kisses become comprehensible only when placed in the context of long-term ill health, at which point they reveal a complex web of affection, solace and dependency, coloured by the inequities and tensions of the mistress–governess relationship. The poignancy of these kisses is echoed in Chapter 8, on kisses between dying men in the First World War. Using memoirs, fiction, poetry and the short story, Das shows that expectations of manly stoicism, strength and self-reliance did not preclude the exchange of kisses between the dying soldiers in the bloody First World War trenches. These moments betray relationships of emotional intensity. As with the kisses between a mistress and her governess, these kisses were not about sex – they were about intimacy. These final kisses call into question claims that civilised 'modernity' virtually erased all possibility of expressions of intimacy between adults of the same sex. After centuries of moralising, and despite recent works of sexology, there were expressions of human intimacy that civilisation failed to silence.

Set against a backdrop of acute international tension, Norbert Elias felt that the world of 1939 was yet to be civilised. Though reversals were possible, the civilising process was likely to continue.[44] As proposed by Keith Thomas later in this book, late twentieth- and twenty-first-century permissiveness suggests that this has not been the case. This book goes no further than the First World War, but the moderate excitement generated in the press by the 2000 conference 'The Kiss in History' allows some brief comment on the kiss in the twenty-first century. The press coverage of the conference could be seen as reflecting the emergence of a permissive society. Several journalists took the opportunity of the conference (from which this book was forged) to pen lively articles, often lavishly illustrated with explicit depictions of mouth-to-mouth kissing and erotic, close-up shots of full red lips. Contrary to the direction of Elias's pattern, the threshold of shame and repugnance seems to have been lowered.

Yet upon closer inspection, the images in the mainstream press were seen to be of chaste, closed mouths.[45] Moreover, despite the apparent superficiality and frivolity of their pieces, these commentators shared something of the approach of cultural historians – they sought to pin down the kiss, even to tame it. Writers discussed the multiple meanings of the kiss and the disparity between an apparently simple act and the complex readings of that act.[46] One article used a cinematic kiss to explore the political and religious world of oppressive regimes.[47] Another presented the kiss as an index of the intimate relationship of a couple.[48] Often delighting in the variability of the kiss, and the obvious liveliness this could lend a newspaper article, journalists nevertheless shared with historians a desire to decipher the kiss and its meanings.

Some of the key themes highlighted by the chapters in this book were absent from these recent comments. Most obviously, mainstream news journalism did not explore the kiss of peace, though this did arouse notable interest in the Church press.[49] Yet there were concerns that had a familiar ring to them. The conference seems to have tapped into (or was born out of) a deep interest in the emotions, the appropriateness of public gestures and British codes of manners.[50] Ambiguity and transgression were key issues, and it is striking that the conference was used as an opportunity to reproduce some of the early modern public debates of the period concerning kissing etiquette and the sincerity of the kiss. Some writers worried over the insincerity of the public kiss and were unsettled by the possibility that a public kiss might not be a reflection of sincere affection or passion.[51] The suggestion was that the kiss should be an authentic and romantic gesture, an act of intimacy (often sexual intimacy) that is a genuine expression of love. Other writers called for guidelines on etiquette, pondering whether to exchange a kiss on one cheek or two, or instead enjoy a hearty handshake.[52]

In all these articles, the focus was not on formal public ritual, in which the kiss now plays little role for most of us (except the marriage ceremony, of course), but on the personal relationships of individuals, albeit the rich and famous. Several writers expressed an unease about those holding positions of power engaging in acts of affection, but reveal an avid curiosity for information on the personal lives of others. Indeed, many accounts of the kiss in popular print culture create a distinction between public and private kissing. A division emerges between the public face of power and the private expression of intimacy. Or, more accurately, we can observe a redefinition of the public to encompass the personal and the emotional, a development which has produced widespread debate about celebrities' right to privacy.[53] This does not reflect state-compelled restraint, because arguably the mass media constitute a public realm of relatively free expression, outside immediate state control. Yet, nor is this quite a permissive society. Keith Thomas asks in his Afterword, 'even today, who would kiss the Queen?' The answer is, only her husband. However, when Prince Philip kissed his wife in public for the first time in fifty years, some elements of the British press were outraged.[54] Our culture does not approve of kissing by all.

The press interest in kissing was not, of course, prompted merely by a historical conference. The event took place just days before National Kissing Day, and in a year when some high-profile kisses attracted considerable media attention.[55] Indeed, the response to the conference was not wholly positive. One radio news journalist wanted to cover the event for a BBC Radio 4 news programme, but he struggled to find a 'hook' because the contributors had no tangible discovery to offer. The responses from people around the globe to a BBC News online feature included those who sympathised with our premise that a kiss can convey social, political and cultural meaning, but there were those who felt it was an utter waste of time. It was the closest lonely academics got to kissing, someone suspected; it was irrelevant compared with cancer research, claimed another. Research in the arts and humanities does not need discoveries or life-saving advances to be valuable, though, and the discussion in the press suggests that we were on to something of human interest. These writers were not much interested in history for its own sake, it is true, though they used it to try to understand the present: the British once engaged in public kissing, one author asserts, so why we are so bad at it now?[56] In analysing the kiss as an embedded and as an exemplary gesture, cultural history can use small gestures to take us to big issues concerning ourselves and others, the past and the present.

## NOTES

I should like to thank Keith Thomas, the anonymous readers for Manchester University Press and particularly Mike Braddick for their helpful comments.

1 C. C. Bombaugh, *The Literature of Kissing, Gleaned from History, Poetry, Fiction and Anecdote* (Philadelphia, 1876); Christopher Nyrop, *The Kiss and its History*, trans. William Frederick Harvey (London, 1901), p. 9.

2 Robert Darnton, 'Intellectual and Cultural History', in Michael Kammen (ed.), *The Past before US: Contemporary Historical Writing in the United States* (Ithaca, 1980), p. 347. Also see Peter Burke, 'Overture: The New History, its Past and its Future', in *idem* (ed.), *New Perspectives on Historical Writing* (Cambridge, 1991), p. 2.

3 Clifford Geertz, 'Religion as a Cultural System', in *The Interpretation of Cultures: Selected Essays* (1973; London, 1993), p. 89. On the impact of Geertz on the humanities, see Sherry B. Ortner (ed.), *The Fate of 'Culture': Geertz and Beyond* (Berkeley, 1999).

4 Patrick H. Hutton, 'The History of Mentalities: The New Map of Cultural History', *History and Theory*, 20 (1981), 238. See also Peter Burke, 'Mentality and Ideology', *History and Social Theory* (Cambridge, 1992), p. 92.

5 Darnton, 'Intellectal and Cultural', pp. 328, 342.

6  Burke, 'Overture', p. 3. See also Victoria E. Bonnell and Lynn Hunt, 'Introduction', in *idem* (eds), *Beyond the Cultural Turn: New Directions in the Study of Society and Culture* (Berkeley, 1999), on the impact of the cultural turn on history and sociology.

7  Marc W. Steinberg, 'Culturally Speaking: Finding a Commons between Post-Structuralism and the Thomposian Perspective', *Social History*, 21:2 (1996), 193–214, at 194.

8  *Ibid.*, 194, 202.

9  Darnton, 'Intellectual and Cultural', p. 348; Hutton, 'The History of Mentalities', 238.

10  Michel de Certeau, *The Practice of Everyday Life*, trans. Steven Rendall (1974; Berkeley, 1984), p. xi.

11  Lynn Hunt, 'Introduction: History, Culture, and Text', in *idem* (ed.), *The New Cultural History* (Berkeley, 1989), p. 7.

12  *Ibid.*, p. 19.

13  E. P. Thompson, 'Anthropology and the Discipline of Historical Context', *Midland History*, 1:3 (1972), 49.

14  Keith Thomas, *Man and the Natural World: Changing Attitudes in England 1500–1800* (1983), p. 16. Quoted in Peter Burke, Brian Harrison and Paul Slack, 'Keith Thomas', in *idem* (eds), *Civil Histories: Essays Presented to Sir Keith Thomas* (Oxford, 2000), p. 20.

15  Hunt, 'Introduction', pp. 10–11.

16  Stephen Greenblatt, 'Towards a Poetics of Culture', in H. Aram Veeser (ed.), *The New Historicism* (New York, 1989), p. 1. On the similarities between new historicism and cultural history see *idem*, 'The New Historicism', in *idem* (ed.), *The New Historicism Reader* (New York, 1994), p. 9.

17  H. Aram Veeser, 'Introduction', in *idem* (ed.), *The New Historicism*, p. xi.

18  Greenblatt, 'Towards a Poetics', p. 9.

19  *Ibid.*, p. 12.

20  Robert Darnton, 'History and Anthropology', in *idem*, *The Kiss of Lamourette: Reflections in Cultural History* (London, 1990), p. 342.

21  Veeser, 'Introduction', p. xv.

22  Thompson, 'Anthropology', 41–55, at p. 45.

23  *Ibid.*, p. 46. On the impact of anthropology on Thomas's work, see Burke, Harrison and Slack, 'Keith Thomas', pp. 8–10.

24  Darnton, 'History and Anthropology', p. 342; Catherine Belsey, 'Reading Cultural History', in Tamsin Spargo (ed.), *Reading the Past: Literature and History* (Basingstoke, 2000), p. 107.

25  Bonnell and Hunt, 'Introduction', p. 26.

26  Roger Chartier, *Cultural History: Between Practices and Representations*, trans. Lydia G. Cochrane (Cambridge, 1988), pp. 5, 6.

27  Hunt, 'Introduction', p. 17.

28  John Tosh, *The Pursuit of History: Aims, Methods and New Directions in the Study of Modern History*, 2nd edn (1984; London, 1991), p. 87; Chartier, 'Introduction', p. 7.

29  David Summers, 'Representation', in Robert S. Nelson and Richard Shiff (eds), *Critical Terms for Art History* (Chicago, 1996), p. 15; Chartier, 'Introduction', pp. 11, 13.

30  *Ibid.*, pp. 13, 14.

31  Keith Thomas, 'Introduction', in Jan Bremmer and Herman Roodenburg (eds), *A Cultural History of Gesture: From Antiquity to the Present Day* (London, 1991), p. 11.

32  Tim Hitchcock, 'Redefining Sex in Eighteenth-Century England', *History Workshop Journal*, 41 (1996), 72–90, at 79.

33  Bonnell and Hunt, 'Introduction', p. 10.

34  Burke, 'Overture', p. 4.
35  Hutton, 'The History of Mentalities', p. 239.
36  *Ibid.*, p. 258.
37  Burke, 'Culture', *History and Social Theory*, pp. 125–6.
38  Norbert Elias, *The Civilizing Process: The History of Manners of State Formation and Civilization*, trans. Edmund Jephcott (1939, 1994; Oxford, 2000), p. 90. Elias was here speaking specifically about table manners.
39  The phrase 'emotional communities' comes from Barbara H. Rosenwein, 'Worrying about Emotions in History, *American Historical Review* (June 2002), www.historycooperative.org/journals/ahr/107.3/ah0302000821.html (accessed 11 November 2003), par. 35. I am grateful to the anonymous reader at Manchester University Press for suggesting this piece.
40  Elias, *Civilizing Process*, p. 89.
41  *Ibid.*, pp. 106, 71.
42  *Ibid.*, p. 71.
43  I am indebted to the generosity of Bridget Nichols, Lay Chaplain to the Bishop of Ely, and the late Alan Bray for discussing these issues with me.
44  Elias, *Civilizing Process*, pp. 446–7.
45  See, for example, Anna Pusglove, 'Go On Then, Just a Quick One', *This is London, Evening Standard* (20 October 2000), 35–6. Many thanks to Amanda Vickery for bringing this piece to my attention. Also see Tony Barrell, 'Lips Wide Shut', *Sunday Times Magazine* (17 October 1999), pp. 52–8.
46  Joan Smith, 'Of Mouths and Men', *G2*, *Guardian* (6 July 2000), 8–9.
47  A. C. Grayling, 'It Started with a Kiss', *G2*, *Guardian* (1 July 2002), 8–9.
48  Pusglove, 'Go On Then, Just a Quick One', 35–6.
49  Rachel Harden, 'Smacker's Backers to Confer', *Church Times* (9 June 2000), 5. This was probably the best title of the press reports.
50  All the scholars participating in the event, except one, worked in the UK.
51  See, for example, Pusglove, 'Go On Then, Just a Quick One', 35.
52  Annalisa Barbieri, 'Whatever Happened to the Hearty Handshake?', *G2*, *Guardian* (28 May 2002), 9; Barrell, 'Lips Wide Shut', 57.
53  The current interest is prompted in part by the Human Rights Act which came into force in October 2000, and which makes provision for individuals' rights to privacy. For an account of many of the recent attempts of celebrities to take advantage of this Act, see Andrew Anthony, 'Public Faces, Private Lives', *Observer* (17 February 2002) http://observer.guardian.co.uk/focus/story/0,6903,651662,00.html (accessed 11 November 2003).
54  Pusglove, 'Go On Then, Just a Quick One', 35. Other writers discuss kissing among the Royal Family. See Barbieri, 'Whatever Happened to the Hearty Handshake?', 9, and Smith, 'Of Mouths and Men', 8.
55  As already mentioned, the Queen and Prince Philip received much attention for kisses they shared in January and April, as did Al and Tipper Gore during the US presidential election campaign. National Kissing Day, for those keen to celebrate, is held on 6 July.
56  Pusglove, 'Go On Then, Just a Quick One', 36. Only one report discussed the historical content of the conference in any detail, and not surprisingly this was in a publication dedicated to higher education. See Harriet Swain, 'A Kiss and Tell Story', *Times Higher Educational Supplement* (23 June 2000), 18.

# PART I

# Worship
# and
# ritual

<>

# I

# The kiss of peace in the German Reformation

<>

Craig Koslofsky

ON 29 OCTOBER 1528 a commission of pastors and lay officials that included Martin Luther questioned the clergy of the Saxon town of Schmiedeberg, near Wittenberg. This was the first systematic Protestant church visitation in Saxony and one of the first in Europe. Armed with the power of the state, this commission sought to reform the church in the Saxon principality by putting into practice the doctrines of Luther and his colleagues. In each town the visitors inventoried the real and movable property of the town's churches. The inventory for the Schmiedeberg parish church included '5 small silver pax-boards [and] 2 good gilded pax-boards'.[1]

Pax-boards like these were passed from the celebrant to the deacons and then among the laity during the canon of the traditional Christian mass. Their moment in the ritual came after the consecration and Lord's Prayer, during the *Agnus Dei* and directly before the priest's communion. Priest, deacons and laypeople kissed the pax in a ritual gesture of peace and devotion: by 1500 such pax-boards were used in almost all churches in the Latin West, replacing the traditional face-to-face kiss of peace. These paxes or pax-boards were rounded or rectangular tablets of wood, ivory, gold or silver with a handle projecting from the back, often bearing an image of the Crucifixion or the *Agnus Dei*.[2] By kissing an inanimate object to evoke the divine gift of peace, medieval Christians performed a public kind of kiss at once more transcendently spiritual and more crudely material than the kiss in the modern West.

The new liturgies that Protestants created and established in the first decade of the Reformation had no place for the traditional pax-boards, or for the kiss of peace given to them. As in all other localities, the Saxon visitation commission ordered that the Schmiedeberg pax-boards be sold and the money placed in a new common fund for the worthy poor. The fate of these pax-boards calls our attention to a question raised by John Bossy in his work on community and the mass.[3] After describing the elimination of the ritual kiss of peace from Christian worship in the Reformation, Bossy asked 'what long-range shifts in European civilization might account for so general a fact as the disappearance of the *Pax* from early modern liturgies'?[4] In this chapter I approach his question by considering specifically the role of the physical kiss in the disappearance of the ritual kiss of peace, the *Pax*.

Bossy argued that the mass in general and the *Pax* specifically had become better at representing the parts of the Christian community than at representing its unity. Reformers sought to 'restore the Eucharist to center of social unity', which meant removing other foci like the *Pax*.[5] Bossy has examined the changing theological and social content of the ritual kiss of peace and unity, but I argue that its form – as a kiss – is equally significant. Building on his cogent arguments, I will show that by the end of the fifteenth century the kiss of peace was caught up in the larger history of gesture. No established Protestant liturgy sought to reform the *Pax*, restore it to its apostolic form (as understood in the sixteenth century) or retain it in a reformed service.[6] Why did Protestants reject the kiss of peace? To answer this question, I will place the liturgical kiss in several contexts, focusing on the headwaters of the Reformation in central and southern Germany.[7]

## THE KISS AS GESTURE

The holy kiss belongs among the oldest practices of the Christian tradition. Mentioned in the letters of Paul (1 Corinthians 16:20, 2 Corinthians. 13:12, Romans 16:16, 1 Thessalonians 5:26) and Peter (1 Peter 5:14), the kiss was an everyday greeting among early Christians, but also a significant part of their communion liturgy. Tertullian (*c*.145–*c*.220) attested to its importance in the liturgy, asking 'What prayer is complete if divorced from the "holy kiss"?' He then referred to 'the kiss of peace' as 'the seal of prayer'.[8] The kiss of peace developed along with the communion rite, as described by Cyril of Jerusalem (*c*.315–386), John Chrysostom (*c*.347–407), Ambrose of Milan (340–397) and Augustine of Hippo (354–430), who described the ideal identity of 'lips' and 'conscience', body and spirit: 'After this [the Lord's Prayer], the "Peace be with you" is said, and the Christians embrace one another with the holy kiss. This is a sign of peace; as the lips indicate, let peace be made in your conscience, that is, when your lips draw near to those of your brother, do not let your heart withdraw from his.'[9] By the fifth century the kiss of peace had assumed its place after the Lord's Prayer and just before communion, for which it was seen as preparation.[10]

Use of this powerful sign of reconciliation and unity spread, and by the High Middle Ages the 'holy kiss' was given or exchanged in Christian rituals

of baptism, ordination, and consecration of bishops, in coronation ceremonies, in the absolution of penitents and in the marriage ceremony.[11] In law, a
kiss could be given or exchanged in rituals of contract-making or dispute
settlement, and in the act of homage.[12] Of all these ritual kisses, the kiss of
peace in the mass was by far the most common and widely experienced.[13]

In the fifteenth and sixteenth centuries the liturgical kiss of peace was
understood as a form of bodily gesture. In his widely circulated moral tract
*Coelifodina* (*Heavenly Quarry*), first published in 1502, the Erfurt Augustinian
monk and preacher Johannes von Paltz (d. 1511) divided 'kisses of the body'
('osculum corporale') into three categories and described as 'praiseworthy'
kisses that create peace and unity among Christians.[14] In 1520 Paltz's fellow
Augustinian Martin Luther spoke of honouring God 'with the mouth, on
bended knee, with kisses or other gestures ("geberden").'[15] On the other side
of the Reformation, in 1535 the Bavarian bishop and theologian Berthold
Pirstinger defended the mass against those who 'mock the kiss of peace and
scorn other Christian gestures'.[16]

Scholars of gesture in the Christian Middle Ages can cite a wide range of
authorities, from Bernard of Clairvaux and Albertus Magnus to Jean Gerson,
to show a fundamental consensus on the subject.[17] Gestures were significant
because they were based on a fundamental connection between inside and
outside, soul and body. Thomas Aquinas provided an especially precise
description of the relationships between body, soul, person, and God in the
*Summa contra gentiles*:

> Man performs certain sensible actions, not to arouse God, but to arouse himself
> to things divine: such as prostrations, genuflexions, raising of the voice and sing-
> ing. Such things are not done as though God needed them, for . . . He looks at the
> affection of the heart, and not the mere movements of the body: but we do them
> for our own sake, that by them our intention may be fixed on God, and our hearts
> inflamed.[18]

'Experience shows', Aquinas concluded, 'that by acts of the body the soul is
aroused to a certain knowledge or affection. Wherefore it is evidently reasonable that we should employ bodies in order to raise our minds to God.'[19]
With a powerful immediacy, gestures could express the movements of the
soul and spirit; the performance of specific gestures could move the soul 'to
a certain knowledge or affection'. Across the history of medieval gesture, this
sense of exchange and mutual influence is never absent.[20]

Ordinary or everyday gestures embodied ordinary or everyday states. The
kiss was something special and could reflect or effect more profound and
abstract values. Bernhard of Clairvaux explained that the kiss could express
the abstract and ineffable, connecting mystical experience, theological understanding and liturgical symbolism. For medieval theologians, the kiss could

express '[such] experiences, in which God is more tasted than seen . . . when [this] taste cannot be explained or described to others.'[21] When faced with communicating the inexpressible, the Augustinian Johann Staupitz (d. 1524) advised that 'We must draw these things out of God's teaching, and when we have drawn them out, bring them alive with representations, models, figures and human visualization.'[22] The kiss was ideal for this kind of visualisation, and Staupitz then quite traditionally presents marriage as a 'figure' for the mutual love of Christ and the faithful soul. This devotional experience is described in richly embodied terms: Christian soul and Saviour encounter one another 'with kissing, embracing, and drawing together, naked to naked'.[23]

The representative power of the kiss came from its special ability to connect inside and outside. As Berthold Pirstinger explained: 'The visible pax-board is kissed by those attending with the mouth, *externally*, to show that they have *internally* in their spirit spiritually sacrificed and received the invisible body and chalice of Christ.'[24] The kiss held a special power to represent spiritual intimacy, communion, peace and unity. The efficacy or effect of the kiss of peace was understood through its role as a gesture in a Christian anthropology that connected internal and external.

In the fourteenth and fifteenth centuries, three trends converged on the kiss of peace in the mass: the spread of the pax-board (also *osculatorium* or *pacificale*), the substitution of the *Pax* for the Eucharist, and concerns about the *Pax* as a source of deceit, desire and pride.

The pax-board was an innovation of the thirteenth century. It originated in England, where it is first mentioned in 1248 in the statutes of The Archbishop of York; later references are found in the statutes of an Exeter synod of 1287 and in an inventory of St Paul's Cathedral in London of 1295.[25] From England the pax-board spread to the continent in the fourteenth century. There is no mention of the pax-board in Durandus's detailed *Rationale divinorum officiorum*, the great guide to liturgical practice and symbolism of 1286, but references to the custom of kissing the pax-board in the mass begin to appear in France in the early fourteenth century.[26] The 1328 inventory of Queen Clemence of Hungary, widow of Louis X, mentions 'ung portepais d'argent'.[27] The first translation of the *Rationale* into the vernacular, a French text by Jean Golein of 1382, inserts a reference to the 'la paix porter' into Durandus's description of the *Pax*.[28] The earliest evidence from the Holy Roman Empire appears in the statutes of a Prague synod of 1355. The synod stated that parish priests should encourage their parishioners to exchange the traditional kiss of peace; if the laypeople were unwilling, however, they could be given a tablet with the image of the Crucifixion to kiss instead.[29]

For the Empire, the vernacular Nuremberg and Augsburg *Messe singen oder lesen*, printed in several editions from the 1480s on, is an especially valuable prescriptive source on the liturgy. This text, the first German-language commentary on the mass, drew upon the many Latin expositions of the mass circulated in the Empire in the fifteenth century.[30] (It is sort of a German counterpart to the *Lay Folk's Mass Book*.[31]) It describes a ritual kiss of peace issued from the celebrant to the deacons and then to the laypeople through the pax-board. After the priest has kissed the pax, 'The deacon or subdeacon carries to the other priests in the choir that pax that he himself has kissed, and they kiss it one after another with devotion ["andacht"]. It is also the custom in many places that the subdeacon carries the tablet he has kissed to all who stand or kneel at the service or mass for each to kiss; that is called "Osculum pacis", the kiss of peace.'[32] The use of the pax-board is described by other fifteenth-century German commentators such as Gabriel Biel and the Leipzig theologian Balthasar von Pforta; by the early sixteenth century pax-boards appear in countless German church inventories and visitation records.[33] The pax-board made tangible the sense of hierarchy and transmission that had developed in the *Pax*. According the *Messe singen oder lesen*: 'It signifies the transmission of the love of Christ as the Lord [gives] love to the Church, the Church to the priests and the priest to those standing by.'[34] Holy peace proceeds out from the celebrant: these commentators present an interpretation that says a lot about hierarchy and very little about community.

By the time of the *Messe singen oder lesen* in the 1480s, laypeople had begun to understand the *Pax* not merely as preparation for receiving communion, but also as a substitute for the sacrament. This fundamental development was explained by Pirstinger in his explanation of the mass for laypeople: 'instead of daily reception [of the Eucharist] those attending mass are given the pax-board or a relic to kiss during the *Agnus Dei* . . . This shows that they receive the selfsame sacrament in faith spiritually, daily, through the kiss of peace and the unity so signified by the *Pax*.'[35] The *Pax* is also described as a substitute for lay receipt of the Eucharist by Ludolf von Sachsen (d. 1377) and by Wilhelm von Gouda (late fifteenth century).[36] This substitution was possible only through the medieval understanding of gesture described above. Again, Pirstinger: 'Whoever seeks to kiss the pax-board with a pure heart proclaims that he wants to meet his neighbour . . . in the unity of faith through our Lord Jesus Christ, who on the altar of the cross was . . . sacrificed bodily, and now on the altar by the priest is sacrificed sacramentally, and by those in attendance is sacrificed spiritually and received spiritually.' The physical gesture, the kiss, made possible the spiritual receipt of the Eucharist: 'And so everyone in attendance shows with such a kiss that he has spiritually sacrificed and received the holy sacrament in true faith and right love.'[37] The power to link the visible (what is 'shown') with the spiritual (the sacrifice) gave the kiss its importance. This power to connect inside and outside could also make a gesture as versatile as the kiss deeply ambiguous.[38]

## 'DETESTABLE KISSES'

In his 1502 *Coelifodina* the Erfurt Augustinian Johannes von Paltz incorporated a sermon of his former teacher Johannes von Dorsten (d. 1481) on kissing.[39] Paltz and Dorsten explained in scholastic fashion that 'kisses of the body' were three-fold: they could be praiseworthy, excusable or detestable.[40] As mentioned above, the kiss of peace was a prime example of a commendable kiss. Kisses were excusable when exchanged between mother and son, for example, or as a simple sign of greeting. Paltz and Dorsten then went on to discuss in more detail the 'osculum detestabile', marked in their analysis by dissimulation, betrayal and lust.[41] Although Paltz and Dorsten distinguished carefully between kisses commendable, excusable and detestable, these categories could not be truly sealed off from one another. In the fifteenth century the sins summarised under the 'osculum detestabile' began to surround the *Pax* as well.

To describe the sinful kiss of 'dissimulation' the Augustinian preachers used the example of Absalom, who kissed his social inferiors to ingratiate himself with them and win support for his rebellion against his father David: with kisses 'Absalom stole the hearts of the men of Israel' (2 Samuel 15:1–6). Dissimulation through kissing receives little discussion in the *Coelifodina* and the other moral literature of the time, however.

Kisses of betrayal and deceit, on the other hand, were a constant concern for commentators on the mass and moralists in general. The late fourteenth-century German translation of Durandus's *Rationale* warns that 'those who kiss one another but are hateful follow the traitor Judas'.[42] In fact, the kiss of peace was explicitly omitted from the traditional mass on Maundy Thursday, and in some cases on Good Friday and Easter Saturday. During the commemoration of Christ's passion, commentators agreed, the kiss of peace would call to mind the kiss of Judas.[43] 'One does not give the *Pax* on Maundy Thursday,' as the German translator of Durandus explained, 'because the wicked greeting [by Judas] was made with a kiss.'[44] On Easter Saturday commentators noted that 'again one does not give the *Pax*, to dishonour that kiss of Judas the traitor.'[45] The *Messe singen oder lesen* describes a similar restriction: the kiss of peace is given 'every day of the year except Maundy Thursday . . . this shows that the Lord was betrayed through the sign of peace with a kiss from Judas'.[46] The traditional Easter week services recognised the ambiguity of the kiss: the same commentaries that forbade the kiss of peace on Maundy Thursday explained that extra opportunities should be given for the *Pax* during the first part of Easter week to reconcile congregants.[47]

Lustful kisses were of course also detestable and receive the longest commentary from Paltz and Dorsten in the *Coelifodina*. From the earliest references to the *Pax* in the second century, we hear that only same-sex kisses were to be exchanged at the mass: 'the baptised should greet each other, men the men and women the women. But the men should not greet the women'.[48] Lay folk attending mass were sometimes separated by sex, but medieval references to the *Pax* as an opportunity for amorous kisses between the sexes are also common.[49] The German translation of Durandus's *Rationale* explained that 'the men and the women do not give one another the kiss, because some might become lustful'.[50] Following the exposition of Gabriel Biel, the early sixteenth-century mass commentary of Johannes Bechofen cited the dangers of lust as the reason for the use of the pax-board instead of face-to-face kissing.[51]

In the fourteenth and fifteenth centuries, however, the most common complaint regarding the *Pax* invoked a different sin: pride. The chain of kisses and the sense that the celebrant received holy peace from God and then passed it down a hierarchy to the lay people fostered disputes about precedence and prestige. Chaucer cited the proud man who wished 'to kiss the pax and be censed' before his neighbour.[52] Christine de Pisan (1365–c.1429) described the same problem: 'Undoubtedly, those of whom we speak fervently kiss the object called the "Peace": however, they do not make peace but rather war, since their hearts are full of anger arising from great pride.'[53] In Pisan's words, the *Pax* 'signifies the communion of peace (which ought to prevail among Christians)' and 'is for the little people just as much as for the great ones'. But the sin of pride transformed the circulation of the pax into a struggle for precedence: 'It is certainly a foul and odious habit these women have of envying each other like this during the Kiss of Peace at mass. It is an obstacle and hindrance to devotion to God, for one person passes it on to another who would feel humiliated to take it.' Pisan asked, 'What do such ceremonies accomplish?' She concluded that 'they should hang it [the pax-board] up on a nail and let whoever wants to kiss it do so'.[54] In 1512 the Synod of Seville agreed, declaring that the pax should no longer be carried through the churches, but placed where the faithful could easily approach it and show their devotion.[55] Thomas More also described 'how men fall at variance for kissing of the pax'.[56] These unedifying struggles to kiss the pax before someone else were certainly a problem, although the numerous Reformation attacks on the traditional mass do not mention these problems with the *Pax*, so perhaps they were not as widespread as the complaints suggest.[57]

Beyond these specific problems surrounding the kiss of peace, ritual gestures in general were in flux in the fifteenth and early sixteenth centuries. The spread of the pax-board and the decline of the face-to-face kiss suggests some intriguing parallels with the rituals surrounding the consummation of marriage in the same period, and with the decline of secular ritual kisses. Michael Schröter has documented the 'intimization of the wedding night', on the basis of a study of fifteenth- and sixteenth-century German ego-documents. He notes a clear shift away from the unashamed observation by family and friends of the physical consummation of the marriage.[58] In the secular rituals of homage and fealty, the negative associations of the same-sex kiss began to outweigh its value as a symbolic gesture, and its use declined sharply in the fifteenth and sixteenth centuries.[59] These examples correspond with the larger picture sketched by Yannick Carré of the slow disappearance of the kiss from sacred and secular rituals from the fourteenth century on.[60]

The bundle of significations that made the kiss in the Middle Ages was coming undone. How could one act be both spontaneous and ritualised, public and private, sacred and profane, spiritual and erotic, a sign of peace and a source of discord? The response of the Reformations of the sixteenth century to the ambiguity of the kiss would decisively transform the kiss as it entered the modern era. As the most venerable and widespread form of sacred kiss, the kiss of peace was at the centre of this transformation.

### REFORMING THE KISS OF PEACE?

In the first years of the Reformation, reformers criticised the kiss of peace directly and as part of their general assault on the traditional mass. By far the angriest words were evoked by the substitution of the *Pax* for the Eucharist. In other words, it was the power of the kiss to signify that was most disputed and most offensive to reformers. This criticism focused on the assumptions about gesture that underlay the kiss, not on the 'corruption' or abuse of the *Pax*.

In 1523 the former Franciscan Johann Eberlin von Günzburg contrasted proper Christian worship with the Roman mass: 'Instead of the proclamation of the Gospel one now reads secretly a piece of the Bible . . . Instead of the common prayer is the shriek of the choir and the blaring of the organ. Instead of receiving the sacrament, we are give the pax-board to kiss.'[61] In a 1520 sermon on the mass Luther made the same comment: 'they want to take the other species [i.e. the bread] away from us and give us a mere monstrance as a relic to kiss'.[62] Given their anger at the replacement of lay communion by the *Pax*, how did reformers like Johann Eberlin von Günzburg and Martin Luther see the kiss? Despite their avowed biblicism, they showed no interest in restoring or reforming the kiss of peace. Considering the prominence of the holy kiss in Christian Scripture and tradition, this lack of interest is in itself significant.

A closer look at Martin Luther's understanding of the kiss and of liturgical gestures in general reveals the basis of the Protestant rejection of the kiss as a sign. In 1523, preaching on 1 Peter 5:14, 'Greet one another with the kiss of love', Luther notes curtly that 'This custom is now gone . . . such was a practice in those lands.'[63] In his 1530–31 lectures on the Song of Solomon he comes up against the *locus classicus* of the kiss as a spiritual metaphor, chapter 1 verse 2, 'Let him kiss me with the kisses of his mouth.' According to Luther's exegesis, 'Solomon here speaks according to the custom of his people.' In both cases Luther described the kiss as historical and contingent rather than as a transcendent sign of peace. He commented that 'Among us kisses are not considered proper', and emphasised their personal and private connotations: 'kisses are however signs of love and favour ["amoris et favoris signa"].' Luther's understanding contrasts with that of Bernhard of Clairvaux, Johannes von Paltz or Berthold Pirstinger: Luther makes no mention of social values like peace or unity, only the more individual and ambiguous 'love and favour'.[64] Conversely, in his *Formula missae* of 1523 Luther left no place for the physical kiss of peace exchanged among congregants. He described the prayer for peace as 'a public absolution of the sins of the communicants'. Any sense of 'horizontal' peace-making among Christians was eliminated, being replaced by a vertical relationship between God and person that was not created through any gesture, but only through 'the Gospel voice announcing remission of sins'.[65]

Taking the evidence from Luther into a broader context, we can examine around two dozen German Protestant liturgies developed and put into use in the 1520s. In all these services, ranging from Wittenberg to Zürich, only one liturgical kiss is described: in Ulrich Zwingli's *Aktion oder Bruch* (1525), the pastor kisses the Gospel book just before communion is distributed.[66] Any sort of physical kiss of peace was eliminated: neither the medieval pax-board nor the ancient face-to-face kiss was mentioned.[67] Instead, most nascent Protestant services included a prayer for peace and response from the congregation – but the body and the kiss could no longer symbolise or evoke this peace.[68]

The uniform omission of the kiss of peace from the Protestant German worship services of the 1520s was a radical step based on new doubts about what public gestures could or should do for the spirit. But the removal of the *Pax* was not entirely unprecedented to the ministers who created these services or the lay folk who participated in them. As described above, the traditional mass carefully omitted the kiss of peace on Maundy Thursday (and on the following two days in many cases) because it would evoke the betrayal of Jesus by the kiss of Judas. We can consider the Protestant rejection of the kiss of peace a radical change, but also as a kind of continuity: it marked the generalisation or expansion of a message conveyed in the celebration of mass during the Holy Week of the traditional Church.

What did the year-round rejection of the *Pax* say to the laity in 1520s? By omitting the kiss of peace, the early Protestants suggested liturgically that all kisses of peace were in fact Judas kisses. The human inability to perform good works such as peace-making without divine grace was underscored by the omission of the *Pax*. John Bossy touched on this in his brief discussion of Luther's troubled relation to the 'moral tradition' of Christian peace-making.[69] The new emphases of the Reformers also revalued peace itself, as the last of Luther's *Ninety-Five Theses* suggests: 'And thus be confident of entering into heaven through many tribulations rather than through the false security of peace.'[70] These Protestant services refused to consider human gestures of peace-making as preparation for communion.

In the first decades of the Reformation, defenders of the traditional Church saw the *Pax*, and liturgical gestures in general, as a significant issue. In 1534 the tireless Catholic apologist Georg Witzel noted that 'the holy Sacrament has fallen into great disrespect' because the Protestant 'sects' preach that 'vestments, the sign of the cross, raising one's hands, kissing, etc. are the work of fools'.[71] As Berthold Pirstinger, bishop of Chiemsee, put it: 'In these false times we daily neglect mass, mock the kiss of peace and scorn other Christian gestures, as if we want to uphold no peaceful ways or orderly love for one another. Then we must suffer war and threats . . . from Turks and heathens, from Lutherans and Zwinglians, from Anabaptists and other heretics.'[72] In Pirstinger's understanding, cause and effect operate along a traditional connection of inside and outside: because the kiss of peace and other Christian gestures are scorned, discord, heresy, war and division result. Gesture links body and spirit, and Pirstinger sees their mutual influence in the Reformation: the neglect of the gestures of peace and unity leads to war and heresy, just as heretics lead people to scoff at ritual gestures.

When we take this sixteenth-century Bavarian theologian seriously, we can see the fate of the *Pax* in a larger history of the body in the fifteenth and sixteenth centuries. I argue that the failure of a specific sign reveals the failure of a whole system of gesture. Luther spoke of honouring God 'with the mouth, on bended knee, with kisses or other gestures ["geberden"],' but for Luther and his followers these gestures could no longer effect anything essential: 'if it is not done in the heart through faith . . . it is nothing but an illusion and . . . trickery.'[73] In his 'Sermon on the New Testament' of 1520, Luther advised that 'if we want to celebrate and understand the mass prop-erly, we must first let go of everything that shows and signifies to the eyes and all the senses, be it vestments, music, song, decoration, prayer, raising up, setting down . . . or whatever may happen in the mass, until we have grasped the words of Christ.'[74] In this view only the Word could connect inside and outside – gestures of the body could not.

Traditional piety saw gestures as public and essential; Luther saw them as private and optional: 'It is of no great importance whether one stands, kneels, or falls to the ground because these are bodily practices, neither prohibited nor commanded as necessary.'[75] In his 1523 tract on the veneration of the Sacrament he described Christian prayer as 'righteous and spiritual so that it is free of all external things. One does not need to have special places or use special gestures.'[76] Gestures could reflect the human will, but they could not create virtues like peace in the inner person.[77] The magisterial Protestant denunciation of the works of the body overrode the clearly scriptural origins of the kiss of peace.

The Church historian Thomas Lentes has shown how the connection of the movements of the body to the state of the soul was also denied by Zwingli and Bucer.[78] He documents the start of this trend in the late fifteenth century, as traditional devotions such as the 'Spiritual chivalry' ('Geistliche Ritterschaft') that included bodily imitation of Christ's Passion gave way to moral and textual understandings of piety.[79] Desiderius Erasmus epitomised this trend away from the body and towards the Word in the foreword to his 1516 edition of the New Testament. 'An image, if it represents anything at all, represents only the form of the body', he explained. The Scriptures on the other hand 'set before you the living picture of his sacred mind, Christ as he actually spoke . . . rendering him so completely present that you would see less of him if you had him directly in front of your eyes'. A relic or image of Christ that one might kiss like a pax could never compare with the Word: 'Should anyone produce a tunic worn by Christ, we would hurry to the ends of the earth to kiss it. But you might assemble his entire wardrobe, and it would contain nothing that Christ did not express more explicitly and truly in the evangelic books.'[80] This devaluation of the body and its gestures would ultimately destroy the kiss of peace.

Of course, the established Protestant churches of the sixteenth century rejected the ritual kiss of peace for a less abstract reason as well: its association with the Anabaptist movement, the persecuted 'radical wing' of the Protestant Reformation. True to their biblicism, the Anabaptists (forerunners of today's Mennonites) greeted one another with a kiss of peace in daily life and in their commemoration of the Lord's Supper. These radicals revived the two ancient roles of the holy kiss, 'salutatory and ritual'.[81] The code of discipline they adopted at Strasbourg in 1568 described the practice: '11. The brethren and sisters, each to each, shall greet each other with a holy kiss; those who have not been received into fellowship shall not be greeted with a kiss, but with the words, "May the Lord help you".'[82] Most of our evidence of the early Anabaptists' use of the holy kiss comes from accounts of imprisonment and martyrdom; the first reference is from the execution of twelve Anabaptists in Austria in 1528.[83] The Anabaptist adoption of the kiss of peace places its rejection by the established Protestant churches in especially sharp focus.

### TOWARDS THE MODERN KISS

By the end of the fifteenth century, a set of larger cultural shifts called into question each aspect of the ritual kiss of peace. It was meant to be a public act, but the face-to-face kiss of peace had been supplanted by the pax-board because clergy and laypeople found the public face-to-face kiss (same-sex or mixed) increasingly troubling. The kiss disappeared from the theory and practice of the related secular ritual of homage in this period as well. The *Pax* was meant to be chaste and spiritual, but the boundaries between praise-worthy and sinful kisses became less secure as concerns about lust and pride surrounded a gesture of peace and concord.

Fundamental to the *Pax* was the belief that public gesture could and should connect body and spirit in mutual influence. But when reformers like Erasmus emphasised sacred texts over pious bodies, they undermined the medieval understanding of gesture. Luther and his followers then explicitly reinter-preted the correspondence between soul and body, inside and outside. Here, as with other aspects of the body, the Protestant Reformation consolidated theologically and institutionally the cultural shifts of the fifteenth century.[84]

German Protestants now tended to see the power of a public gesture to affect the inner person as transgressive, to be either denied, concealed or forbidden. When an ailing Lutheran youth in the Spanish Netherlands, far from his Nuremberg home, viewed the famous procession of the Holy Sacrament in Brussels in 1577, he described in his diary the monstrance carried in the procession as a 'gimmick' ('Gauckelwerk') – but he also joined the hundreds who kissed the monstrance, perhaps in hopes of healing.[85] This otherwise devout Lutheran's act reveals two contradictory but coexisting Prot-estant attitudes towards the public ritual kiss: it could be seen as a meaning-less gesture, but also as a transgressive connection between body and spirit.

The Protestant separation of inside and outside made it much more difficult for the kiss to connect social values like peace, Christian unity or political order with the individual: its versatile range of meanings was lost. The Easter week services of the traditional Church affirmed the ambiguity of the kiss by providing extra opportunities for the *Pax* to aid the reconciliation of parishioners during the first part of the week; on Maundy Thursday, in memory of a kiss of betrayal, the *Pax* was explicitly omitted from the mass. By universalising this omission, Protestant liturgies suggested that public kisses were always treacherous. The resulting shift of the kiss from the social to the erotic, and from the communal to the private, is fundamental to its place in the modern West.

## NOTES

1 Karl Pallas (ed.), *Die Registraturen der Kirchenvisitationen im ehemals Sächsischen Kurkreise* (Halle, 1906–18), ii:1, pp. 299–305 (Schmiedeberg, 1528): 'Anno domini 1528 donerstags nach Simonis und Judae [29 October] ... in der stat Schmidberg ... 5 kleine silberne pacem; 2 gute ubergult pacem'. Also published in Emil Sehling (ed.), *Die Evangelischen Kirchenordnungen des XVI. Jahrhunderts* (Leipzig und Tübingen,

1902– ), i, p. 662. For other reports of the destruction of pax-boards see Pallas (ed.), *Registraturen*, ii:1, pp. 365–70 (town of Zahna, 1528) and ii:2, p. 3 (Bitterfeld, 1531).

2 Following the usage of Bossy, *Pax* refers to the ritual kiss; 'pax-board' refers to the liturgical object so kissed, also called the pacificale or *osculatorium*. See also John P. Hardy, 'What is a Pax?', *The Connoisseur*, 131 (1953), 37.

3 John Bossy, 'The Mass as a Social Institution 1200–1700', *Past & Present*, 100 (1983), 29–61.

4 *Ibid.*, 58.

5 *Ibid.*, 59. Bossy also argues (p. 56) that 'the Reformers ... abolished it from their eucharistic rites ... on more theoretical grounds ... notably for its suggestion of a contractual element in the salvation of Christians'.

6 The related abandonment of the *Pax* by the Roman Catholic Church in the early modern period is discussed by Bossy, 'Mass', 58–60, and Joseph Braun, *Das Christliche Altargerät in seinem Sein und in seiner Entwicklung* (Munich, 1932), p. 560. On the kiss of peace in the Roman Catholic Church since the Second Vatican Council, see Thomas J. Reese, 'In the Catholic Church, a Kiss is Never Just a Kiss', *America*, 172:13 (1995), 12–20.

7 On the kiss in the Middle Ages see Yannick Carré, *Le Baiser sur la bouche au Moyen Age: Rites, symboles, mentalités, à travers les textes et les images, XIe–XVe siècles* (Paris, 1992); Klaus Schreiner, ' "Er küsse mich mit dem Kuß seines Mundes" (Osculetur me oscolo oris sui, Cant. 1,1): Metaphorik, kommunicative und herrschaftliche Funktionen einer symbolischen Handlung', in Hedda Ragotzky and Horst Wenzel (eds), *Höfische Representation: Das Zeremoniell und die Zeichen* (Tübingen, 1990), pp. 89–132; and the material in James R. Reusser, 'The History of the Ordinance of the Holy Kiss until the Reformation', research paper, Mennonite Biblical Seminary, Chicago, 1952. A copy is held in the Mennonite Historical Library, Goshen College, Goshen, Indiana.

8 Tertullian, 'On Prayer', in Alexander Roberts and James Donaldson (eds), *The Ante-Nicene Fathers* (New York, 1925), iii, p. 686 (ch. 18, 'Of the Kiss of Peace').

9 Augustine of Hippo, 'Easter Sermons', in Saint Augustine, *Sermons on the Liturgical Seasons*, trans. Mary Sarah Muldowney, The Fathers of the Church: A New Translation, 38 (New York, 1959), pp. 197–8 (sermon 227). See Carré, *Baiser sur la bouche*, pp. 222–5 on the *Pax* in the ancient Church.

10 Gregory Dix, *The Shape of the Liturgy* (London, 1945), pp. 105–10, and Adrian Fortescue, *The Mass: A Study of the Roman Liturgy* (London, 1922), p. 372.

11 Carré, *Baiser sur la bouche*, pp. 221–307, Schreiner, 'Funktionen einer symbolischen Handlung', pp. 92–102, and Rudolf Suntrup, *Die Bedeutung der liturgischen Gebärden und Bewegnungen in lateinischen und deutschen Auslegungen des 9. bis 13. Jahrhunderts*, Münstersche Mittelalter-Schriften, 37 (Munich, 1978), pp. 362–78. The symbolism of the kiss in Christian ritual is, as Klaus Schreiner has noted, 'ein Thema ohne Grenzen'.

12 Carré, *Baiser sur la bouche*, pp. 153–219, Schreiner, 'Funktionen einer symbolischen Handlung', pp. 113–29, and J. Russell Major, ' "Bastard Feudalism" and the Kiss: Changing Social Mores in Late Medieval and Early Modern France', *Journal of Interdisciplinary History*, 17 (1987), 509–35, and Hans-Wolfgang Strätz, 'Der Kuss im Recht', in Gisela Völger and Karin von Welck (eds), *Die Braut: Geliebt, Verkauft, Getauscht, Geraubt: Zur Rolle der Frau im Kulturvergleich* (Cologne, 1985), i, pp. 286–93.

13 It was practised in the liturgies of the heretical Cathars and Waldensians, for example. See Schreiner, 'Funktionen einer symbolischen Handlung', pp. 101–2 n. 30.

14 As discussed in Schreiner, 'Funktionen einer symbolischen Handlung', pp. 108–10. See Johannes von Paltz, *Werke*, ed. Christoph Burger and Friedhelm Stasch (Berlin, 1983), i, pp. 154–7: 'Decimum osculum commendabile dicitur christianae unionis, quod forte est complementum omnium praedicatorum osculorum et forte ab ipsis quasi omnibus

figuratim, et dicitur "osculum sanctum" 1 Ad Corinthios 16 et 2 Ad Corinthios 13. Hoc etiam significatur in osculo pacis.'

15 'mit dem mund, knye bogen, kussen, odder ander geberden wirt geehrt, szo das nit im hertzenn durch den glaubenn in gottis hulde tzuvorsicht geschicht, ist es doch nichts, dan ein schein und farb der gleissenery'. Martin Luther, *D. Martin Luthers Werke: Kritische Gesamtausgabe* (Weimar, 1883–) (hereafter WA), vi, p. 218.

16 Berthold Pirstinger, Bishop of Chiemsee, *Keligpuchel: Ob der Kelig ausserhalb der Mess zeraithen sey* (Munich [?], 1535), §7: 'des Pacem kuß verspotten und ander christenliche gepär verachten'. On Pirstinger see Ernst Walter Zeeden, 'Berthold von Chiemsee (1465–1543)', in Erwin Iserloh (ed.), *Katholische Theologen der Reformationszeit* (Münster, 1986–88), i, pp. 65–75 and the literature cited there.

17 On Gerson see Martin Nicol, *Meditation bei Luther* (Göttingen, 1984), p. 72.

18 Thomas Aquinas, *The Summa contra gentiles of Saint Thomas Aquinas*, trans. English Dominican Fathers (London, 1928), iii:2, p. 102 (bk 3, cap. 119). For the Latin text see www.unav.es/filosofia/alarcon/amicis/ctintroi.html (accessed June 2002).

19 Aquinas, *Summa contra gentiles*, iii:2, p. 102.

20 See the studies of Jean-Claude Schmitt, 'The Rationale of Gestures in the West: Third to Thirteenth Centuries', in Jan Bremmer and Herman Roodenburg (eds), *A Cultural History of Gesture: From Antiquity to the Present Day* (Ithaca, 1991), 59–70, and his Introduction to Jean-Claude Schmitt (ed.), *Gestures*, History and Anthropology, 1 (London, 1984), pp. 1–28. See also Volker Saftien, 'Rhetorische Mimik und Gestik: Konturen epochenspezifischen Verhaltens', *Archiv für Kulturgeschichte*, 77:1 (1995), 197–216, and the articles in *Sénéfiance*, 41 (1998), 1–624, a special volume on 'Le Geste et les gestes au Moyen Age'.

21 Johann von Staupitz, *Sämtliche Schriften: Abhandlungen, Predigten, Zeugnisse*, ed. Lothar Graf zu Dohna and Richard Wetzel (Berlin, 1979), ii, p. 189: '[solche] erfarnheit, in dero got mer geschmeckt dann gesehen wirdet . . . den andern seins geschmacks mit verstendigen noch volliglich berichten mag'. From the German translation of the *De exsecutione aeternae predestinationis* (1518).

22 Staupitz, *Sämtliche Schriften*, ii, p. 189: 'Darumb müsen wir diese dingk aus der leer gots schöpfen und, das geschöpft ist, erquicken mit gleichnüsen, ebenbilden, figuren, und menschlicher einbildung.'

23 *Ibid.*, ii, p. 193.

24 Pirstinger, *Keligpuchel*, §7: 'Entlich wirdt das sichting Pacem durch die umbstender außwendig mit dem mund gekußt / dadurch anzezaigen daß sy inwendig im gemüt unsichtigen leib und kelig Christi geistlich geopffert und genossen haben.'

25 Braun, *Das Christliche Altargerät*, p. 558. See also Joseph A. Jungmann, *The Mass of the Roman Rite: Its Origins and Development* (*Missarum sollemnia*), trans. Francis A. Brunner (New York, 1955), ii, pp. 328–30, and Schreiner, 'Funktionen einer symbolischen Handlung', p. 101.

26 See Guillaume Durand, Bishop of Mende (c.1230–1296), *Rationale divinorum officiorum*, ed. A. Davril and T. M. Thibodeau, Corpus Christianorum: Continuatio Mediaevalis, 140 (Turnholt, 1995–2000); Braun, *Das Christliche Altargerät*, p. 558.

27 *Ibid.*, p. 558.

28 Guillaume Durand, *Le Racional des divins offices* . . . (Paris, 1503), fol. 133ᵛ.

29 Braun, *Das Christliche Altargerät*, p. 558.

30 The modern edition of the *Messe singen oder lesen* is Franz Rudolf Reichert (ed.), *Die älteste deutsche Gesamtauslegung der Messe*, Corpus Catholicorum, 29 (Münster, 1967). See also *Sequitur expositio misse multum utilis pro regentibus curam animarum clericis simplicibus necnon et laycis qui se informare possunt ex eadem salutifera expositione, ut*

*patet in processu. Hyenach volget gar ein lobliche heylsame ausslegung der heyligen messe* ... (Augspurg, 1484), British Library, London, IB.5716, and Adolph Franz, *Die Messe im deutschen Mittelalter* (Darmstadt, 1963), pp. 711–17.

31 See Bossy, 'Mass', 30.

32 Reichert (ed.), *Gesamtauslegung der Messe*, p. 184: 'Der diacon oder altar diener der tregt denn hin das selbe gekueste tefelein den andernn priesternn, die in dem kore sein, zekuessen. Und das kuest einer nach dem andernn mit andacht. Es ist auch an vil enden sith, das der altar diener umb tregt das selbe gekueste tefelein allen den, die hinder dem ambt oder messe stan oder knyen, einem yeden zekuessen. Und das heyst osculum pacis – der kuß des frides.'

33 Bossy, 'Mass', 30, citing Gabriel Biel, *Canonis misse expositio*, ed. Heiko Oberman and W. J. Courtney (Wiesbaden, 1963–69), iv, p. 43, and Franz, *Messe im deutschen Mittelalter*, p. 587, citing the 1494 Leipzig edition of the *Expositio misteriorium misse* of Balthasar von Pforta, fol. D4. See also Braun, *Das Christliche Altargerät*, pp. 559–62, on the use of the pax.

34 Reichert (ed.), *Gesamtauslegung der Messe*, p. 184: 'Und bedeut die verwandlung der liebe Cristi: als der Herre hat liebe zu der kirchen, und die kirch zu dem priester, und der priester zu den umsteenden.'

35 Pirstinger, *Keligpuchel*, §6: 'an stat täglicher speisung den umbständern und andern leuten underem Agnus dei das pacem oder ain heilthumb zeküssen geraicht werde ... Zu ainem anzaigen / daß ir dasselb sacrament im glaub geistlich wollet täglich empfahen / durch den kuß des frids und der ainigkait so bey dem pacem bedeyt ist.'

36 See Patricius Schlager, 'Über die Meßerklärung des Franziskaners Wilhelm von Gouda', *Franziskanische Studien*, 6 (1919), 323–36. On substitution, see Miri Rubin, *Corpus Christi: The Eucharist in Late Medieval Culture* (Cambridge, 1991), pp. 73–7.

37 Pirstinger, *Keligpuchel*, §7: 'Welcher aber auß rainem hertzen das Pacem zeküssen sucht / derselb bekent daß er gegen seinem negsten wölle fridlich und gut freundlich sein / ime auch begegenn in ainigkait des glaubs durch unsern herren Jesum Christum / der auffm altar des creutzes vorzeiten leiblich geopffert ist und yetz auffm altar durch den priester sacramentlich / daneben durch die umbstender geistlich geopffert und genossen wirt. Deßhalb yglicher umbstender sich mitt solchem kuß erzaigt daß er hab das heylig sacrament geistlich geopffert und genossen in warem glaub und rechter lieb.'

38 On the dangerous ambiguity of the kiss, see Beatrix Bastl, 'Intimität und Höflichkeit: Gesten und Orte der Intimität und deren Ambivalenz in der Zeit', in Christa Tuczay, Ulrike Hirhager and Karin Lichtblau (eds), *Ir sult sprechen Willekomen: Grenzenlose Mediävistik: Festschrift für Helmut Birkhan zum 60. Geburtstag* (Bern and New York, 1998), pp. 361–415, esp. pp. 363–74.

39 Paltz, *Werke*, ed. Burger and Stasch, i:XVII, XXXV, pp. 147, 154–7. The comments of Paltz and Dorsten on the kiss are discussed briefly in Schreiner, 'Funktionen einer symbolischen Handlung', p. 110.

40 Paltz, *Werke*, i, p. 155: 'osculum corporale est triplex: Quoddam est commendabile, quoddam excusabile, quoddam destabile'.

41 *Ibid.*, i, p. 156. The authors did not mention the *osculum infame* discussed in Chapter 2 below.

42 G. H. Buijssen (ed.), *Durandus' Rationale in spätmittelhochdeutscher Übersetzung: Das vierte Buch nach der Hs. CVP 2765*, Studia theodisca, 6 (Assen, 1966), p. 329: 'Darumb, welich sich chuzzent und sind hessig, di voligent nach den vorreter Juda.' The German translation of Durandus's *Rationale* was completed c.1406. In the original, 'qui ergo se

odientes osculantur, Iude proditoris osculum imitantur.' Durand, *Rationale divinorum officiorum*, ed. Davril and Thibodeau, p. 545 (bk 6, ch. 53).

43 Suntrup, *Liturgischen Gebärden*, p. 377, citing twelve commentaries on the mass from Amalarius of Metz (775–852) to Durandus.

44 G. H. Buijssen (ed.), *Durandus' Rationale in Spätmittelhochdeutscher Übersetzung: Die Bücher V–VIa nach der Hs. CVP 2765*, Studia theodisca, 15 (Assen, 1983), p. 295 (bk 6, ch. 69): 'Auch an den drin tag spricht man nicht DOMINUS VOBISCUM ... Darumb geit man auch nicht daz paecz, der böz gruez geschach mit dem chuz.'

45 G. H. Buijssen (ed.), *Durandus' Rationale in Spätmittelhochdeutscher Übersetzung: Die Bücher VIb–VIII nach der Hs. CVP 2765*, Studia theodisca, 16 (Assen, 1983), p. 49 (bk 6, ch. 82): 'Man geit auch nicht daz pecz, zw einer smach des chus Jude, dez vorretter.'

46 Reichert (ed.), *Gesamtauslegung der Messe*, p. 182: 'Und das altag im jare ane an dem gruenen donerstag ... Und das bedeut, das der Here durch das zeychen des frids durch Judam in dem kuß verraten und gegeben ward dem Juden in dem Tod.'

47 Suntrup, *Liturgischen Gebärden*, pp. 377–8.

48 Jungmann, *Mass of the Roman Rite*, ii, p. 322, quoting Hippolytus of Rome (d. c.236). See also Major, ' "Bastard feudalism" and the kiss', pp. 510–11, citing Clement of Alexandria (d. c.215).

49 See the reference in Bossy, 'Mass', p. 56 to Biel, *Canonis misse expositio*, ed. Oberman and Courtney, iv, pp. 30–2, and Johan Huizinga, *The Autumn of the Middle Ages*, trans. Rodney J. Payton and Ulrich Mammitzsch (Chicago, 1996), p. 147.

50 Buijssen, (ed.), *Durandus' Rationale in spätmittelhochdeutscher Übersetzung: Das Vierte Buch*, p. 329 (bk 4, ch. 40): 'Auch die man und die weiber nicht gegen einander den chuzz reichent, daz icht villeicht ettleichew gailheit auffderstet.'

51 Johannes Bechofen, *Quadruplex missalis expositio* ... (Basel, 1505), fol. F3ʳ as quoted in Franz, *Messe im deutschen Mittelalter*, p. 594: 'Licet autem olim sicut et hodie in plerisque locis hoc osculum pacis a sacerdote per ministrum porrectum fideles sibi mutuo imprimat, tamen honestior est cautela, ut per pacificale sive tabulam imaginem Christi aut sanctorum reliquias continentem fiat, ne sub specie boni aliquid carnalitas diabolico inflatu surripiat.'

52 H. Maynard Smith, *Pre-Reformation England* (New York, 1963), p. 97, citing Chaucer and Thomas More.

53 Christine de Pisan, *The Treasure of the City of Ladies, or, The Book of the Three Virtues*, trans. Sarah Lawson (Harmondsworth, 1985), p. 136.

54 *Ibid.*, p. 136.

55 Braun, *Das Christliche Altargerät*, p. 560.

56 Smith, *Pre-Reformation England*, p. 97. Huizinga also describes a related practice, the hyper-courteous refusal to kiss the pax before someone else, in *Autumn of the Middle Ages*, pp. 48–9.

57 Bossy, 'Mass', p. 56.

58 Michael Schröter, 'Zur Intimisierung des Hochzeitsnacht im 16. Jahrhundert: Eine zivilisationstheoretische Studie', in Hans Jürgen Bachorski (ed.), *Ordnung und Lust: Bilder von Liebe, Ehe und Sexualität in spätmittelalter und früher Neuzeit* (Trier, 1991), pp. 359–414, esp. pp. 378–404.

59 Major, ' "Bastard feudalism" and the Kiss', 514–21.

60 Carré, *Baiser sur la bouche*, pp. 322–36. See also J. C. Bologne, 'Du sacré à l'Intime: Rituels, sacrés, officiels', in Gérald Cahen (ed.), *Le Baiser: Premières leçons d'amour*, Autrement: Série mutations, 169 (Paris, 1997), pp. 45–66: 'A partir de la Renaissance, le baiser va perdre peu à peu sa fonction officielle et sacrée' (p. 45).

61 Johann Eberlin von Günzburg, *Ain kurtzer geschrifftlicher Bericht etlicher Puncten halb Christlichs Glauben, zügeschickt der Cristen zü Ulm . . .* (Augsburg, 1523), fol. c1ʳ: 'Von der Meß / Für die verkündigung des Evangelii lißt man yetz haymlich ain stück von der biblia . . . Für gemain gepet ist das gschray der Korsinger und dß bombeln der orgeln. Für enpfahung des sacraments / gibt man dß pacem zeküssen.'

62 Martin Luther, 'Eyn sermon von dem newen Testament, das ist von der heyligen Messe', WA, vi, p. 374: 'mit der weyße mochten sie uns auch die ander gestalt nemen und die ledige monstranzen fur heylthumb zu küssen geben.'

63 '"Grusset euch untereynander mit dem kuss der liebe." Dieser brauch ist ytzt abgangen. Im Evangelio lieset man klar, das Christus seyne junger mit dem kuss empfangen hatt, und ist solchs gewest eyne weyse ynn den lendern.' WA, xii, p. 399.

64 Luther's lectures on the Song of Solomon were printed in 1539. See WA, xxxi:2, p. 594: 'Loquitur pro more illius populi. Apud nos minus honesta oscula habentur. Sunt autem oscula amoris et favoris signa.'

65 See the *Formula missae* of 1523, WA, xii, p. 213; Eng. trans. in R. C. D. Jasper and G. J. Cuming, ed., *Prayers of the Eucharist: Early and Reformed*, 2nd edn (New York, 1980), p. 138. Echoing Luther's 'vertical' sense of peace, the Prussian church ordinance of 1525 described the prayer of peace as 'absolution': 'then the pastor turns to the people immediately and gives them the evangelical absolution or peace and sings in German "the peace of the Lord etc."' See Sehling (ed.), *Kirchenordnungen*, iv, p. 32.

66 See Leonhard Fendt, *Der Lutherische Gottesdienst des 16. Jahrhunderts: Sein Werden und sein Wachsen* (München, 1923), pp. 82–101, and Julius Smend, *Die Evangelischen deutschen Messen bis zu Luthers deutscher Messe* (Göttingen, 1896), pp. 198, 209. Zwingli retained this practice from the traditional mass: see Suntrup, *Liturgischen Gebärden*, p. 362.

67 It is true that fifteenth-century mass rubrics did not always specifically call for the *Pax*, but the occasional absence of the *Pax* in traditional liturgical texts does not mean that the kiss itself was absent (as is confirmed by other evidence, such as the use of the pax-board). The Protestant liturgies sought to eliminate any arbitrary embellishments of the service, so that the absence of the *Pax* in Protestant liturgy meant that it was certainly excluded.

68 In Reformation visual propaganda, most influentially in the 'Passional Christi und Antichristi' of Lucas Cranach and Luther, we see the kiss in the direst and most perverted contexts, and again, there is no interest in restoring a 'proper' kiss between the Pope and a king or an emperor. See Karl-August Wirth, 'Imperator pedes papae deosculatur: Ein Beitrag zur Bildkunde des 16. Jahrhunderts', in Hans Martin Freiherrn von Erffa and Elisabeth Herget (eds), *Festschrift für Harald Keller, zum sechzigsten Geburtstag, dargebracht von seinen Schülern* (Darmstadt, 1963), pp. 175–221, and Schreiner, 'Funktionen einer symbolischen Handlung', pp. 117–29.

69 John Bossy, *Peace in the Post-Reformation* (Cambridge and New York, 1998), pp. 56–7.

70 WA, i, pp. 229–38, 'Disputatio pro declaratione virtutis indulgentiarum.' Luther draws on Acts 14:22, 'exhorting them to continue in their faith, and saying that through many tribulations we must enter the Kingdom of God', but has added 'rather than through the false security of peace'.

71 Georg Witzel, *Von der Heiligen Eucharisty odder Mess, nach Anweisung der Schrifft . . .* (Leipzig, 1534), fol. oᵛ, which emphasises the importance of gesture in the conflict: 'ja es ist dardurch eben das heilig Sacrament ynn grosse unacht gefallen. Wie viel wirt itzt gehört? . . . Kleydung / Creutz zeychen . . . hende heben / küssen rc. ist narrenwerck.' On Witzel see Barbara Henze, *Aus Liebe zur Kirche Reform: Die Bemühungen Georg*

*Witzels (1501–1573) um die Kircheneinheit* (Münster, 1995), and the literature cited there.

72 Pirstinger, *Keligpuchel*, §7: 'Nachdem wir aber in diser unrichten zeit / teglich meß versaumen / des Pacem kuß verspotten und ander christenliche gepär verachten / gleich als wollen wir kain fridliche verwandtnuß noch ordenliche lieb gegeneinander halten. Darumb müssen wir leiden krieg und beschwärung auch ander ungesell von Turcken und unglaubigen / von Lutherischen und Zwinglichen / von Zwytauffern und ander ketzern . . .'

73 Martin Luther, 'Von den guten Werken', 1520, WA, vi, p. 218.

74 *Idem*, 'Eyn Sermon von dem newen Testament', 1520: 'Wollen wir recht mess halten und versteen so mussen wir alles faren lassen was die augen und alle synnen in diesem handel mogen zaigen und antragen / es sey klaid / klang / gesang / zierd.' WA, vi, p. 355.

75 From Luther's sermons on the Gospel of John, 1528: 'Da ligt nu kein grosse macht an, ob man stehe, knie oder niederfalle, denn es sind leibliche weise wider verworffen noch geboten als noetig . . . allein das man sie nicht verachte, weil sie die schrift und Christus selbst lobet.' WA, xxviii, pp. 74–5.

76 *Idem*, 'Von Anbeten des Sakraments des heiligen Leichnams Christi', 1523: 'Das ander anbeten ist rechtschaffen unnd geystlich, das ist ynn allen euserlichen dingen frey, also das man nicht von notten muesse sondere ortter haben odder sondere geperde furen.' WA, xi, p. 445.

77 In his writings against the spiritualists, Luther did stress the scriptural basis of some personal prayer gestures. See Nicol, *Meditation bei Luther*, pp. 72–3.

78 Thomas Lentes, ' "Andacht" und "Gebärde": Das religiöse Ausdrucksverhalten', in Bernhard Jussen and Craig Koslofsky (eds), *Kulturelle Reformation: Sinnformationen im Umbruch 1400–1600*, Veröffentlichungen des Max-Planck-Instituts für Geschichte, 145 (Göttingen, 1999), pp. 29–68. These reformers were echoed by John Marbeck, in *A Book of Notes and Common Places* (London, 1581), who remarked that 'Some foolishly imagine that praier is made either better or worse by the jesture of our bodyes', as quoted in Keith Thomas, 'Introduction', in Bremmer and Roodenburg (eds), *A Cultural History of Gesture*, p. 6.

79 Lentes, ' "Andacht" und "Gebärde" ', pp. 58–61 and illustrations 5 and 6.

80 Desiderius Erasmus, *The Praise of Folly and Other Writings: A New Translation with Critical Commentary*, ed. and trans. Robert M. Adams (New York, 1989), p. 127.

81 Reusser, 'History of the Ordinance of the Holy Kiss', p. 14: 'Thus is preserved, or rather revived, the apostolic twofold use of the holy kiss – ritualistic and salutatory.' The Anabaptists did not elaborate on a theology of gesture and spirit to 'explain' the holy kiss, referring to it always as a divine commandment.

82 Harold S. Bender, 'The Discipline Adopted by the Strasburg Conference of 1568', *Mennonite Quarterly Review*, 1:1 (1927), 61, 65.

83 Reusser, 'History of the Ordinance of the Holy Kiss', p. 15.

84 See Jussen and Koslofsky (eds), *Kulturelle Reformation*.

85 Steven Ozment, 'The Private Life of an Early Modern Teenager: A Nuremberg Lutheran Visits Catholic Louvain', *Journal of Family History*, 21:1 (1996), 22–43, at 25: 'Hab ich die Procession gesehen und das Gauckelwerk geküst.'

# 2

# *The* osculum infame: *heresy, secular culture and the image of the witches' sabbath*

<>

Jonathan Durrant

[W]hen the dance finished, one bent before the ram sitting in the chair and
had to kiss [it] reverently on the behind.[1]

THIS QUOTATION is taken from the answer given by the witch-suspect
Walburga Knab to a series of questions asked by her interrogators about
whether she worshipped the Devil, what honour she did him and in what
manner, who instructed her in this and whether she did this alone or with
others. It is a simple statement of an event which historians of the early
modern witch persecutions would probably expect to recur in any sequence
of witch-trial documents. The *osculum infame* or kiss of shame had by 1621,
when Knab was arrested, long been associated with medieval heretics. It can
be found too in the demonology which gave the witch persecutions their
theological basis, in the illustrations to these works and in the pamphlet
literature by which news of the more spectacular witch trials circulated.
A secular version of the kiss of shame appears in fictional literature, in
Chaucer's 'Miller's Tale', for example, and in Grimmelshausen's *Simplicissimus*.
Despite the established history of the obscene kiss, however, and the variety
of contexts in which it appears, Knab's short description of it is one of the
few surviving mentions of this kiss in the fairly extensive documentation
generated during the witch persecutions in Eichstätt, a prince-bishopric in
south-eastern Germany which experienced a particularly intense period of
witch-hunting between 1617 and 1631. The *osculum infame* is not the only
significant demonological detail missing from the Eichstätt witch-confession
narratives. An analysis of why it among these others was omitted offers an
alternative explanation of how a confession was constructed to the prevailing
acculturation theories which seem to imply that the witch-suspect simply
regurgitated a standard demonological version of the sabbath under duress.

## A HISTORY OF THE KISS OF SHAME

The origins of the stereotypical image of the early modern witches' sabbath have been traced in detail by Norman Cohn, Carlo Ginzburg and Stuart Clark.[2] Only in Cohn's work, however, does one get a sense of the history of the kiss of shame because it happens to be repeated in the descriptions of the nocturnal gatherings of heretics. Cohn's references to this kiss highlight the consistency with which the image recurs in texts concerning heretical groups. His history begins with the late second-century apologist for Christianity Minucius Felix. In his *Octavius*, Felix has a pagan character set out the various rumours about the practices of his Christian neighbours. Among these he reported that they worshipped the head of a donkey, and reverenced the genitals of their priests.[3] Here we have separated the two essential elements of the kiss of shame which were later conflated into one idea, the worship of an animal which was considered abject in the dominant culture and the adoration of an unclean part of the body. Felix's pagan also attributed ritual infanticide, cannibalism and orgies to the early Christians. Similar accusations were made against Jews and conspirators in the Roman Empire, and they continued to be utilised, although apparently with less voracity, in Christian propaganda against other dissident groups in the early medieval period.[4]

The kiss of shame, alongside the murder and eating of children and promiscuity and sexual abandon, then re-emerged strongly towards the end of the twelfth century in the propaganda first against the Cathars and then against the Waldensians. By this time it was the Devil in the form of an abject animal who received both the worship and the adoration of the heretics. In his *De nugis curialium* (*c*.1180), the English cleric Walter Map wrote of the 'synagogues' described by some former French heretics:

> About the first watch of the night, when gates, doors, and windows have been closed, the groups sit waiting in silence in their respective synagogues, and a black cat of marvellous size climbs down a rope which hangs in their midst. On seeing it, they put out the lights. They do not sing hymns or repeat them distinctly, but hum through clenched teeth and pantingly feel their way toward the place where they see their lord. When they have found him they kiss him, each the more humbly as he is inflamed by frenzy – some the feet, more under the tail, most the private parts.[5]

Not long afterwards, in 1233, Pope Gregory IX described the initiatory rites which were supposedly performed by novices being received into the heretical sect of the Waldensians. During these rites, a novice had to kiss three creatures. The first was a huge toad (or a goose or a duck) which he kissed on the behind or on the mouth. There followed a mysterious being whose eyes were coal-black, who was so pale and thin that he seemed merely skin and bone, and whose body was ice-cold to the touch; on kissing him, the novice forgot his Catholic faith. At some later point during the feasting, singing and orgiastic sex, a black cat descended from a statue about which the heretics had gathered, and this cat was offered the homage of a kiss on the feet, under the tail or on its genitalia by both the novice and his fellow heretics.[6] The belief that the Waldensians worshipped the Devil in the form of an animal continued well into the fifteenth century, when manuscript editions of Johannis Tinctoris's tract *Contra sectam Valdensium* were illustrated with miniatures showing members of the sect (mainly male) kneeling before a goat, one about to kiss its anus (see Figure 1).[7]

1 Waldensians adoring the Devil in the form of a he-goat. From Johannis Tinctoris, *Contra sectam Valdensium* (c.1460).

In the later Middle Ages therefore the image of the nocturnal gathering of the heretical sect – at which the Devil was worshipped and travesties of Christian liturgy were performed – had become a widely applicable stereotype. Philip IV of France, for example, found it expedient to accuse the Knights Templar of such sacrilegious practices in 1307. His aim was to break the power of this crusading military order, whose base was their house outside Paris, and confiscate its vast wealth. He could not use the secular judiciary to achieve this because these knights were subject only to the Pope; and to engage such experienced and wealthy warriors in battle would have been foolhardy and expensive. Philip chose therefore to surprise the order and arrest the knights on charges of heresy. In this way he could present himself as acting on the behalf of Pope Clement V and secure his co-operation. Among the charges levelled at the Knights Templar were that they engaged in sodomy, worshipped an idol in the shape of a head and revered a Satanic cat by removing their hats, bowing to it and kissing it on the anus.[8]

Against this historical background it is not surprising that the practices attributed to these previous sects were incorporated into the literature on the new heresy of witchcraft from the late fifteenth century onwards. In the works of theologians and jurists, for no clear reason, the kiss of shame itself did recede from the foreground. The only mention of something like the obscene kiss to be found in the most notorious of the works on the witch sect, the *Malleus maleficarum* (*c.*1486), is the anecdote that a woman whom the author had not been able to bring to trial added the words 'Give me the tongue in the arse' to the blessing bestowed on the people during mass.[9] 'Kissing the divels bare buttocks', as the English critic Reginald Scot put it, did, however, retain a central position in images of the witch sect.[10] The miniature representation of the Waldensians kneeling before their goat-god re-emerged in the late sixteenth century in forms which took account of the new context (the persecution of the largely female witch sect) and which were aimed at a much wider audience than that available for an illuminated manuscript written in Latin. A prominent image in the illustrations to a news-sheet of 1570 reporting the witch trials in Geneva was a woman (rather than a man) bending to kiss the backside of the Devil or a demon (see Figure 2).[11] And a goat sits on a stool to have its anus kissed by a woman in the highly developed representation of the Blocksberg sabbath in Johannes Praetorius's *Blockes-Berges Verrichtung* of 1668 (Figure 3); in this illustration it takes centre stage.[12]

The kiss of shame might occasionally be received, instead of given, by the witch, as shown in an early sixteenth-century woodcut by Hans Baldung Grien of a young witch with a dragon (Figure 4). The dragon sticks its long tongue into the witch's vagina from behind.[13] The kiss might also be omitted

2 Detail of 'Witches' sabbath in Geneva, 1570'. From a coloured news-sheet in Johann Jakob Wick's *Nachrichtensammlung*.

completely, as in Jan Ziarnko's detailed image of the witches' sabbath which illustrates Pierre de Lancre's *Tableau de l'inconstance des mauvais anges* of 1613, although the worship of the Devil as a goat still appears in this as a central image.[14]

Despite Scot's inclusion of the kiss of shame among the rituals performed by the alleged witch, there are no English images of this kiss from the period of intense witch persecution, and indeed the references to the witches' sabbath in English literature are not as detailed or salacious as those in contemporary European works. The lack of torture in English interrogation procedures probably accounts for this difference.[15] This is not to say that the obscene kiss was not known to English observers. The pamphlet account of the Scottish witches' seditious attack on James VI in 1590, commonly called *News from Scotland* and published in London in 1591, introduced its English readers to various elements of a continental-style witches' sabbath, including the kiss of shame. This pamphlet reports the confession made by the witch Agnes Sampson, that the Devil 'seeing that they [the North Berwick witches] tarried overlong, he at their coming enjoined them all to a penance, which was that they should kiss his buttocks in sign of duty to him; which being put over the pulpit bar, everyone did as he had enjoined them.'[16] Earlier in this pamphlet, the author reported that it had lately been found in Scotland 'that the Devil doth generally mark them [the witches] with a privy mark, by reason the witches have confessed themselves that the Devil doth lick them with his tongue in some privy part of their body before he doth receive them to be his servants'.[17] Here we have a literary description of the less common form of obscene kiss (from Devil to witch) depicted by Baldung in his woodcut of the witch and the dragon. Despite the early date of this pamphlet and the presence of James VI, who was to publish his *Daemonology* in 1597 and whose early reign in England saw the introduction of a revised witchcraft statute at the North Berwick trials, the sabbath never gained currency in English witch confessions.

3 'Witches' sabbath on Blocksberg'. From Johannes Praetorius, *Blockes-Berges Verrichtung* (1668).

4 Hans Baldung Grien, 'Young Witch with Dragon' (1515).

## CONVENTIONAL INTERPRETATIONS OF THE KISS OF SHAME

If the kiss of shame pervaded theological and pictorial representations of the heretics' gatherings, especially in Catholic Europe, what did it mean to the authors of those descriptions? Stuart Clark has noted that '[a] single ritual act such as the anal kiss perverted religious worship and secular fealty, dethroned reason from a sovereign position on which individual well-being and social relations (including political obligation) were thought to depend, and symbolised in the most obvious manner the defiant character of demonic politics as well as its preposterousness'.[18] The nineteenth-century theologian Johann Joseph von Görres regarded this kiss as a sign of the heretic's promise of eternal servitude to the Devil, suggesting that the perversion of normal Christian rituals could not disguise a similarity of function.[19] Norman Cohn has likewise suggested that for their opponents the rituals at the heretics' gatherings affirmed the solidarity, and therefore the potential danger, of the group of conspirators who partook of them.[20] These interpretations of the heretics' rituals are complementary, but they are not exhaustive.

Theologians and orthodox Catholic propagandists could conceive of heretical gatherings only in ritual form. Like Map, they may have used the terms 'synagogue' and 'sabbath' pejoratively to align the heretics with the Jews, but these gatherings were still understood as ritualised religious occasions. In this context the kiss of shame might be regarded as having the same function as the kiss of peace or *osculum pacis* while being also a parody of that Christian ritual. The kiss of peace derived from Paul's friendly injunctions in his epistles to the early Christians, that the brethren should greet each other with a holy kiss.[21] It was incorporated into the sacrament of the Eucharist early in Christian history as a symbol of *compaternitas* or god-brotherhood.[22] The Eucharist was the natural home of the kiss of peace as it too signified the unity of Christians. For the mass to retain its meaning, one had to be at peace with God and one's fellow Christians, and this required confession of one's sins and the laying aside, if not the resolving, of disagreements. The witches' sabbath was an inverted Eucharist (hence the modern term 'black mass'). To be worthy of partaking of the cannibalistic feast, including the obscene kiss (and here one might note the cannibalistic element of transubstantiation, the literal eating of Christ's flesh and the drinking of his blood), a witch was meant to 'confess' her evil deeds. The kiss of shame was therefore transformed into a symbol of devil-brotherhood, or, in the case of witches, sisterhood.

But the kiss of shame was more than just a parody of the kiss of peace and a symbol of the heretics' solidarity. The physical act of putting one's lips to the anus, buttocks or genitalia revealed other attributes of the witch sect and the character of the witch. It is interesting that descriptions of the *osculum infame* give an alternative site of kissing: the feet. This detail has its origins in the Gospel episode in which a sinner, usually identified as Mary Magdalene, washed Christ's feet with her tears. After she had dried them with her hair and anointed them with perfume, she kissed them.[23] The whole ritual was one of adoration and reverence, and the kiss element of it became incorporated into the rituals of greeting the Pope.[24] The kiss offered by Mary Magdalene to Jesus, king of the Jews, also reflected the kiss given by Samuel to Saul after he had anointed him king of Israel, a kiss which found its way into European coronation ceremonies.[25] In this sense the kiss could be interpreted as an act of fealty and honour. Alternatively, the kissing of feet could be used as a sign of humility not to sovereigns, but to God. Until James II's exile after the Glorious Revolution of 1688, the English monarch kissed the feet of those among whom Maundy money was distributed.[26] In this performance it was the monarch who was demonstrating his humility before

God, an act of fealty in itself. In kissing the Devil, therefore, his acolytes were adoring him, showing him fealty and rejecting Christ as well as signifying their unity as a community of believers.

## PUNISHMENT AND HUMILIATION

The kiss of shame did not only serve these religious functions. In her notes to *News from Scotland*, Barbara Rosen has observed that the kiss demanded by the Devil from his followers was a humiliating punishment.[27] They were forced to do it because they 'tarried overlong'. This function of the kiss also has a long tradition. As Rosen points out, the anal kiss described in Chaucer's 'Miller's Tale' is also forced upon the giver as a humiliation.[28] Importuned at night by her hapless suitor Absalon to satisfy his lust for her by granting a kiss, Alison, the adulterous wife, agrees to oblige him. Instead she sticks her 'hole' (Chaucer's terminology) out of the window; and Absalon 'Put up his mouth and kissed her arse / Most savorously before he knew of this'.[29]

In this story the kiss is comic, but in Grimmelshausen's *Simplicissimus*, a fictional autobiography of a soldier set in the Thirty Years' War (1618–48) and published in 1668, this humiliating kiss is deployed in a sinister fashion. It occurs twice, and in both cases the consequences for the characters involved are serious. In the first of these episodes, Simplicissimus watches an encounter between a party of soldiers and some peasants whom they have caught burying something. When challenged the peasants run away. The soldiers decide to dig up whatever has been buried, and it turns out to be a comrade of theirs, still alive sealed in a barrel. He recounts that he and five other foragers were captured by the peasants on the previous day. These peasants had lined their captives up one behind the other and shot at them. The interred soldier had survived because he was at the back of this line and the bullet never reached him. The peasants then cut off his ears and nose, both of which were contemporary punishments used to brand criminals and were therefore another form of humiliation,[30] but first he had to lick the 'arses' of five of his captors. He begged then to be killed with a bullet, but they refused and buried him alive. While the soldier is telling his story, the fleeing peasants have been captured. The responses of the soldiers who find the mutilated forager are interesting. Two are made to speak: the treatment by the peasants 'brings shame on all soldiers,' says the first; but the other observes that it was the trooper's cowardice in performing the act that dishonoured the military. Finally, the soldiers agree that their dishonour, regardless of who caused it, should be avenged by forcing the peasants to perform the same act on some of them. The peasants (towards whom the author is sympathetic throughout the novel) maintain their own honour by

obstinately refusing. As the hero leaves the scene the peasants are being pun-
ished with torture (having ropes rubbed across their backsides until they
bleed), but he does not know what the soldiers then did to them.[31]

In the second episode, Simplicissimus exacts revenge on another soldier
who has been impersonating him and terrorising the local countryside.
Simplicissimus tricks the impostor into rustling some sheep and in the ensu-
ing encounter makes him believe that he is accompanied by the Devil (a
comrade 'dressed in a horrible Devil's costume with huge goat's horns').[32]
The impostor, too afraid to take up the challenge to a duel, shits in his
trousers and agrees to kiss the arses of three sheep he has intended to steal.[33]
Simplicissimus also scratches his face all over, which is, like the disfiguration
of the soldier in the first episode, an act designed to inscribe the man's
dishonour on his body in a way that could not easily be disguised.[34] It was
also the very opposite to a recognisable scar of the wound an honourable
soldier might receive in battle or in a duel such as that from which the
impostor escaped.

### THE KISS OF SHAME AS AN ACT OF DISHONOUR

In its religious and literary contexts, the kiss of shame demonstrated a lack of
integrity and honour on the part of the performer. The function of this kiss
resonated more widely than that, however, in early modern popular culture.
It was a sodomitical, unnatural, adulterous and unsocial act. In the kiss of
shame the world was turned upside down in a more comprehensive way than
in contemporary portrayals of Phyllis riding Aristotle or disorderly dancing
at the witches' sabbaths.

There is a clear symbolic connection in both the demonological and literary kisses of shame between uncleanliness and abjection on the one hand and
dishonour on the other. The function of the anus makes it literally unclean
and consequently a site of symbolic uncleanliness. A certain scatological genre
of early modern literature manipulated this connection to comic and satirical
effect. The impostor in the second description of the kiss of shame in
*Simplicissimus* shitted in his trousers, something which the hero had done
out of fear earlier in the novel.[35] Many of the adventures recounted in
another German text, *Till Eulenspiegel*, involved baring buttocks to mock and
humiliate, and defecating on food and religious objects and in important
buildings.[36] Pollution with excrement in this text became a means through
which the author could comment on and criticise seemingly inviolable elements of early modern life. In later representations of the witches' gatherings,
the Devil can also sometimes be seen defecating. One of the larger figures in
the image of the Blocksberg sabbath of 1669 is the black Devil at the bottom
of the scene, wings spread, shitting into a chamber pot.

To kiss the anus therefore was to pollute oneself, but from our modern hygienic perspective we may not appreciate the full extent of this pollution. Other early modern figures were polluted in a symbolic sense by the practices of their profession. An obvious example is the executioner. His trade brought him into direct physical contact with the social excrement of society – criminals – and through this association it was considered that merely touching his clothing or dancing with his daughter could rob someone of their honour.[37] It is not surprising therefore that the executioner performed other dishonourable tasks. The late eighteenth-century executioner of Bremen, Johann Christian Göppel, for example, was also the local knacker; in addition he buried suicides, castrated dogs and, significantly in the context of this discussion on anuses, removed human excrement.[38]

To kiss an anus, whether it was human, animal or diabolical, was to align oneself symbolically with polluted characters like the executioner. Jonas Liliequist's research into bestiality in early modern Sweden shows how this worked in practice. For reasons which remain unclear, bestiality seems to have been prosecuted more frequently in Sweden than elsewhere at this time – between 1635 and 1754, about 1500 cases of bestiality came before the Swedish courts.[39] In contrast, there were only eight cases of same-sex male acts (like bestiality classed as 'sodomy' or 'buggery') over the same period.[40] In my own research on the prince-bishopric of Eichstätt, I have come across only one confession of bestiality which was neither solicited nor prosecuted by the judges trying that particular case of witchcraft.[41] In most agrarian communities, however, it is more than likely that boys lacking other opportunities to release sexual tension at least fantasised about sex with the animals with which they worked closely and which they watched copulating.[42] The range of bestiality recorded in the Swedish trial depositions included penetrative sex with cows and, more often, mares, as well as kissing a mare's pudenda. In two episodes which would not have been out of place in Grimmelshausen's novel, soldiers and servants forced other men to kiss the vulva of a mare.[43] In doing so, they humiliated their real victims, just as Simplicissimus humiliated his fictional one.

In the context of this chapter, suspicion or knowledge that a person, usually an adult male, had 'sodomised' an animal led to the imposition of the social sanctions normally reserved for the executioner onto the 'bugger'. Family, colleagues and neighbours distanced themselves from him as far as possible, to the extent that brothers and sons would sever kinship ties, and they symbolised and articulated this distance by refusing to eat or drink with that person.[44] Although everyday social relations between executioners and their neighbours did not always entail the extreme sanction of exclusion from ordinary meals, these men would not have been tolerated at the tables of the social elite at public festivities, and their children were not permitted to marry into 'honourable' households.[45] They were polluted by their actions as the bugger was polluted by his action, and that pollution could spread by association, particularly by the sharing of food; it was contagious and threatened the moral well-being of the whole community, like the excrement which threatened its physical and social well-being through disease if it was not cleared away. In the same way, the witch, who had also kissed a bestial figure, could seduce her neighbours into the witch sect (that is, pollute them with heresy), sometimes through the gift of food. Several Eichstätt witches, for example, confessed that their seductions took place at baptismal or wedding celebrations.[46] It is no coincidence, either, that Snow White was corrupted by her witch stepmother when she accepted the invitation to eat of the poisoned apple, or, indeed, that Eve's taste of the fruit of the tree of knowledge led to the fall of man.[47]

A second reaction to a 'bugger' was to assume that the Devil had somehow been involved. In Sweden, bestiality was 'Devilry', and witnesses to it often declared to the perpetrator, 'The Devil has taken you', or a similar comment.[48] At the moment of the encounter between the witness and the bugger, the former must sometimes have had in mind an image of the witch's seduction by a Devil with cloven feet or horses' hooves. This is an image with a strong presence in the demonology of witchcraft and its pictorial representations. The simple seduction depicted in the woodcuts illustrating, for example, Ulrich Molitor's *De lamiis et phitonicis mulieribus tractatus pulcherimus* (1489) continued to be reproduced until the late seventeenth century, where it appears, for example, as the first of a series of illustrations to a broadsheet of 1669 describing the crimes and trial of the witch Anna Ebeler.[49] In these woodcuts, a man and woman are seen alone out in the countryside, and the man is about to embrace the woman or take her hand. The only indication that he is the Devil are his bird's claws or hooves and, in the seventeenth-century example, also the horns poking out of his hat. The embrace or holding of hands in these images indicates a further context in which one can place the kiss of shame. Leaving aside their bestial and diabolical elements, these encounters with the Devil were illicit in one of a number of ways depending on the status of the woman involved.

If the woman depicted was unmarried she would have been a fornicator, an unchaste woman having sex with someone whom she could not marry, even if marriage had been promised. This would not have been unusual. There is plenty of evidence of sexual activity before marriage and attempts to get rid of unwanted pregnancies throughout early modern Europe. Eva Susanna Moringer, an Eichstätt witch-suspect, confessed to meeting her lover, a huntsman, in a wood and spending the night with him there. This relationship with the hunter had been encouraged by Moringer's mother and her neighbours, but did not end in marriage. Indeed, under interrogation, the huntsman became a convenient form for the Devil to assume as Moringer's diabolical seducer.[50] Another Eichstätt witch-suspect, the healer Anna Harding, treated many young clients who had become pregnant. They came to her – sometimes more than once – with their mothers, and the female members of the community did not censure young women for seeking abortions.[51] Theoretically, however, public knowledge of unwise pre-marital sexual activity or the failure to terminate a pregnancy which would not later be legitimised by marriage to the father could lead to permanent dishonour.[52]

Married women who embraced the Devil were committing adultery, a serious crime in itself and often legislated against as a form of petty treason. Rather than resort to the law, however, neighbours might attempt to punish one or other party to the adultery by subjecting them to 'charivari', the 'Skimmington ride' or some other local variant of this public humiliation.[53] Through the symbolism of some of its elements, this performance was connected to the witches' sabbath. The discordant music which represented the social disharmony and danger created by the adultery (because it undermined the basic unit of political and economic stability in early modern society, the household) was also an element of the demonological versions of the witches' gatherings, where it represented the disorderly inverted world of the Devil. The adulterer might also be paraded around backwards on a donkey. This has a certain religious resonance because Christ entered Jerusalem on an ass, an abject animal in Roman symbolism, shortly before his death.[54] But the donkey in a Skimmington ride was present to underscore not the humility of the rider but rather his or her humiliation. The goat, in which form the Devil was frequently said to appear before his followers in order to receive their shameful kisses, was also an abject animal. As in the punishments and humiliations inflicted by the fictional and real characters described above, kissing the goat's anus served to reinforce the humiliation of the witch. This humiliation had begun with the purchase of her chastity for nothing more than the horse-shit or leaves into which the Devil's money had turned after he had had sex with her.

Social attitudes towards sex between a widow and another man depended on the age of the woman. Unless she was beyond child-bearing age, a widow would be expected to re-marry, several times if necessary. In these circumstances, sex with a man was inappropriate but otherwise little more than the fornication in which younger women might indulge. The sexually active postmenopausal widow was, however, deemed to be unnatural, and might be subject to the same communal punishments as the adulterer. In demonological terms she was a powerful witch, seeking to destroy the fertility of her sexual partner in the act of coitus, and to suck life from the infants she might attempt to suckle with her withered breasts.[55] She was, therefore, a woman to be feared.

In all the circumstances in which the Devil and a prospective witch might have sex, there lurked the furtive, passionate kiss of young or illicit lovers. The kiss of shame placed on the 'secret parts' of the Devil evoked this real, secret version. The sex between the Devil and his witch did not, however, only lead to sexual immorality or pollution, humiliation and heresy. It was also unnatural. The bestial element of sex with the part-animal, part-human, part-demonic Devil was, as Liliequist has argued in his study of sex with animals, clearly a transgression of the boundaries between what was considered human (because it was based on rational premises), what was natural (because it was instinctive) and what was demonic (because it came from the Devil).[56] This unnaturalness was also expressed in the sexual practices in which witches were understood to engage. The dragon's tongue pushing between the legs of Baldung's young witch as she pushes out her backside to allow penetration of her vagina from behind is a sexual and, to modern eyes, stereotypically pornographic image. It is a depiction of oral sex, the means by which the Devil also inscribed his mark on the Scottish witches in the 1590s. In another of Baldung's works, three witches of different ages touch and look at their own genitals, again a sexually provocative image.[57] Elsewhere witches copulate with demons in 'unnatural' positions. Hans Schäuffelin depicted a witch, clothed, lying on top of a demon and embracing him in one of his illustrations for Ulrich Tengler's *Der neü Layenspiegel* (1511). In this woodcut there are clear echoes of Phyllis riding Aristotle, of the world turned upside down, but presented in an overtly sexual and demonic way.[58] Schäuffelin could not, however, represent penetrative sex with the freedom permitted to Baldung. His audience consisted of a literate public who bought books and broadsheets, but who were engaged in the processes of reform and moral welfare as municipal councillors; Baldung produced his works for a wealthier clientele who purchased them for their private collections. But the images created by Schäuffelin and others evoke unnatural sexual positions in the way in which the couple are positioned, an interpretation confirmed by the presence of the kiss in the picture: the woman is leaning forward, her lips about to meet the demon's.

There is one other kiss of shame which I will examine here: the abused social kiss. In his study of village life in early modern Germany, *Power in the Blood*, David Sabean examines the case of Georg Gottfrid Bregenzer, a Württemberg pastor whose personality constantly got him into trouble with the authorities and his parishioners. Among the accusations laid against the pastor during the investigations into his behaviour were that he kissed some musicians, forced a neighbour to kiss his wife, attempted to kiss the *Schultheiss* of Hattenhofen, Johann Jacob Übelin, and kissed the wife of a furrier whom he had met in an inn.[59] Kissing was an accepted way of greeting relatives and colleagues; it signified close kinship, friendship or political or craft ties, even if it did not always signify affection. In each of these accusations about Bregenzer, however, he had allegedly overstepped the social boundaries which delimited the types of people one might legitimately kiss and when. In the case of the musicians, Bregenzer had crossed a class division. These men were of lower social status than the pastor and his guests, and they were strangers in his house.[60] They had no relationship with the pastor that permitted him to kiss them as equals. In doing this he would have dishonoured himself in the presence of the more important parishioners who had attended this gathering.

Allegations of forcing a neighbour to kiss his wife at a party and kissing the wife of a furrier several times in the presence of others in an inn were designed to hint at the pastor's sexual impropriety. If he was not an adulterer himself, then he was encouraging others to see his wife as one, and he was presenting an image of himself as unchaste. In publicising his own or his wife's adultery, Bregenzer was advertising his own dishonour as a man incapable of controlling himself or his household. Attempting to kiss Übelin the *Schultheiss* was a more ambiguous action. In certain circumstances this might have been an acceptable thing to do. The *Schultheiss* was, however, one of Bregenzer's enemies, and the attempt to kiss him occurred during a gathering in a tavern when the pastor was drunk. The *Schultheiss* had also just refused to share a toast with him. The failed kiss was out of place, and the *Schultheiss* attempted to use it to dishonour Bregenzer. Übelin reported that he had 'said he did not kiss women let alone men'.[61] This would seem to be a reference to kisses between unmarried lovers, because the *Schultheiss* presumably kissed his wife. The inference, in conjunction with the refusal to drink with the pastor, seems to have been that Bregenzer was a 'sodomite', and therefore had no more personal credit than the bugger who defiled animals or the executioner. The illegitimate kiss, the one which brought shame on Bregenzer or his wife, appeared frequently in the accusations against the pastor, alongside his alleged sexual harassment of and adultery with other female parishioners, because it sent a powerful message to those investigating this case that he was a dishonourable man. Those who deployed the kiss in this fashion clearly thought that it was more likely to impress the investigators than allegations about other character traits or the content of his preaching.

### THE KISS OF SHAME AND THE WITCH-SUSPECT

The kiss of shame resonated widely throughout early modern Europe and is to be found in several overlapping contexts in which honour was at stake. Why, then, are there so few explicit references to it in the confessions made by witch-suspects in Eichstätt? There are two possible answers to this question which would seem to be related. The first is that the authorities failed to impress the reality of the witch sect and its dangers on the inhabitants of the principality. The second is that the witch-suspects, as far as was humanly possible under torture and psychological duress, attempted to present themselves as honourable women.

Until the election of Johann Christoph von Westerstetten as prince-bishop in 1612, Eichstätt had not experienced the full impact of Tridentine reform. The cathedral chapter, the most important ecclesiastical and political institution in the principality, had resisted the public promulgation of the decrees of the Council of Trent regulating marriage, for example, or banning *Fastnacht* (carnival). The Society of Jesus had been active in neighbouring Catholic states, notably in the Duchy of Bavaria, seeking to inculcate Catholic belief in the population and using its mission stations there as bases from which to recatholicise local Protestant areas, but the Eichstätt chapter had simply refused to admit the order onto its territory. And the canons clung to the old local rites, ignoring calls to take up the Roman rite which the delegates to the Council of Trent had hoped would unify the Church.[62] The bishops had also been concerned to live peaceably with their Protestant neighbours. Johann Conrad von Gemmingen, for example, corresponded with Joachim Ernst, the Lutheran Margrave of Ansbach, a territory on his western border, about his famous garden.[63] He also refused to join the Catholic League, headed by Maximilian I of Bavaria and formed in 1609 to protect the Catholic states within Germany from Protestant aggression.[64]

Westerstetten's arrival in the spring of 1613 radically changed this situation. Tridentine decrees were introduced and enforced, Eichstätt joined the Catholic League, the Jesuits were invited in, and local Protestant rulers were encouraged to convert to the Catholic faith. Part of this package of reform and recatholicisation was the eradication of the witch sect, a policy which Westerstetten had pursued as prince-provost of Ellwangen (1603–13). Although there had been minor outbreaks of witch persecution in Eichstätt in 1590–2 and 1603, it was Westerstetten who introduced a commission to oversee a systematic hunt for witches. This was successful in executing over 270 alleged witches between 1617 and 1631. It did not, however, receive any help from the local population. With one exception, no one seems to have used the witch trials to resolve local conflicts or express concerns about this or that woman rumoured to be a witch. Husbands and neighbours were incredulous that these particular women, mainly from the patrician and craft elites, were being arrested for the crime of witchcraft, and where they could they made considerable effort to get the suspects out of custody. Abraham Windteis employed a clerk to write letters on his behalf testifying to his wife's innocence and arguing that the circumstances of her interrogation contravened the *Constitutio criminalis Carolina* (Imperial Law Code) of 1532. The clerk also cited the tenth-century *Canon episcopi* which argued that witchcraft was illusory, a point of view contradicted by the later authorities adopted by the Eichstätt witch commissioners.[65] Maria Magdalena Windteis was, however, released. Georg Mayr, on the other hand, bribed his way into the town hall, where the witch-suspects were held in custody, and attempted to get his wife pregnant. She appears to have miscarried shortly after telling her interrogators that she was expecting a baby. The subsequent investigation into the circumstances of her meeting with her husband led to the dismissal of the entire town hall staff and the discovery of the systematic abuse of prisoners and servants in the building.[66] Maria Mayr was executed.

Others, women especially, are known to have also bribed the town hall staff for access to suspects in custody. Raffelin, a butcher's wife, for example, took the opportunity of her visit to the town hall to settle a meat bill, to persuade Barbel Halm, the wife of the *Oberamtsknecht* (the official responsible for the care of the building and its occupants), to allow her up into Maria Mayr's quarters. She stayed for about an hour and the pair drank beer together. The witch, of course, was a dishonourable person. She disrupted the harmony of the community, endangered its members, rejected Christian values and was believed to perform rituals like kissing the Devil on the anus. Once identified, the witch attracted similar sanctions to those which were imposed on the executioner and the bugger: exclusion from ordinary shared activities. There was also the additional physical danger that being in her presence entailed because she embodied evil, and her touch, look or words were enough to cause harm. If Raffelin or her neighbours had believed that Mayr was really a witch, then her successful attempt to visit Mayr and share drink with her could have cast Raffelin as a dishonourable person in the community by association. As the butchers were one of the dominant secular political groups in the town of Eichstätt, she would have been corrupting her own household and the status of her husband in choosing to spend so much time with Mayr. Raffelin, her kin or her property could also have been harmed as a result of the visit. Worse still, Raffelin herself could have become suspected as a witch. It is unlikely that Raffelin or the other women who secured clandestine visits to other prisoners would have risked their honour, health and family by visiting a suspect who was commonly reputed to be a witch.

Raffelin's visit confirms the general scepticism about the presence of the witch sect in the principality in another way, too. Barbel Halm testified that during Raffelin's meeting with Mayr, she had asked her whom she had denounced. Mayr had not confessed to being a witch at this point in her interrogation, but the question shows that her neighbours had grasped the dynamic by which the persecution was escalating. They were aware that suspects were being identified in the naming of accomplices under torture; and they wanted to know who was being denounced in this process. Raffelin was not the only neighbour to demonstrate that she had understood this feature of the interrogation process; two clients of Anna Harding sought to bribe her, unsuccessfully, against naming them as witches. The significance of these examples is that they come from the first two years of the persecution of 1617–31. The witch-suspects' neighbours had not become disillusioned with the hunt as time went on, and an apparently never-ending stream of neighbours found themselves locked up in the town hall. They were sceptical of the persecution from its very beginning.

If husbands sought to get their wives released and neighbours drank with supposed witches, the witnesses subpoenaed to confirm a suspect's confessions of malevolent witchcraft invariably failed to do so. In the winter preceding Walburga Knab's arrest, for example, Hans Alter's wife had been seized with great pains as the condition of her ulcerated leg deteriorated. This was a result, Knab claimed, of an indiscriminate attack on the population in which she 'scattered her powder out of enmity towards the people'.[67] In his statement about his wife's painful leg, Alter did not mention any enmity between his family and Knab's, nor did he attribute a supernatural cause to the ulcers. Instead, he outlined his wife's medical history: four years ago she had lain ill, but she had survived; this last winter, the time at which Knab allegedly attacked the woman, his wife had suffered great pains in her afflicted limb, but these were the result of a condition which had persisted for the previous two years.[68] Alter's failure to corroborate Knab's testimony was typical of the Eichstätt experience of witch persecution. The extant trial transcripts show that almost every witch was convicted, when it came to this element of her witchcraft, solely of the harm she committed against her own livestock and children for which no other witness was necessary.

It seems, therefore, that the communities of the prince-bishopric of Eichstätt did not engage in the process of witch-hunting. This may have been because the most socially disruptive element in the territory at this time was regarded not as the witch sect and the misfortune caused by its members (unseasonable weather, inexplicable deaths and other disasters), but as Westerstetten and the reformist activities of the Jesuits after half a century of relaxed episcopal rule. There is certainly evidence of the tension caused by his arrival. The cathedral chapter, dominated by the local minor nobility, persisted in its reluctance to allow the Jesuits a foothold in the territory. The canons did give in, but only by degrees and only under pressure from the Society's General. The largest occupational group in the principality, the clothworkers, on the other hand, successfully petitioned the chancellor to hold their traditional procession at carnival in 1613, even though the local chapter had just issued decrees against *Fastnacht* and mummeries in anticipation of Westerstetten's arrival. It seems that the chancellor granted their request only because the new bishop had yet to take up residence in the territory. After 1613, it is unlikely that they were again allowed to parade about the town on this date. Because they did not subscribe to the idea that the witch sect was operating in the territory, therefore, and had other preoccupations, the suspects failed to confess to any demonological aspect of the witch heresy, including the obscene kiss, in detail.

The suspects may also have omitted the lewd and lurid elements of the demonologists' fantasies, such as the kiss of shame, for another reason: to present themselves as honourable. There is a tendency among historians of the witch persecutions to assume that once an individual had finally broken under torture and confessed to being a witch, the rest of her confession simply flowed along uninterrupted in answer to her interrogators' questions. This is not the case. The Eichstätt trial transcripts are unusual in that they present a session-by-session account of the encounters between the suspect and her judges. The flow of testimony was hindered by declarations of innocence, revocations, digressions and inconsistent stories, breaks for torture, lunch or sleep and adjournments which could occasionally last for months or years. The confession was a process of negotiation framed by the witch commissioners' interrogatory, and in this process the witch played her role.

The standard questions asked by the Eichstätt interrogators covered a range of issues from the witch's personal history to her seduction, the sabbath, harmful magic and the names of her accomplices. They began innocuously enough – 'What is your name?', 'Where were you born?' and so on – but these questions were quickly replaced by others which probed more deeply into the suspect's personal life: 'Did you marry of your own will or with the knowledge of your parents and friends?'; 'Did you have an unseemly love for him [your husband] when you were single, did you mix carnally with him, or do this willingly?'; 'Did you or others not use superstitious things at your wedding, either before or after it?'; 'Did you not win the unseemly love of others during your marriage?'[69] These questions dealt not just with the suspect's personal circumstances, but with her morality. They are similar to those found in two other contexts, the visitation and the trial for slander.[70] In Westerstetten's reign in Eichstätt, the visitation became a principal tool through which to identify areas of moral laxity and superstition, two issues which concerned him greatly as the architect of Catholic reform in the territory. The questions about morality were therefore ones which most inhabitants of Eichstätt would have to answer during the course of his episcopate. In order to avoid trouble, it was a good strategy to learn to answer them appropriately. In the context of the witch trial, they allowed the defendant to present herself to her interrogators as pious and honourable. It was vital that she established her good character at this early stage of the proceedings, as this was the only real, if extremely slim, chance of being released. Most suspects understood what was being offered to them in these questions and took the opportunity to underline their moral standing. Thus Anna Harding did not tell her interrogators at this point that she was a healer and prostitute. She also stated before God that she was as innocent as our Saviour on the cross (of what specific sin she did not say – witchcraft had not yet been mentioned). Once the subject of witchcraft was brought up Harding declared that she would be 'as pious as God in Heaven' and that 'one cannot say anything unjust about her'.[71]

After these initial declarations, a battle of wills ensued as the suspect tried to maintain her profession of innocence in the face of the evidence against her (often rehearsed in personal confrontations with her denouncers) and the threat or use of torture. Most of the suspects in Eichstätt lost this battle and confessed to being witches. They continued, however, to present themselves as integrated, and therefore honourable, members of the community. Margretha Bittelmayr, for example, began her first story of her seduction by telling of a trip to a wedding in a local village. About fifteen years before her arrest she had travelled there with four other women, all of whom had since been executed for witchcraft. On the way they had drunk wine and entered the village carousing. She then refused to continue with this tale.[72] Bittelmayr and her companions were women of the territory's patrician elite and of about the same age. It is not surprising that they had gone to a wedding together. In fact, weddings (and other celebrations) and companionship were the central themes of the Eichstätt confession narratives. When she named the accomplices whom she had seen at the nocturnal gatherings of the witch sect, Bittelmayr named her closer associates. Only three of the twenty-nine persons she identified as witches were not councillors, their wives or senior clergymen, that is, individuals with whom she would have associated at weddings, baptisms and funerals. The three exceptions were not marginalised old crones, but cooks in the households of clergymen.[73] Although she was asked about the conduct of these people and worship of the Devil, her answers were cursory and usually repeated the phraseology of the question. In fact, the gathering was an orderly affair.

The confession narratives consistently emphasise the orderliness and normality of the sabbath. In most testimonies, salt – a commodity which symbolised hospitality – was present, and the wine, of which the best in the real world was reserved for celebrations, was good; they should have been absent and bad respectively. The dancing and other arrangements were organised well – Peter Porzin, for example, was one of several men identified as a 'Platzmeister' (seemingly a master of ceremonies).[74] Not one of the Eichstätt suspects described an orgy or a wild and disorderly dance. Food was prepared by the professional cooks of leading clerical or patrician households, as it would often have been in real life, and did not consist of unpalatable food. Indeed, the witches commonly ate fish, a staple food of celebration in central

Europe. And people turned up with companions who were of the right status. Bittelmayr observed, for example, that Egina Penner attended the sabbath with a 'Bürger' (citizen), which would not have been unusual as her husband was a 'Bürgermeister' (mayor).[75] A gathering of Eichstätt witches did not accord with conventional images of the sabbath as the world turned upside down. It is hardly surprising that Walburga Knab, among others, described the scene 'as at a wedding'.[76]

Nor is it surprising in this context that the kiss of shame and other travesties of Catholic rites rarely appear in the Eichstätt confessions, despite their widespread cultural resonance. If the gathering was presented by the suspect as an ordinary wedding or similar occasion, then it was imagined as an integrative event which served to promote her honour by her inclusion in it among her kin, neighbours and friends. She refused to engage with the fantasies of her prosecutors and exclude herself from the community alongside the executioner who had tortured her. In this respect, the conventional theories of witchcraft confession narratives appear too simplistic and schematic. In Eichstätt, the suspects' confessions did not represent an authoritative mixture of negative demonological and popular conceptions of witch beliefs which had become standardised through a process of acculturation a century or more before the main period of persecution began, at least in central and Western Europe.[77] If they could not withstand the aggressive questioning and torture, most witch-defendants did at least assert enough control over their testimonies of harmful magic and the witches' sabbaths to retain some degree of honour for themselves and their households. They did so by containing their self-confessed successful attacks on people and property within their own households, and therefore by refusing to disrupt and corrupt the wider community. The suspects' neighbours likewise refused to cast doubt on the honour of the alleged witches by accusing them of such malevolent acts; they refused to align these women with the executioner and the bugger. The witch-suspects also refused to admit voluntarily to participating in the excesses of heretical ritual, such as kissing the Devil on the anus, and when they were forced to confess such details they did not elaborate beyond a simple statement of each act. Again the suspect was refusing the role of the social outcast, while also retaining an image of herself as a pious Catholic. In a world in which personal credit in the eyes of one's neighbours was a commodity which had a significant influence on one's social and economic prospects, and those of one's spouse, children and other relatives, it is not surprising to find that women sought to uphold their honour as far as was humanly possible under the extreme circumstances of the witchcraft trial. Each Eichstätt witch therefore died honourably not only because she had confessed her sins committed as a witch and been reconciled to the Catholic faith, but also because she took the opportunities offered by the interrogation process to assert her integration in the wider community. She was not a shameful person and refused to commit a shameful act.

## NOTES

1 Staatsarchiv Nürnberg (hereafter StAN), Hexenakten 45 (W. Knab), 7 August 1621.

2 Norman Cohn, *Europe's Inner Demons: An Enquiry Inspired by the Great Witch-hunt* (London, 1975); Carlo Ginzburg, *Ecstasies: Deciphering the Witches' Sabbath* (1989), trans. Raymond Rosenthal (London, 1990); and Stuart Clark, *Thinking with Demons: The Idea of Witchcraft in Early Modern Europe* (Oxford, 1997).

3 Cohn, *Europe's Inner Demons*, p. 1.

4 *Ibid.*, pp. 16–20.

5 Quoted in Jeffrey Burton Russell, *Witchcraft in the Middle Ages* (Ithaca, NY, 1972), p. 131.

6 For the text of this papal bull, see 'Pope Gregory IX: *Vox in Rama*', in Alan Charles Kors and Edward Peters (eds), *Witchcraft in Europe 400–1700: A Documentary History*, 2nd edn (Philadelphia, 2001), pp. 114–16.

7 Cohn, *Europe's Inner Demons*, pp. 32–42.

8 *Ibid.*, pp. 85–8.

9 Heinrich Kramer [and Jacob Sprenger], *Malleus maleficarum: The Classic Study of Witchcraft* (*c.* 1486), trans. Montague Summers (1928; repr. London, 1986), p. 219. Both Kramer and Summers left the quote in its original German: 'Kehr mir die Zung im Arss umb'.

10 Reginald Scot, *The Discoverie of Witchcraft* (1584; repr. Mineola, NY, 1972), p. 24.

11 The image is reprinted in Richard van Dülmen (ed.), *Hexenwelten: Magie und Imagination* (Frankfurt am Main, 1987), p. 352.

12 *Ibid.*, p. 365.

13 *Ibid.*, p. 395.

14 *Ibid.*, p. 352.

15 Because heresy did not flourish in England as it did in Languedoc or the Vaudois, the tradition of anti-heretical tracts was also much weaker.

16 *News from Scotland*, repr. in Lawrence Normand and Gareth Roberts (eds), *Witchcraft in Early Modern Scotland: James VI's* Demonology *and the North Berwick Witches* (Exeter, 2000), pp. 309–24; quotation at p. 315. In her dittay, Sampson merely confessed that 'before they departed they kissed his arse'. See 'The Trial of Agnes Sampson', *ibid.*, pp. 231–46, at p. 243.

17 *News from Scotland*, p. 313.

18 Clark, *Thinking with Demons*, p. 92.

19 Richard van Dülmen, 'Imaginationen des Teuflischen: Nachtliche Zusammenkünfte, Hexentänze, Teufelssabbate', in Dülmen (ed.), *Hexenwelten*, pp. 94–130, at p. 124.

20 Cohn, *Europe's Inner Demons*, p. 73.

21 For example, Romans 16:16.

22 On the kiss of peace, see L. Edward Phillips, *The Ritual Kiss in Early Christian Worship* (Cambridge, 1996), and John Bossy, 'The Mass as a Social Institution 1200–1700', *Past & Present*, 100 (1983), 29–61. My thanks to the late Alan Bray for these and other references on this kiss.

23 Luke 7:38.

24 C. C. Bombaugh, *The Literature of Kissing, Gleaned from History, Poetry, Fiction and Anecdote* (Philadelphia, 1876), pp. 70–1.

25  1 Samuel 10:1.

26  Bombaugh, *Literature of Kissing*, pp. 59–60. In this context the ritual would seem to be an imitation of the episode in which Jesus washed the feet of his disciples. See John 13:5–10.

27  Barbara Rosen (ed.), *Witchcraft in England, 1558–1618*, rev. edn (Amherst, MA, 1991), p. 195 n. 7.

28  *Ibid.*

29  Geoffrey Chaucer, 'The Miller's Tale', in *The Canterbury Tales* (late fourteenth century), trans. Nevill Coghill (1951); rev. edn (Harmondsworth, 1977), pp. 105–22, at p. 119.

30  Richard J. Evans, *Rituals of Retribution: Capital Punishment in Germany, 1600–1987* (London, 1997), pp. 31–2.

31  Johann Jakob Christoffel von Grimmelshausen, *The Adventures of Simplicius Simplicissimus* (1668), trans. Mike Mitchell (Sawtry, 1999), pp. 47–50.

32  *Ibid.*, p. 204.

33  *Ibid.*, p. 205.

34  On the disfiguration of the face and its symbolic meaning, see Valentin Groebner, 'Losing Face, Saving Face: Noses and Honour in the Late Medieval Town', *History Workshop Journal*, 40 (1995), 1–15.

35  Grimmelshausen, *Simplicissimus*, pp. 205 and 98 respectively.

36  Thirteen of the ninety-five chapters of the earliest complete edition of *Till Eulenspiegel* (1515), trans. Paul Oppenheimer (Oxford, 1995), involve such acts, for example pp. 6–7.

37  Evans, *Rituals of Retribution*, p. 57.

38  *Ibid.*, p. 61.

39  Jonas Liliequist, 'Peasants against Nature: Crossing the Boundaries between Man and Animal in Seventeenth- and Eighteenth-Century Sweden', in John C. Fout (ed.), *Forbidden History: The State, Society and the Regulation of Sexuality in Modern Europe* (Chicago, 1992), pp. 57–87, at p. 59.

40  *Ibid.*, p. 60. In contrast, bestiality was hardly prosecuted in other Western European countries: *ibid.*, p. 60 n. 5.

41  Georg Gutmann confessed that 'when he was still young . . . when he lodged with a horse-herd, he had [sex] not only with horses, but also with cattle': StAN, Hexenakten 45 (G. Gutmann), 31 January 1618.

42  Liliequist subscribes to this observation made by Havelock Ellis and Richard von Krafft-Ebing. See 'Peasants against Nature', pp. 74–8.

43  *Ibid.*, p. 82.

44  *Ibid.*, p. 68.

45  Evans, *Rituals of Retribution*, pp. 56–60.

46  Thus, Peter Porzin was seduced at a wedding while away from home on business: StAN, Hexenakten 45 (P. Porzin), 13 September 1627.

47  Diane Purkiss makes a similar comparison of the role of food in the stories of witches and ancient folk-tales, including 'Snow White', in *The Witch in History: Early Modern and Twentieth-century Representations* (London, 1996), p. 277.

48  Liliequist, 'Peasants against Nature', p. 65.

49  These images are reproduced in Dülmen (ed.), *Hexenwelten*, pp. 356 and 386 respectively.

50  StAN, Hexenakten 48 (E. S. Moringer), 14 February 1619 (a.m. and p.m.).

51  StAN, Hexenakten 45 (A. Harding), 20 February 1618 (a.m.) and 21 February 1618 (a.m.).

52 On the connections between pre-marital sex and (dis)honour, see, for example, Sandra Cavallo and Simone Cerutti, 'Female Honor and the Social Control of Reproduction in Piedmont between 1600 and 1800', in Edward Muir and Guido Ruggiero (eds), *Sex and Gender in Historical Perspective* (Baltimore and London, 1990), pp. 73–109.

53 On this custom, see, for example, E. P. Thompson, 'Rough Music', in *idem*, *Customs in Common* (London, 1991), pp. 467–538.

54 Matthew 21:1–11.

55 This point is made by Lyndal Roper in 'Witchcraft and Fantasy in Early Modern Germany', in her *Oedipus and the Devil: Witchcraft, Sexuality and Religion in Early Modern Europe* (London, 1994), pp. 199–225, at p. 207.

56 Bestiality itself was a transgression of the boundaries between man and animal and of masculinity. See Liliequist, 'Peasants against Nature', pp. 83–4.

57 See Dülmen (ed.), *Hexenwelten*, p. 394.

58 *Ibid.*, p. 358.

59 David Warren Sabean, *Power in the Blood: Popular Culture and Village Discourse in Early Modern Germany* (Cambridge, 1987), pp. 121, 124, 130–2.

60 *Ibid.*, p. 121.

61 *Ibid.*, p. 130.

62 The Counter-Reformation in Eichstätt is discussed in Jonathan Durrant, 'Witchcraft, Gender and Society in the Early Modern Prince-Bishopric of Eichstätt', PhD dissertation, University of London, 2002, pp. 6–96.

63 Nicolas Barker, *Hortus Eystettensis: The Bishop's Garden and Besler's Magnificent Book*, corrected edn (New York, 1995), pp. 1–9.

64 Simon Adams, 'The Union, the League and the Politics of Europe', in Geoffrey Parker (ed.), *The Thirty Years' War*, 2nd edn (London, 1997), pp. 22–34, at p. 31.

65 The texts used by the Eichstätt commissioners included Francis Agricola, *Gründtlicher Bericht ob Zauber- und Hexerey die argste vnd gravlichste sünd auff Erden sey* (Cologne, 1597), Peter Binsfeld, *Tractatus de confessionibus maleficorum et sagarum* (Trier, 1589) and Kramer, *Malleus maleficarum*.

66 Durrant, 'Witchcraft, Gender and Society', pp. 243–84.

67 StAN, Hexenakten 45 (W. Knab), 4 August 1621.

68 StAN, Hexenakten 45 (W. Knab – Inquisitio), article 4.

69 StAN, Hexenakten 49 (interrogatory – fair copy), questions 9, 12, 14, 17.

70 On the 'witch' slander cases heard at the Imperial Chamber Court in Speyer, see, for example, Ralf-Peter Fuchs, *Hexerei und Zauberei vor dem Reichskammergericht: Nichtigkeiten und Injurien* (Wetzlar, 1994).

71 StAN, Hexenakten 48 (A. Harding), 19 January 1618 (p.m.).

72 StAN, Hexenakten 45 (M. Bittelmayr), 16 October 1626 (a.m.).

73 *Ibid.*, 29, 30, 31 October and 2, 5, 7 November 1626.

74 StAN, Hexenakten 45 (P. Porzin), 18 September 1627.

75 StAN, Hexenakten 45 (M. Bittelmayr), 29 October 1626.

76 StAN, Hexenakten 45 (W. Knab), 7 August 1621.

77 This view of witch beliefs is presented in, for example, Richard Kieckhefer, *European Witch Trials: Their Foundations in Popular and Learned Culture, 1300–1500* (London, 1976). Although it has been critised by historians of witch persecutions outside central and Western Europe, notably by Ginzburg in his *Ecstasies*, pp. 6–7, there has been little debate about the origins of witch beliefs in areas such as Germany.

# PART II

# Ambiguity
# and
# transgression

## 3

# Lawful kisses? Sexual ambiguity and platonic friendship in England c.1660–1720

<>

Helen Berry

THIS CHAPTER considers the way in which printed texts during the half-century after the Restoration focused upon the uncertainties attendant upon the gesture of kissing. In the past, as today, the kiss could be essentially ambiguous in many social encounters. Requiring as it does a form of unusually intimate touch, often on the face or hand, with at least one person's lips (loaded with cultural freight and erotic potential),[1] the gesture contained within it a dimension of sexual ambiguity (specifically, in this context, a dimension of sexual attraction) in a way which other more impersonal forms of greeting such as a handshake never could, at least not in Western European societies.[2] Nuanced discourses about the kiss from the 1660s onwards deliberately focused upon the ambiguity of the gesture of a kiss as a shorthand for exploring a range of possible feelings and emotions evoked between individuals, from platonic friendship to erotic love. The sources under consideration here are among the cheapest forms of popular literature that were available in England at the time – the mass-produced periodicals and miscellanies that provided guidance to their readers on the conduct of life. It is in these that we find some of the few surviving contemporary discussions of frequently experienced bodily gestures such as the kiss, which were (and are) commonplace occurrences, yet extremely difficult to reconstruct in a historical context.

What was a 'lawful kiss' in the context of early modern society? The holy kiss of peace has been widely recognised in England at least since the early medieval period as one of the few physically intimate gestures legitimised and acceptable according to Christian teaching.[3] Though manifested through bodily contact, the sacred kiss of peace between friends denoted a harmony of spirits, an expression of the biblical idea that there were 'no sexes in souls'.[4] One result of this is that our early modern ancestors tended to deploy the kiss as a mutually acceptable form of greeting much more readily than we would do today. As Lawrence Stone observed, visitors to England in the sixteenth century commented upon the frequency with which kisses were exchanged as a greeting; Erasmus found it 'a most attractive custom'.[5] The customary greetings of three hundred years ago were indeed startlingly different from those of our own time in that kisses at that time were commonly exchanged between men, a phenomenon that would be regarded with anxiety and suspicion, if not hostility, in many English-speaking countries today.[6] It may seem paradoxical to the modern eye that more 'everyday' kissing took place in early modern society, where the rituals of Christian worship were more formally observed and greater social pressure was applied to the regulation of sexual conduct (in, for example, stigmatising bastardy).[7] This, however, merely illustrates the preoccupations of our own post-Freudian era, in which signs of affect are collapsed into a narrowly sexual reading. The kiss, as Keith Thomas argued some years ago, may be more usefully considered in a broader interpretative framework as a physical embodiment of an ongoing negotiation of power between individuals that could indicate an unspoken range of feelings and intentions.[8]

Indeed, kisses have always assumed a wide range of meanings in English history. They could be a mark of submission or domination, as well as indicating status, sexual desire, friendship or the sealing of a pact or contract such as an intention to marry, or even a truce. In the thirteenth century, for example, a day of reconciliation (or 'love day') was ordered in village courts in the event of a dispute between neighbours, 'sealed by a kiss (the kiss of peace)', which would be blessed by a priest and witnessed by friends and kinsmen.[9] There is evidence of continuity into the early modern period of this model of a lawful kiss of peace between individuals who neither were married to each other, nor were blood kin. In December 1727, the Northumberland gentleman George Liddell wrote to Robert Cotesworth, the nephew and heir of his deceased business partner. He addressed the young man as 'Dear Bob', and directed the letter to London from his country seat at Ravensworth Castle. The subject of the letter was the state of the Newcastle coal trade. Liddell's primary purpose was to communicate the news that relations with their former rival, Lady Clavering (who had engaged Robert's uncle William Cotesworth in a series of protracted and expensive law suits), had improved. 'I last Wednesday breakfasted with [Lady Clavering] & took leave,' recorded George Liddell in his letter, 'we had a little talk, & she told me she would have 2000 Tons [of coal]. I told her I wished ye trade would allow it, but I was sure it could not. That tho' I should not talk more of the Trade, I would visit her as a friend, & so we parted after a hearty kiss'.[10] This documented gesture signified the termination of their discussion of business, and the transition of their relationship from public commercial rivalry to personal friendship. One senses Liddell's satisfaction, in the aftermath of the death of his friend, that his dealings with their powerful neighbour were concluded thus; the implication was that they had not been on 'kissing terms' in the past, but that the exchange of a 'hearty kiss' set a seal on their future alliance. This actual early eighteenth-century kiss serves to illustrate how the gesture could be perfectly apt and unambiguous. In this situation, the status of both parties was equal, and their primary interest was in signalling the ultimate resolution of a former animosity. Liddell's edification at the freely given heartiness of their kiss defines it as a sign of mutual affection, evoking the kiss of peace prescribed by St Paul as a mark of Christian fellowship.[11]

The example of the kiss between George Liddell and Lady Clavering was one type of lawful kiss, set in a commercial context akin to that of warring factions, where it signified a truce after a long struggle to gain mastery over the economic fortunes of the region. It is just one example of many scenarios where kisses must have been exchanged without sexual connotation. It was crucial for people to be judicious in their deployment of the gesture, however, since in the wrong context, it could be entirely inappropriate, evoking social embarrassment, public censure, or indeed illicit pleasure. Yet there were no written rules or failsafe guidelines. Conduct literature was traditionally unhelpful in as much as it provided little specific advice on the subject of kissing. If we trace the genre in England back to the early seventeenth century, we can see that Puritan authors such as Gouge, Dod and Cleaver discussed heterosexual relations strictly within the framework of marriage. There is no discussion of the kiss *per se*, but a more general admonition to keep all forms of bodily contact within the bounds of matrimony.[12] The tradition was taken up by Presbyterian conduct writers of the Restoration such as Richard Allestree, who warned women in *The Ladies Calling* (1676), 'Marriage is God's Ordinance . . . And it may well be presum'd one cause why so few Matches are happy [is] that they are not built upon a right Foundation. Some are grounded upon Wealth, some on Beauty, too sandy bottoms God knows to raise any felicity [up]on.'[13] Throughout the early modern period, the modest virgin knew that she should not allow men to get too close – the *Ladies Dictionary* (1694) presented a piece of proverbial wisdom in the following couplet: 'In part to blame is she that has been tride / He comes too near that comes to be denied'.[14] In general, there was little specific guidance about kissing directed at young people. In the misogynistic diatribes of the mid-seventeenth-century writer Francis Osborne, for example, the author warned unmarried men about the danger of passion in general, as a slippery slope to 'rendering Him subject to slavery, that was born free'. Lust, Osborne warned, 'after a few enjoyments grows tedious'.[15] Hannah Woolley's advice in the *Gentlewoman's Companion* (1675) considered how ladies should regulate 'the Gait or Gesture' and warned that outward gestures were indicators of a woman's inward moral state: 'Light occasions', she observed, 'are often-times grounds of deep aspersions'.[16] Woolley cautioned her female readers against 'wanton Gesticulations' and lures to sensuality such as 'Sloth, Words, Books, Eyes, Conforts [sic] and luscious fare'.[17] She provided a fascinating list of injunctions against whispering, laughing loudly and entering and leaving a room noisily, and concerning etiquette in speech and addressing social inferiors and superiors, but again, there is nothing specific about kisses.

Some writers were more forthcoming. In a posthumous publication of 1686, the lawyer Henry Swinburne attempted to clarify the confused tangle of law and custom over spousals promises, the ambiguity of which (as he put it) had been the 'Mother of many Quarrels' among the 'ruder sort'. He confirmed that a promise of marriage was binding if certain words or signs were made between the parties '[such] as if they lye together, imbrace or kiss each other, or give and receive Gifts and Tokens either of them'.[18] Kisses in the early modern period could be cited in court as evidence of a spousals promise, and were therefore not to be given or received lightly by unmarried men and women in situations where a sexual meaning might be imputed. Laura Gowing concluded from her study of sixteenth- and seventeenth-century court records that outward gestures and "familiarities" were under constant scrutiny among local communities.[19]

There were thus a whole range of situations where the giving or receiving of a kiss was a complicated business, and it was this potentially perilous area of social conduct that was exploited by a new genre of popular literature. In periodicals from the 1690s onwards such as the *Athenian Mercury*, the *Ladies Mercury*, the *Athenian Oracle*, the *British Apollo* and the *Post-Boy Robb'd of his Mail*, and their more famous literary descendants, the *Tatler* and *The Spectator*, we find detailed first-person narratives representing the concerns of a growing tier of society, the middling sorts.[20] Questions in these texts regarding the parameters of lawful kissing between the sexes created a new public space in which a range of possible relationships could be explored. In contrast to the austere voices of earlier conduct writers, the new question-and-answer periodicals responded to individual questions concerning how to choose a spouse, how to conduct oneself with the opposite sex and whether to take parental advice in such matters. These were a new departure from the didactic tone of single-author works by writers such as Osborne, Woolley and the Marquis of Halifax – a new genre in which an ongoing dialogue was represented between author and reader in the form of questions and answers on matters of personal scruple.

The process of asking questions in print was a twist upon the casuistical or case-by-case reasoning that is most often associated with the Jesuits. Counter-Reformation casuistry entailed the bringing to bear of all relevant evidence in cases of moral and doctrinal confusion through a process of philosophical and moral inquiry.[21] This theological practice was not confined to Catholicism. Following the Restoration in England, nonconformist divines such as Dr Samuel Annesley, and Richard Baxter, adopted casuistry as a method of practical instruction for their flocks.[22] Baxter's *A Christian Directory* (1673), enjoyed considerable popularity in the last decades of the seventeenth century, and ran through several editions.[23] John Dunton, the editor and publisher of the *Athenian Mercury*, had been apprenticed to Thomas Parkhurst, 'the most eminent Presbyterian bookseller in the three kingdoms', and was married to Dr Annesley's daughter, Elizabeth. It is likely that his idea for a popular 'casuistical' publication that would address matters of personal scruple was inspired by the success of the pragmatic nonconformist approach to resolving commonly experienced problems. The idea was later taken up in *The Spectator* by a correspondent who offered his services as a 'Love Casuist', a kind of 'agony uncle', who announced his intention of giving judgement 'on the most nice and intricate Cases which can happen in an Amour'.[24] Here again, the advice offered was to centre upon the appropriateness or otherwise of certain gestures, such as 'Whether a Lady, at the first Interview, may allow an humble Servant to kiss her hand'.[25]

We therefore see the genre of conduct literature developing new features in the last decades of the seventeenth century, with some publications breaking away from the conventional didactic format and moving towards an increasingly personal address to individual problems. It was here that specifics, such as the meaning of a kiss, came under consideration. The following anonymous questions, for example, appeared in the *Athenian Mercury* in 1691, and were apparently from an unnamed male reader. The questions were about the best tactics to pursue in courtship, such as the following: 'What behaviour and carriage in the progress of an Amour will be most Winning and Acceptable to a lady of Ingenuity and Fortune?' and 'What Expression's fittest for a lover to make use of to declare his Passion?' The fifth question in this series was concerned specifically with kissing: 'Quest: Whether Interrupting Discourse by repeated Kisses ben't [*sic*] rude and unmannerly, and more apt to create Aversion than love?' 'Not so hasty, Good Sir!' replied the periodical's authors, the self-styled 'Athenian Society'. They quoted Horace and translated the poet's observation that 'Kissing is a lushious Dyet' which is 'extreamly apt to surfeit'. They advised a courting man to feed cautiously upon kisses 'as if he were eating Mellons'. The general principle was that a man should 'Kiss as well as Talk with Discretion'.[26] Underlying this statement was clearly the long-standing belief that being in thrall to a woman jeopardised a man's reason, the particular quality which distinguished him from the female sex. According to Robert Burton, to be in love was to be 'full of fear, anxiety, doubt, care, peevishness, suspicion'; furthermore, he warned, 'it turns a man into a woman'.[27] The risk of lapsing into effeminacy which a man faced if he was in love was an oft-repeated maxim in early modern England,[28] but it is notable that here is a reworking of the theme which focuses upon the kiss as a moment of seductive and possibly addictive danger. The reference to Horace, and elsewhere in the text to classical authors such as Ovid, Martial and Juvenal, suggests the expectation of a shared episteme of classical works between author and reader, at a time when a growing volume of such texts was available to wider audiences in cheap translated editions.[29] The reworking of ancient themes was the life blood of Grub Street, where every aspiring hack writer had a classical pseudonym (in Dunton's case, he was 'Philaret', and in his wife's, 'Iris').[30] The fascination with kisses as a literary trope was therefore not new (as seventeenth-century readers of the poet Catullus would have been only too aware), but it resurfaced and reached new audiences among these easily accessible forms of popular print culture.

The examples of 'kissing questions' cited above clearly had the potential to entertain and invoke pleasure; the tone is satirical. It is notable however that popular periodicals did not usually enter into the sensual descriptions of romantic encounters we associate with the novel or the more heightened language of erotica.[31] The authors of periodicals were asked to arbitrate on the parameters of lawful kissing, since this licensed them to explore the ambiguities of the gesture, and provided entertaining scenarios for the edification of their readers. The popular appeal of this theme is not difficult to fathom. A renewed interest in discussing the meanings of gestures, especially the kiss, was one feature of a society more socially mobile than before, concerned about how to behave in the presence of social equals and superiors (there has never been much doubt expressed that kissing one's social inferiors was a perilous and undesirable degree of familiarity). At approximately the same time as Lady Clavering and George Liddell were setting a seal upon their truce with a kiss, many aspects of social conduct in England were undergoing profound change. The rise of what some historians have called 'polite society' was producing a new breed of literate self-improvers who sought guidance on the latest fashions in dress, deportment and conversation. Knowing whom to kiss, and in what circumstances, and indeed when to refrain from kissing, was an important marker in society of that elusive quality of 'breeding' which so many were seeking to acquire.[32] Paul Langford argues that, owing to lack of differentiation in dress and deportment in early to mid-eighteenth-century England, it became virtually impossible to judge social status from outward appearance alone 'below the rank of peer of the realm and above the level of the labouring man'.[33] 'Appraising each other', he argues, 'accordingly became a complicated, nuanced task'.[34] Strict rules on kissing were applied according to gender, supplementing the often rigid codes that had traditionally governed hierarchical status relationships. As the eighteenth century progressed, there is evidence that new types of behaviour were disrupting established customs. There is anecdotal evidence of contemporary awareness that customary rules of gesture were changing, even if there was general confusion as to precisely what types of behaviour were now acceptable, even in simple matters such as exchanging a greeting. The unwritten nature of the rules of kissing, and the hazards in exchanging customary greetings, provoked what was no doubt a widespread demand in the early eighteenth century for some guidance on this most delicate of matters. One pseudonymous correspondent, 'Philagnotes', described in *The Spectator* a scenario whereby he had enraged a wealthy citizen of London by kissing the latter's wife, to whom he was related, with 'the usual Salutations of Kindness' that were customary in their home county.[35] 'The parting kiss', observed Philagnotes of his kinswoman's husband, 'I find mightily nettles him'. This entertaining narrative was doubtless a satirical commentary upon London society, where deportment was 'more strict than the common Rules of our Country [i.e. county] require'. It was also illustrative of how metropolitan polite society differentiated its manners from those living in provincial England.[36]

It is no coincidence that *The Spectator* distilled all that was seen as backward about rural society in the early eighteenth century through the representation of social scenarios where kisses were inappropriately bestowed by country gentlemen unaware of the rules of polite conduct in town. One 'Rustick Sprightly', a country gentleman, complained of the 'unhappy Arrival of a Courtier' at assemblies in his area.[37] While it was his habit to kiss all the ladies in his company ('I never came in publick, but I saluted them') this new 'Town-Gentleman' substituted bows for kisses. 'This he did with so good a Grace and Assurance', complained the rustic gentleman, 'that it is taken for the present fashion; and there is no young Gentlewoman within several Miles of this Place has been kissed ever since his first Appearance among us'.[38] *The Spectator* was asked to deliberate 'for or against kissing, by way of Civility or Salutation', a request which the editor ignored. The story had presumably served its purpose in cautioning readers against over-effusion of manner.

This was not just a matter of pragmatic guidance on how to behave in society, however. Talking about kisses was, on another level, an eroticised metaphor for the articulation of sexual desire, which also licensed multiple readings and fantasies regarding the scenario as described. Though the didactic periodicals could claim to be on a mission to improve public morality (a project lent authority by no less a person than Queen Mary during the Reformation of Manners campaign of the 1690s) they were also instrumental in articulating those desires that they professed to be policing.[39] The *Athenian Mercury* described the suitor's dilemma: when in company with honest young

LAWFUL KISSES? ENGLAND C.1660–1720

women, was it acceptable to 'kiss em in a Frolick'?[40] Here, the reader was invited to consider this merry scene, before being invited to consider the sobering question 'Whether tis a sin or no?' The Athenian Society argued that there was a distinction between 'a Civil Kiss, & an Uncivil' one, and left it up to the individual to judge according to circumstance what was appropriate behaviour. A woman who refused to kiss her suitor even after several years' courtship was chastised for her 'singularity', which suggests that it was considered normal for a couple to have reached the 'kissing stage' by this time:

> Quest: 'Gentlemen, I have long made my Application to a certain Lady yet after many Years Services cannot arrive to that slight inconsiderable favour call'd a Kiss, is not the party . . . severe, not to say cruel?[41]

The boundary between lawful and illicit kisses was also explored in the same periodical with the following question about whether it was ever acceptable to kiss another man's wife:

> Quest: Whether it be lawful for a marry'd Man to kiss his Neighbours Wife, out of real respect & affection?

> Answ: Yes undoubtedly, out of respect none will deny, & if not real, so much the worse; out of affection too, for we are to Love our Neighbour . . . tho' we may thus love our Neighbours Wife, we mayn't Covet our Neighbours Wife.[42]

Again, the custom of the Primitive Christians who exchanged the 'kiss of peace' was invoked as the rule for judging appropriate kisses. In spite of these frequent and troubling questions, few could have been unaware that the lawful kiss was one which did not threaten or pre-empt the proper regulation of sexuality through marriage, suggesting that it was the pleasure of contemplating the question, and not the rather predictable answer, which elicited public interest in such scenarios.

When mentioned within a literary context, the kiss was also ambiguous in that it could be an apparently careless gesture that none the less touched upon deeper issues. It is significant that just at the moment when the *Athenian Mercury* was pondering the meanings and implications of kisses, women writers such as Mary Astell were provoking public debate at this time over the role of women in society. In Astell's case, this led to her *Serious Proposal to the Ladies* (1694), a tract which challenged the necessity of marriage for all women and revived the Renaissance humanist debates about whether women should be educated. This was a period in which we find evidence of gender roles being scrutinised and challenged: silencing troublesome women with a kiss was one strategy to put an end to their protests of equality. Rather than beat them into submission (hardly the polite method of discipline), the Athenian Society advised the husbands of unruly wives: 'stop her mouth with a Kiss, & show you are no Coward, by not being conquer'd by a woman's anger, & if you can kiss her whether she will or no, 'twill be a convincing argument that you are still the stronger . . . if you cou'd but conclude all at home by such a private arbitration . . .'[43] Here the seemingly lighthearted dismissal of women's protests of equality belied a darker history of enforced submission.[44]

The potentially threatening prospect of greater sexual equality was at this time only hinted at: however, there was undoubtedly a growing interest within these earliest forms of printed mass media in publicly discussing the nature of relationships other than conventional marriage. This included the possibility of friendship without sexual desire between men and women. The vogue for platonic friendship at this time, as exemplified in the literary correspondence between Mary Astell and Dr John Norris, was anomalous in the context of widely held assumptions about the compulsory nature of heterosexual attraction. Astell promoted the idea of 'noble, Vertuous, and Disinterest'd Friendship' for pious and studious young women, for whom 'idle Novels and Romances' were anathema.[45] Emma Donoghue has suggested that in the early years of the long eighteenth century, there was a literary fascination with friendships between men and women, since 'platonick' relations raised 'anxieties about the pervasiveness of sexual desire, the instability of male authority, and the socially constructed nature of traditional gender roles'.[46] Indeed, we need to look more closely at the idea of platonic love as a cultural leitmotif that provoked many of the discussions about the meaning of a kiss in this historical context. Plato himself did not give the eponymous term its modern meaning – 'of a purely spiritual character, not sexual'.[47] The totalising theory of love posited in the *Symposium* was a means of more fully apprehending truth: indeed, the philosopher regarded sexual longing as one of the primary manifestations of true love.[48] It was only in the early fifteenth century that platonic love came to mean chaste love. It is now widely accepted that this happened because Italian scholars, unable to accept the explicit treatment of homosexuality in these classical texts, reasoned that Plato's love for boys must have been of a non-sexual kind.[49] Renaissance scholars like Ficino systematically rendered Plato's philosophy of love palatable within the dominant Christian morality of their own time. The re-orientation of the platonic ideal within a heterosexual framework, so that the love-object was no longer a boy but a woman, was accomplished in Castiglione's formulation of platonic courtly love according to this new and chaste definition.[50] In England, these ideas were disseminated by humanist writers such as Vives and Erasmus, and through the translation of Castiglione's *Book of the Courtier* by Thomas Hoby (1561), which was to prove highly influential in court circles.[51] Meanwhile, the Cambridge Platonists (often referred to as 'Neo-Platonists'), influenced by the Florentine academy of

Ficino, sought to marry Platonic philosophy with Christian doctrine, and writers such as Ben Jonson in *The New Inn* (1629) celebrated platonic love between the sexes.[52]

In June 1634, the courtier James Howell wrote a letter to Sir Philip Warwick in Paris relaying all the gossip from the court of Charles I. In this letter, we find evidence that the discussions of platonic love had reached royal circles, and had even started a new vogue; he reported that there was:

> Little news at present, but there is a Love call'd Platonick Love which much sways there of late. It is a Love abstracted from all corporeal, gross impressions and sensual appetite, but consists in contemplations and ideas of the mind, not in any carnal fruition. This Love sets the Wits of the Town on work, and they say there will be a Masque shortly on it, whereof her Majesty and her Maids of Honour will be a part.[53]

Not long afterwards, there followed a masque called 'The Temple of Love' in which Henrietta Maria and her entourage did indeed appear in celebration of this newly defined platonic love. The Queen's fondness for masques was vilified by her enemies in the short term as proof of her 'Papist' dissipation.[54] In the long term, however, she established a fashion for female performance at court and the memory of a fashion for platonic 'love games' that was resumed after the Restoration, this time disseminated to a wider audience.[55]

Tracing the intellectual inheritance of how the idea of platonic love passed into common usage goes some way to explaining how it came to be discussed by the end of the seventeenth century beyond the educated elite and courtly circles. Indeed, in spite of an overall diminution in the influence of the court in setting artistic and cultural trends at this time,[56] it appears that in this respect at least here was something which caught the popular imagination. Discussions of platonic friendship between the sexes elicited a fascinated response from the reading public. The subject touched upon a common point of reference: the battle of the sexes, and whether a truce could ever be imagined. There was much mileage to be gained from this subject in popular literature, with endless permutations that tested the boundaries of 'authentic' platonic relations. Here the gesture of the kiss emerges as a sort of litmus test of the 'authenticity' of the platonic friendship, as the following question in the *Athenian Mercury* illustrated:

> Quest: Whether Kisses and Chast Embraces may be admitted into that Friendship between different Sexes, which you have formerly mention'd?

> Answ: Hold, good Mr. Platonique! Not a Lips breadth further, till you have answer'd these Questions . . . 1. Because all agree there are no Sexes in Souls, d'ye think there are none in Bodies? 2. Or are you of Marble? 3. Or is your Friend of the same substance, or kin to St. Francis's Wife of Snow: If not, Hands off, unless en passant, as you may embrace a sister or a Neighbour.[57]

Paradoxically, the Athenian Society thus celebrated platonic friendship as a noble ideal, but simultaneously valorised the power of heterosexual attraction as inevitably conferring a sexual dimension upon any kiss that was likely to take place between platonic friends. The Athenian Society's advice echoed Margaret Cavendish's *Convent of Pleasure* (1668) with reference to the tenets of platonic friendship, and the power of kisses to unmask the 'true' nature of a relationship. In this complex and sexually ambiguous play, the character of a princess garbed in 'Masculine Shepherd's Clothes' asserts the innocence of her platonic love for Lady Happy. She urges that they should take pleasure from their friendship 'as harmless Lovers use to do, as, to discourse, imbrace and kiss, so mingle souls together'. The other woman objects, 'But innocent Lovers do not use to kiss'.[58]

The idea of platonic love, and its boundaries, was certainly explored in same-sex friendship: for example, in Sir Thomas Browne's *Religio Medici* (1642), in which the author declared the superiority of his friendship with another man to the relationship with his wife, in Richard Flecknoe's *Relation of Ten Year's Travells* (1654), a tragic-comic play which echoed Herodotus in depicting a 'Commonwealth of Amazons' bound by ties of platonic love,[59] and in the literary correspondence between 'Lucasia' and Katherine Philips, the 'Matchless Orinda'.[60] The majority of examples from popular periodicals cited here have, however, focused upon relationships between men and women, and these inform our understanding of how a dominant discourse of 'compulsory heterosexuality' was shaped through print.[61] It is evident that the message fostered by popular literature was that men ought to understand that a woman's kiss was never entirely platonic, but was imbued with sexual meaning. Moreover, men were discouraged from entering into a non-sexual friendship with a woman through the discomforting idea that those of their sex who adhered to platonic love did so out of impotence. *The Spectator* recounted a cautionary tale of one Tom Tulip, who slyly commended the 'Doctrine of *Platonick* Love' to his rival, Richard Crastin, while at the same time casting a 'laughing Eye' at Crastin's 'thin leggs, meagre Looks and spare Body', contrasting them with the 'Vigour of his [own] Person, the sinewy Force of his Make', which hinted at Tulip's own lusty sexuality. Crastin got the joke, and challenged him to a duel, protesting he was no dupe: 'I understand very well what you meant by your Mention of *Platonick* love'.[62] The idea that a claim of platonic love was an excuse for impotent men to mask their inadequacy was expressed in other types of popular literature from the late seventeenth century onwards. A collection of seventeenth-century ballads called 'The Loyal Garland' contained two songs on 'Platonick Love'. The first of these elided 'Platonic' with 'Puritan', in ridiculing the idea of non-sexual love between men and women, and casting doubt upon the virility of any man who would pursue a platonic friendship with a member of the opposite sex:

> Then be no more so fond
>    As to think a woman can
> Be satisfied with complements,
>    The frothy part of a man;
> Oh no, she hates a Puritan.
>
> Then venture to embrace,
>    'Tis but one or two,
> I'm confident no woman lives,
>    But sometimes she will do;
> The fault lies not in her, but you.[63]

In a similar reflection upon innocence and folly, *The Spectator* observed, 'when a Man is made up wholly of the Dove, without the least Grain of Serpent in his Composition, he becomes ridiculous in many Circumstances of Life, and very often discredits his best Actions'.[64] Emblematic of this, too, was St Francis, who according to legend discovered a 'young Fellow with a Maid in a Corner'. 'The Innocence of the Saint', mocked *The Spectator*, 'made him mistake the Kiss of a Lover for a Salute of Charity'. It was an error which presumably no less saintly a man would ever make.

The difficulty in conceptualising friendship without desire between the sexes is seen in the doubts which were raised about the ulterior motives of those who claimed to be devotees of platonic love. This theme was explored upon the stage in Sir William D'Avenant's play *The Platonick Lovers* (1636, reprinted 1665) and in Susannah Centlivre's *The Platonick Lady* (1707). D'Avenant originally published his 'Tragi-Comedy' two years after Queen Henrietta Maria's masque on the theme of platonic love, and it constitutes evidence that this 'ideal passion' was still popular in court circles. Revived after the Restoration, and dedicated to Henry Jermyn, who had been created Earl of St Albans by Charles II, the play was set in Sicily among aristocrats, and tells of the platonic love between the young duke Theander and his mistress Eurithea ('lovers of a pure / Celestial kind, such as some style Platonical; / a new court epithet scarce understood').[65] Their sexless love is ridiculed throughout the play, and summarised in the verdict of Phylomont, Eurithea's brother, thus: 'Whining and puling love is fit for eunuchs, / And for old revolted nuns'.[66] As Amadine, Eurithea's servant, observes, this platonic couple may 'whine and kiss' but 'That's all they do'.[67] In Centlivre's play *The Platonick Lady*, the character of Lucinda claims to be 'devoted to Platonick Notions', but the worthlessness of this idea in the face of her desire for the hero, Belvill, is also exposed by a serving maid, Betty:

> Lucinda: What shou'd be the reason of Bevill's stay, Betty? I wish I had not sent to him, I'm very uneasie: How calm my Hours were before I knew this Man.

Betty:     I thought Platonick Love never disturb'd the Mind, Madam.

Lucinda: Yes, when the Friendship is nice and particular.

Betty:     Nay, nay, I never knew Friendship in different Sexes but came to particulars at Last.[68]

The words of plain honest Betty were located here in counterpoint to the
fashion for platonic friendship. Betty's commentary exposed the folly of
sophisticated posturing, and the 'truth' of male–female friendship – that it
was intrinsically and universally no more than a mask for heterosexual desire.
Centlivre's play appealed to the notion that there was no such thing as a
platonic kiss between a man and a woman, and to the widely held suspicion
that literary friendships between the sexes were actually of an illicit sexual
nature. Charles Richardson elaborated upon this idea when he wrote in the
Post-Boy Robb'd of his Mail to unmask the adulterous relationship between
one of the authors of the Athenian Mercury, Richard Sault, and a woman
who he had claimed was his platonic friend and muse.[69] 'Kissing goes by
Favour', observed Richardson, 'and I have seen an Ugly Fellow embrac'd by
a Pretty Lady . . . certainly when a Muse is pregnant she must bring forth
no less than an Orpheus'. Similarly, The Spectator reported how a suspected
pregnancy resulted from an avowedly platonic relationship (he 'observed the
Waste [sic] of a Platonist lately swell to Roundness which is inconsistent with
that Philosophy').[70]

The problem with platonic friendship, as we have seen, was that in spite of
its fashionability, it was an anomaly within the dominant culture: it presented the alarming possibility that men and women could enjoy a balanced
non-sexual relationship of equals.[71] The extracts from late-seventeenth-
century literary sources presented here attempted to sexualise the idea of
non-erotic, and thus erroneous, platonic friendships between men and women.
It was thus not just 'deviant' and illicit sexual behaviour that presented a
challenge to the heterosexual norm,[72] but the possibility that genuinely chaste
friendship between the sexes might be both achievable and desirable. We
have seen how attempts to police sexual behaviour were entirely within the
remit of those who subscribed to the Reformation of Manners campaign,
yet simultaneously there was a growing interest in exploring the ambiguous
axis of friendship, love and desire, between individuals of the opposite sex,
not only within the pages of the novel or the pornographic print, but in the
periodicals read in public every day in private houses and at the local coffee
house. Through the popular literature of this period, platonic love became
re-sexualised within what was seen as the natural order. Thus, what started a
century earlier as a high-minded attempt to fuse Cartesian rationality with
Christian ethics among the Cambridge Neo-Platonists ended up as titillating
discussions in the eighteenth-century press about whether kisses were permissible between platonic friends. If philosophers and the literati frowned at

such debasement, they could do little to control public appetite for opening up the realm of personal and affective relationships to general scrutiny.

We have seen how literary interest in the meaning of gestures was significant in that it both reflected and informed the renegotiation of manners in changing social circumstances. The appearance of new forms of literature at a moment of profound social and cultural transition during the period in question was constitutive of the rise of 'polite society' in London, and may be interpreted as an important part of what Norbert Elias famously called the 'civilizing process': the gradual suppression of outward bodily habits towards self-restraint, especially the suppression of 'passionate impulses' which damped down 'extreme fluctuations in behaviour and emotions'.[73] As a result of this process, he argued, substitutes were created to compensate for a lack of direct 'release of pleasure', with the violent and erotic impulses of the bourgeois sublimated via literature and (later) film, to be experienced by proxy. The literary vogue for platonic friendship could be regarded as one manifestation of the sophisticated aspirations of a civilizing society. Was this a form of substitution, as envisaged by Elias? Did contemporary discussions of platonic friendship indicate a sublimation of sexual pleasure to within the literary realm, and were people increasingly inclined more to read about kisses than to exchange them? Certainly, contemporary sources suggest that as the eighteenth century progressed, there may have been less kissing among polite company, at least in London; effusive displays of affection upon greeting came to be associated with provincial backwoodsmen. Yet, as the contributors to this volume, and their readers, would no doubt acknowledge, reading and writing about the kiss did not necessarily indicate a substitution for experience. Instead, the ambiguity of platonic friendship invoked a pleasurable moment of uncertainty for the early eighteenth-century reader, one which would never be definitively resolved, in spite of the attempts of didactic authors to unmask such relationships as covertly sexual through the gesture of the kiss.

## NOTES

The author would like to thank Scott Ashley for his invaluable help in supplying additional suggestions and advice on this chapter.

1 The association between the mouth and eroticism is not a constant across time and cultures. For the improvement of oral hygiene, and eroticisation of the mouth in late-eighteenth-century France, see Colin Jones, 'Pulling Teeth in Eighteenth-Century Paris', *Past & Present*, 166 (2000), 100–45, and Roy Porter, *Bodies Politic: Disease, Death and Doctors in Britain, 1650–1900* (London, 2001), pp. 197–9, on how cosmetic dentistry became a more 'refined and remunerative' trade in Georgian England.

2 Even a cursory glimpse at modern guidebooks for the business traveller will illustrate the variable meaning of gestures across the globe; see, for example, Terri Morrison, Wayne A. Caraway and George A. Border, *Kiss, Bow or Shake Hands: How to do*

*Business in Sixty Countries* (Holbrook, MA, 1994). This contains invaluable advice such as 'Do not prop your feet up on anything other than a footstool in the Czech republic' (p. 81) and 'Venezuelans often touch each other's arms or jackets' (p. 423).

3 For a fascinating series of essays on the body and spirituality in the medieval church, see Caroline Walker Bynum, *Fragmentation and Redemption: Essays on Gender and the Human Body in Medieval Religion* (New York, 1991), esp. pp. 190, 194 and 198 for the 'holy' kisses from God envisioned by female mystics.

4 Galatians 3:28. For references to the idea of the sexless soul in the Gospels, see Matthew 22:30; Mark 12:25 and Luke 20:34–6.

5 Lawrence Stone, *Family, Sex and Marriage in England, 1500–1800*, abridged edn (Harmondsworth, 1979), p. 325.

6 Alan Bray, 'Homosexuality and the Signs of Male Friendship in Elizabethan England', *History Workshop Journal*, 29 (1990), 1–19, at 4; see also Alan Bray and Michel Ray, 'The Body of the Friend: Continuity and Change in Masculine Friendship in the Seventeenth Century', in Tim Hitchcock and Michèle Cohen (eds), *English Masculinities, 1660–1800* (London, 1999), pp. 65–84, esp. pp. 66–7 on kisses bestowed by James I upon his favourites.

7 For the extensive literature on this subject, see for example Richard Adair, *Courtship, Illegitimacy and Marriage in Early Modern England* (Manchester, 1996), pp. 129–48; David Cressy, *Birth, Marriage and Death: Ritual, Religion, and the Life Cycle in Tudor and Stuart England* (Oxford, 1997), pp. 233–81; Martin Ingram, *Church Courts, Sex and Marriage in England, 1570–1640* (Cambridge, 1987), pp. 128–43, 189–218; Robert Shoemaker, *Gender in English Society, 1650–1850: The Emergence of Separate Spheres?* (New York, 1998), pp. 91–101.

8 Keith Thomas, 'Introduction', in Jan Bremmer and Herman Roodenburg (eds), *A Cultural History of Gesture: From Antiquity to the Present Day* (London, 1991), p. 7, on gesture and social differentiation.

9 Michael Clanchy, 'Law and Love in the Middle Ages', in John Bossy (ed.), *Disputes and Settlements: Law and Human Relations in the West* (Cambridge, 1983), pp. 58–9.

10 Tyne and Wear Record Office, Newcastle Upon Tyne, CP/5/51, George Liddell to Robert Cotesworth, 8 December 1727.

11 2 Corinthians 13:12.

12 For examples of this genre, see Robert Cleaver and John Dod, *A Godly Form of Household Government* (London, 1614) and William Gouge, *Of Domesticall Duties*, 3rd edn (London, 1634).

13 Richard Allestree, *The Ladies Calling* (London, 1676), p. 178.

14 N. H., *Ladies Dictionary* (London, 1694), p. 9.

15 Francis Osborne, *Advice to a Son*, 6th edn (Oxford, 1658) pp. 49, 61.

16 Hannah Woolley, *The Gentlewoman's Companion; or, A Guide to the Female Sex* (London, 1675), pp. 96–7.

17 *Ibid.*

18 Henry Swinburne, *A Treatise of Spousals, or Matrimonial Contracts* (London, 1686), pp. 21, 69.

19 Laura Gowing, *Domestic Dangers: Women, Words and Sex in Early Modern London* (Oxford, 1996), pp. 164–5 and *passim*.

20 For the emergence of this genre, see J. Paul Hunter, 'The Insistent I', in *Novel: A Forum on Fiction*, 13:1 (1979), 19–37. See also Richmond P. Bond (ed.), *Studies in the Early English Periodical* (Chapel Hill, 1957), pp. 75–101.

LAWFUL KISSES? ENGLAND C.1660–1720

21 G. A. Starr, 'From Casuistry to Fiction: The Importance of the *Athenian Mercury*', *Journal of the History of Ideas*, 28 (1968), 17–32. See also Lowell Gallagher, *Medusa's Gaze: Casuistry and Conscience in the Renaissance* (Stanford, 1991).

22 Starr, 'From Casuistry to Fiction', pp. 17–18. A quarto volume entitled *Casuisticall Morning Exercises*, iv (London, 1690) featured in Dunton's personal library. See Stephen Parks, *Sale Catalogues of Libraries of Eminent Persons*, v: *Poets and Men of Letters* (London, 1972), item 1538.

23 Richard Baxter, *A Christian Directory; or, A Summ of Practical Theology and Cases of Conscience* (London, 1673).

24 *The Spectator*, 591 (8 September 1714).

25 *Ibid.*

26 *Athenian Mercury*, 4:3 (6 October 1691). For background on the Athenian Society, see Helen Berry, *Gender, Society and Print Culture in Late-Stuart England: The Cultural World of the Athenian Mercury* (Aldershot, 2003).

27 Robert Burton, *Anatomy of Melancholy* (Oxford, 1651), p. 510.

28 Elizabeth Foyster, *Manhood in Early Modern England: Honour, Sex and Marriage* (London, 1999), p. 55.

29 Françoise Waquet, *Latin, or The Empire of a Sign from the Sixteenth to the Nineteenth Centuries*, trans. John Howe (London, 2001), pp. 85–8, 126–7 and *passim*.

30 John Dunton, *Life and Errors of John Dunton, Late Citizen of London* (London, 1705), pp. 79–80, 143–4 and *passim*. This was symptomatic of what Brean S. Hammond has called the 'Mock-heroic moment' in the 1690s, a 'growing imperative to mediate classical texts to English readers through translation and imitation': see his *Professional Imaginative Writing in England, 1670–1740: Hackney for Bread* (Oxford, 1997), pp. 105–44.

31 Karen Harvey, 'Gender, Space and Modernity in Eighteenth-Century England: A Place Called Sex', *History Workshop Journal*, 51 (2001), 158–79, and *idem*, 'Representations of Bodies and Sexual Difference in Eighteenth-Century English Erotica', PhD dissertation, University of London, 1999.

32 See Anna Bryson, *From Courtesy to Civility: Changing Codes of Conduct in Early Modern England* (Oxford, 1998), pp. 107–150 on civility and social change.

33 Paul Langford, *Englishness Identified: Manners and Character, 1650–1850* (Oxford, 2000), pp. 260–1. Langford contrasts this relatively egalitarian state of affairs with the end of the eighteenth century, when he notes an increasing emphasis from 1770 upon the language of exclusion (p. 268).

34 *Ibid.*, pp. 260–1.

35 *The Spectator*, 527 (4 November 1712).

36 *Ibid.* For another interpretation of this particular incident, see Chapter 4 by David M. Turner on adulterous kisses, p. 80.

37 *The Spectator*, 240 (5 December 1711).

38 *Ibid.*

39 See Nancy Armstrong and Leonard Tennenhouse, 'The Literature of Conduct, the Conduct of Literature and the Politics of Desire: An Introduction', in *idem, The Ideology of Conduct: Essays on Literature and the History of Sexuality* (London, 1987), pp. 1–24.

40 *Athenian Mercury*, 15:24 (24 November 1694).

41 *Ibid.*, 7:2 (2 April 1692).

42 *Ibid.*, 6:7 (23 February 1692).

43 *Ibid.*, 19:23 (14 January 1696).

44 See for example Elizabeth Foyster, 'Male Honour, Social Control, and Wife Beating in Late Stuart England', *Transactions of the Royal Historical Society*, 6th series, 6 (1996), 215–24.

45  Mary Astell, *A Serious Proposal to the Ladies* (London, 1694), pp. 70, 86.

46  Emma Donoghue, 'Male–Female Friendship and English Fiction in the mid-Eighteenth Century', PhD dissertation, University of Cambridge, 1996, pp. 7–8. Donoghue suggests that the 'platonic' was 'euphemised to the point of innuendo': see pp. 24–58, 226 and *passim.*

47  *New Shorter Oxford English Dictionary*, 4th edn (Oxford, 1993).

48  Thomas Gould, *Platonic Love* (London, 1963), p. 17.

49  Frances A. Yates, *The Occult Philosophy in the Elizabethan Age* (London, 1979), pp. 76–8.

50  *Ibid.*

51  Anna Baldwin and Sarah Hutton (eds), *Platonism and the English Imagination* (Cambridge, 1994).

52  Ernst Cassirer, *The Platonic Renaissance in England*, trans. James P. Pettegrove (London, 1953), pp. 8–9, 24–8 and *passim.*

53  Quoted in James Maidment and W. H. Logan, prefatory note and memoir on Sir William D'Avenant, in *The Dramatic Works of Sir William D'Avenant*, ii (Edinburgh and London, 1872), pp. 1–2.

54  On the influence of Henrietta Maria, see Sophie Tomlinson, ' "My brain the stage": Margaret Cavendish and the Fantasy of Female Performance', in Clare Brant and Diane Purkiss (eds), *Women, Texts and Histories, 1575–1760* (London, 1992), pp. 141–2; see also E. Veevers, *Images of Love and Religion: Queen Henrietta Maria and Court Entertainments* (Cambridge, 1988).

55  Germaine Greer, 'Introduction', in Germaine Greer, Susan Hastings, Jeslyn Medoff and Melinda Sansome (eds), *Kissing the Rod: An Anthology of Seventeenth-Century Women's Verse* (London, 1988), p. 18.

56  See Susan E. Whyman, *Sociability and Power in Late-Stuart England: The Cultural World of the Verneys 1660–1720* (Oxford, 1999), pp. 47, 89.

57  *Athenian Mercury*, 6:17 (22 March 1692).

58  As Sophie Tomlinson points out, the stage direction for the two characters at this moment to 'imbrace and kiss, and hold each other in their Arms' is 'at once trangressive and salacious'; see ' "My brain the stage" ', pp. 154–5.

59  Herodotus, *The History*, trans. David Grene (Chicago and London, 1987), 4.108–17, pp. 321–2.

60  On Flecknoe, see Tomlinson, ' "My brain the stage" ', pp. 141–2; on Philips, see Lillian Faderman, *Surpassing the Love of Men: Romantic Friendship and Love between Women From the Renaissance to the Present* (New York, 1981), pp. 68–70.

61  For another anomalous challenge to 'compulsory heterosexuality', see Bridget Hill, *Women Alone: Spinsters in England, 1660–1850* (New Haven and London, 2001).

62  *The Spectator*, 90 (30 June 1711).

63  'The Loyal Garland', in J. O. Halliwell (ed.), *Early English Poetry, Ballads and Popular Literature*, The Percy Society, 29 (London, 1850), pp. 56–7.

64  *The Spectator*, 245 (11 December 1711).

65  D'Avenant, *The Platonick Lovers*, Act I, Scene i, in D'Avenant, *Dramatic Works*, p. 17.

66  *Ibid.*, Act V, Scene i, p. 104.

67  *Ibid.*, Act II, Scene i, p. 50.

68  Susannah Centlivre, *The Platonick Lady: A Comedy* (London, 1707), Act II, Scene ii, p. 16.

69  *Post-Boy Robb'd of his Mail*, 2nd edn (London, 1706), letter 63, p. 156.

70  *The Spectator*, 400 (9 June 1712).

71 The literature on the subject of women's subordination in early modern society is extensive. See for example S. D. Amussen, *An Ordered Society: Gender and Class in Early Modern England* (Oxford, 1988); Margaret R. Sommerville, *Sex and Subjection: Attitudes to Women in Early Modern Society* (London, 1995); Bernard Capp, 'Separate Domains? Woman and Authority in Early Modern England', in Paul Griffiths, Adam Fox and Steve Hindle (eds), *The Experience of Authority in Early Modern England* (Basingstoke, 1996); Anthony Fletcher, *Gender, Sex and Subordination in England 1500– 1800* (New Haven, CT, and London, 1995); Shoemaker, *Gender in English Society*.

72 An influential example of this approach to the historiography of sexuality is Randolph Trumbach, *Sex and the Gender Revolution*, i: *Heterosexuality and the Third Gender in Enlightenment London* (Chicago, 1998), whose subject is sodomites, sapphists and extramarital sexual relations.

73 Norbert Elias, *The Civilizing Process*, ii: *State Formation and Civilization*, trans. Edmund Jephcott (Oxford, 1982), p. 240 and *passim*.

# 4

## Adulterous kisses and the meanings of familiarity in early modern Britain

<>

David M. Turner

IN NOVEMBER 1712 a correspondent writing to *The Spectator* periodical under the pseudonym 'Philagnotes' related the unfortunate consequences that had arisen from a recent visit to see his female cousin in London. The three hours they had spent alone together had sent the cousin's husband, 'a wealthy citizen', into a jealous rage. Believing his wife to be conversing not with an innocent 'beardless stripling', but with a rakish 'gay Gentleman of the Temple', the jealous spouse had listened at the door, straining to hear any incriminating word or sound that would confirm his suspicions. But it was the cousins' 'parting kiss' that, the correspondent believed, 'mightily nettles him and confirms him in all his Errors'. Ever since that 'fateful afternoon', his cousin had been 'most inhumanely treated' by her partner, who had 'publickly storm'd' that he had been made a cuckold.[1]

At what point does the kiss as a social gesture become loaded with sexual meaning? What level of familiarity causes suspicion? What amount of intimacy constitutes infidelity and at what point does adultery actually begin? Rather than being a trivial gesture, the kiss raises important questions about the boundaries of acceptable contact between the sexes in early modern Britain. The contested interpretation of the gesture provided an occasion for debating and defining the limits of licit and illicit behaviour, friendship and betrayal, virtue and deceit. This chapter explores these issues by examining representations of kissing in late seventeenth- and early eighteenth-century narratives of marital infidelity. Its purpose is to analyse kissing not only as a metaphor or symbol of sexual transgression, but also as a social practice that was integral to adulterous relationships, examining the manifold ways in which this gesture might be used to initiate unlawful sexual relations.

The study of early modern intimacy has been influenced by the theories of Norbert Elias, whose seminal work *The Civilizing Process* (1939) identified a

rising threshold of shame surrounding all kinds of social (and sexual) behaviour taking place across Europe between the sixteenth and eighteenth centuries.[2] Historians have highlighted the development of new inhibitions on
kissing as the early modern period progressed. For instance, Paul Langford
has pointed to the increasing restraint of kissing habits and the marginalisation
of the gesture from the social to the sexual sphere as being symptomatic
of new perceptions of English reserve emerging by the eighteenth century.[3]
It is certainly true that there was increasing public debate during the late
seventeenth and early eighteenth centuries about the limits of acceptable
conduct as writers of prescriptive literature and periodicals sought to codify
practices of civility and politeness.[4] Not only sexually suggestive, kissing was
condemned as effeminate and as a sign of boorish rusticity.[5] Philagnotes's
letter, which called upon *The Spectator*'s editors to 'lay down Rules' by which
he and others might know what kind of 'Distinctions are to be given or
omitted' in kissing to avoid further offence, may thus be seen as part of the
broader project of drawing up a taxonomy of kissing at this time, explored
elsewhere in this volume.[6]

This cultural development provides the backdrop to this chapter. However, while it is concerned with exploring the boundaries of conduct and
familiarity, its goal is not primarily a history of inhibition. To view kissing
purely from the perspective of restraint is an insufficient method for understanding its social and cultural complexity. Anna Bryson has argued that the
Eliasian paradigm of rising inhibition necessarily 'obscures analysis of the
expressive content' of gestures and manners, masking the ways in which
they might be appropriated in different contexts. As Bryson's work has convincingly shown, the process of codifying social practices brought to the
fore tensions between competing modes of behaviour.[7] As we shall see, though
moralists and exponents of polite manners increasingly emphasised the sexual
danger and social impropriety of kissing, adulterous lovers developed a different lexicon of kissing that might appropriate official rules of conduct to
very different purposes.

Drawing principally on official and didactic sources, the first part of this
chapter looks at the context in which kissing was interpreted and understood, exploring the ways in which distinctions between acceptable and transgressive kisses were established. The thin line between social and sexual kisses,
at the crux of Philagnotes's letter to *The Spectator*, provides a point of departure for this survey, since the complexity of a gesture becomes particularly
visible at moments when it is misinterpreted. While it was broadly recognised that kissing should be bound by social convention, contemporaries
also saw that the interpretation of kisses could be influenced by a variety of
more subjective and circumstantial factors. Indeed, in spite of Elias's theory
of rising levels of psychic restraint surrounding intimacy, contemporaries in

late seventeenth- and early eighteenth-century Britain were intrigued by aberrant situations in which the rules of engagement were not fixed or were open to different readings, and occasions when apparent civility might hide darker intentions.[8] This discussion of dissimulation leads on to a more detailed study of a range of transgressive kisses, exploring the ways in which kissing acted as a symbol of betrayal and tool of seduction. The focus of analysis thus moves away from literary representations and prescriptive sources to descriptions of kissing within personal testimonies of illicit sexuality found in diaries and court records. Though they are scattered and incomplete records of intimate behaviour, these sources none the less enable us to analyse the place of kissing in adulterous relationships and consider the ways in which the practice and meaning of unlawful embracing was shaped by gender and social status.

To foreign observers, sixteenth- and early seventeenth-century English society was remarkably free in its kissing habits. Visitors often remarked on the apparent lack of inhibition among its inhabitants, illustrated above all by Englishmen's willingness to allow other men to kiss their wives and female kin. The Greek traveller Nicander Nucius, visiting England in 1547, commented on the 'great simplicity and absence of jealousy' in the way Englishmen approached women, 'for not only do those who are of the same family and household kiss them on the mouth with salutations and embraces, but even those too who have never seen them' – a practice that was apparently considered 'by no means indecent'. In 1574 Hieronymous Turler remarked that visitors to citizens' houses were invited to take the master's wife or daughter 'by the arm and to kiss them', and 'if any one does not do so, it is regarded and imputed as ignorance and ill-breeding on his part'.[9] The English reputation for allowing others to kiss their wives was regarded with some incredulity by Jonson's Volpone, who was prompted to 'wonder':

> . . . at the desperate valour
> Of the bold English, that they dare let loose
> Their wives to all encounters![10]

Evidence from travellers' accounts and the stage all seemed to confirm Erasmus's opinion of England that 'wherever you move there is nothing but kisses'.[11]

Nevertheless, while it is evident that kissing was a common mode of salutation, it was clearly expected to take place within acceptable boundaries and limits. Taking their cue from Solomon's maxim that 'whosoever toucheth . . . his neighbour's wife . . . shall not be innocent', authors of early seventeenth-century guides to personal conduct treated kissing with some suspicion.[12] Puritan moralists took a broad understanding of the Seventh

Commandment's injunctions against sexual immorality, to include 'not alone the grosse act of adultery, but all such over-familiar and light behaviours' – such as dancing, reading lewd books and plays or excesses of diet and apparel – that might act as incentives to lust.[13] It was as one of these manifold 'species of uncleanness' that threatened to lead to more serious sexual sin that kissing entered moral debate.[14] The authors of religious conduct literature argued that adultery began at the point of intent rather than at the moment of actual consummation.[15] Though they did not seek to outlaw kissing completely, recognising its heritage as a virtuous means of conveying affection, they none the less emphasised that salutation had to be carefully moderated to prevent it from becoming 'wanton' or 'lascivious'. Thus John Downame advised that kissing and embracing were to be tolerated as long as they were 'used after a civill and honest manner to expresse our love one to another'. Yet kisses that went further than 'civil curtesie' were apt to 'inflame impure hearts with burning concupiscence'.[16] William Gouge likewise urged careful government of the lips, so that they 'delight not in wanton kisses', as part of a whole regimen of bodily control to combat sin.[17]

This moral rhetoric found its corollary in the regulatory activities of the ecclesiastical courts, which in the sixteenth and seventeenth centuries functioned as guardians of acceptable morals. The Church's canons of 1604 gave the ecclesiastical authorities the power to present any kind of 'uncleanness and wickedness of life'.[18] Nevertheless, as Ingram has shown, cases of lewd behaviour – including lascivious kissing – were usually presented to the courts only if they involved otherwise acceptable behaviour getting out of hand, or if they were supported by other incriminating evidence or the poor reputations of those involved.[19] Evidence of kissing was more often used to support more serious allegations of sexual immorality. Ecclesiastical lawyers argued that the act of a man and woman being alone in a 'suspected Place, kissing and embracing each other in a very immodest Posture' might be used to enmesh a suspected couple in a web of incriminating evidence if direct proof of their adultery or fornication was not forthcoming, especially if they had 'both [been] suspected before of incontinency'.[20]

However, such evidence was notoriously slippery, and defendants might appeal to concepts of civility to contest the meanings of kisses. This may be seen in the defence strategy employed by Robert Foulkes, vicar of Stanton Lacy in Shropshire, in the correction-of-morals case commenced against him in the Hereford Consistory Court in 1676 for his suspected adultery with a spinster, Anne Atkinson. Although Foulkes had been observed to kiss Atkinson on various occasions, it was argued in mitigation that this behaviour was perfectly normal and well-mannered behaviour in the context of a respectable social relationship since, as one witness pointed out, 'he might salute her by way of courtesie'.[21] Though the act of kissing an unmarried parishioner might be interpreted as a scandal to Foulkes's function as a vicar, Foulkes appears to have been left guardian to Anne by her father, the former incumbent of Stanton Lacy, and therefore he was able to claim that his kisses were an acceptable form of civility in the context of that relationship.[22] In order to make evidence of kissing stronger, witnesses were encouraged to give other kinds of supporting evidence. References to garments touching, hands on parts of the body (especially the waist or knee) during the kiss, faces touching and, as we shall see in more detail later, a reaction of surprise and embarrassment on discovery were all used to demonstrate that the suspected couple were engaged in a kiss of unlawful intimacy rather than mere respect or affection.[23]

As the seventeenth century progressed, moralists and social commentators became more expansive in their attempts to delineate lawful and unlawful kisses. To the general warnings of the dangers of 'wanton' or 'lascivious' kissing present in the Puritan conduct literature of the early seventeenth century were added more specific rules regarding particular relationships and circumstances. For instance, greater concern was shown towards the effects of immoderate displays of affection between married couples in public. The *Ladies Dictionary* (1694) condemned the 'public billing' and 'open smacking' of lips practised by married couples, which, it argued, 'sheweth the way to unexperienc'd youth to commit riot in private'. Thus 'little by little, chastity [is] abolished'.[24] *The Spectator* likewise criticised the 'unseasonable Fondness of some Husbands, and the ill-tim'd Tenderness of some Wives', who 'talk and act, as if Modesty was only fit for Maids and Batchelors'.[25] As the burgeoning literature of politeness emphasised the importance of virtuous social interaction between the sexes as a means of cultivating good manners, so increasing care had to be taken about one's appearance in public and about gestures towards others. Women in particular were advised to avoid all 'kinds of civility, as may be mistaken for an Invitation to what is unseasonable' and behave with modesty and discretion.[26] As authors of conduct literature began to emphasise that the chief dangers to a woman's chastity came from the flattery and insinuation of men rather than her own lustful nature, they emphasised that special care had to be taken to read men's behaviour.[27] In this context, more explicit counsel was given on how to distinguish between different types of kisses. A man's intentions were evident in 'the very manner of his address', counselled one early eighteenth-century advice book, thus 'if he tongues you when he kisses, 'tis an Argument of his Lust'.[28]

But in spite of these attempts to draw up general rules on salutation, it was evident that the interpretation of kissing depended on a variety of incidental factors.[29] Periodicals of the late seventeenth and early eighteenth centuries drew attention to the ways in which context and circumstances might alter moral judgements. The interpretation of kissing, as we have already seen, was influenced by the relationship between the parties involved and the social setting in which kissing took place. While some commentators were urging greater restraint in the use of kisses, it is evident that the kiss remained a powerful symbol of trust and friendship. The apparent reserve demanded in the developing social spaces of polite society – parks, pleasure gardens, assemblies and theatres – might be at odds with more traditional values of neighbourliness. Codes of restraint could create situations of awkwardness and anxiety, as may be seen by a dilemma submitted to the *Athenian Mercury* periodical in April 1695. The correspondent described how the wife of 'a very intimate acquaintance' would insist on being very 'familiar' in her behaviour towards him, 'insomuch that if I don't kiss her, she'll kiss me, and other great familiarities'. Her husband, 'an infirm man', seemed 'very well pleas'd with our conversation', but the correspondent felt uncomfortable, for he was a 'single man, and wou'd not be rude'. Here, 'rude' has a double meaning – to discourage her kisses might be interpreted as a social rebuff, yet the correspondent was anxious to avoid imputations that their kissing implied 'rude' behaviour of another kind, the cuckolding of a man who was, by all accounts, incapable of satisfying his wife sexually. Although such kisses were not 'directly criminal', the editors responded, 'yet the consequences of 'em are so dangerous, and so plain in view' that the correspondent should try 'by all means to change such a course of life' for the sake of his 'own Honour or Happiness'.[30] Nevertheless, as this case shows, while moral prudence and politeness might require restraint, to refuse to kiss the wife of a neighbour or trusted acquaintance, at least when invited to do so, might imply a lack of respect.

The interpretation of kissing was also influenced by the part of the body that was kissed. While mouth kisses were seen as more obviously dangerous and signs of lust, hand-kissing was a more formal, ceremonial practice that carried connotations of distance and respectability. However, even these kisses might carry a double meaning. As manuals of polite behaviour proliferated from the late seventeenth century, so writers became increasingly fascinated with the ways in which social civilities might function as a cloak for sin. 'These little freedoms now make people foolishly question women's virtue', remarks Sir Lively Cringe in Charles Burnaby's comedy *The Modish Husband* (1702), as Lord Promise kisses his wife's hand, comically unaware that his lordship's motives a more sinister.[31] Problems of interpreting such kisses were depicted as driving some husbands to violence or even madness. Writing in despair to the *British Apollo* periodical in 1708, one such husband described how he was liable to 'go distracted' at the conduct of his 'brisk young wife' who 'salutes (as they say) civilly' every 'handsome Fellow' who came to their house. The editors' response, that such behaviour was 'an

Argument of her Confidence in your Opinion of her Modesty', was unlikely to provide much comfort.[32]

It is this potential for kisses to deceive, seemingly to communicate signs of deeper intimacy, that provides a key to their trangressive capabilities. However, the cultural heritage of the gesture gave it a firmer association with matrimonial betrayal. The Judas kiss was a powerful metaphor for alienated affections in early modern culture, especially – given its association with death – in stories of crimes of passion. Such tales were popular in the pamphlet literature of early modern England, not least because in what was effectively a divorceless society, it was feared that an errant spouse might resort to drastic measures to marry a lover.[33] In a pamphlet account of John Marketman, a ship's surgeon of West Ham in Essex, who killed his wife in 1680 believing her to be having an affair with a neighbour, it was reported that he had taken his wife 'about the neck Judas like as if he intended to kiss her', before thrusting a knife into her heart.[34] In a ballad account of John Chambers, 'The Bloody-Minded Husband', who ordered his servant to shoot his wife so that he might enjoy 'sinful pleasures' with his 'wanton Harlot', Chambers is depicted as making to 'salute' his wife as she lay dying:

> But she (alas) refus'd his Judas kiss
> And with her dying voice, she told him this:
> By Murther now you have procur'd my death,
> And with those words she yielded up her breath.[35]

The Judas kiss represented betrayal in its strongest and most dramatic terms. It signalled that justice was imminent and also drew attention to the spiritual dimension of marital breakdown.[36] Marriage was viewed not just as a bond between husband and wife, but also as a covenant between the couple and God, analogous to the union between Christ and his Church. The image of the Judas kiss emphasised that the breach of wedlock was more than a private matter, but a great affront to God and society at large with potentially devastating consequences.[37]

The association between kissing and marital betrayal also revealed itself in less dramatic circumstances. In personal accounts of infidelity from the seventeenth century, it appears that the knowledge that one's spouse had kissed his or her lover could be especially distressing for the deceived partner. This may be inferred from Samuel Pepys's accounts of his wife's reaction to her discovery of his fondling the maidservant Deb Willet in October 1668.[38] While Elizabeth Pepys had grounds to suspect her husband's sexual misconduct with Willet, what appeared to hurt her most was the thought of the smaller intimacies of kissing and hugging that the couple had enjoyed. On 26 October 1668, the day after the discovery, Pepys recorded that around midnight his wife woke him from his sleep 'and there [fell] foul on me . . . affirming that she saw me hug and kiss the girl; the latter I denied and truly; the other I confessed and no more'.[39] Elizabeth's anger was fuelled by the conviction that her husband was lying about kissing Willet and that he was therefore trying to trivialise his relationship with the maid. On 10 November 1668, Elizabeth was again 'troubled' with her husband's story, berating him for his 'unkindness and perjury' for having 'denied . . . ever kissing' Willet.[40]

Pepys's denials were indeed disingenuous. While he may well have thought truthfully that his wife had not *seen* him kiss Willet, he had in fact recorded in his diary on 22 December 1667 that the basis for his relationship with Willet was laid when 'this time I first did give her a little kiss'.[41] That this 'little kiss' became a matter of such importance once the affair had been detected signals once more the gesture's power as a symbol of betrayal. In spite of the unequal relations of authority within patriarchal marriage, religious conduct writers emphasised that matrimony ideally represented a bond of perfect friendship and a partnership of equals, that husband and wife were 'yoke fellows' and that a wife was her husband's 'second self'.[42] The kiss, an important gesture in the making of marriage, symbolised this equality between husband and wife.[43] In Elizabeth's eyes, her husband's kissing Willet represented her displacement both in her spouse's affections and in the household order by a domestic inferior. Equally symbolically, Elizabeth eventually signalled her willingness to mend their broken relationship by permitting the kiss of peace. On 20 November 1668, Pepys recorded that after he had written to Willet (who had been dismissed from service), formally breaking off the relationship and calling her (on Elizabeth's instruction) a 'whore', his wife 'begun to be kind' to him, and they were 'to kiss and be friends'.[44]

To lovers, the kiss carried a different set of meanings and served a variety of purposes in extramarital relationships. First and foremost, kissing provided a means of breaking down inhibitions as a pathway to further sexual relations. This was evidently a tactic used by Samuel Pepys in his relationship with Deb Willet, and his diary as a whole provides numerous other examples of kisses used for this purpose. In a manner that seems to confirm the cultural anxieties raised in the period's conduct literature and plays, Pepys's kissing practices richly demonstrate how rituals of salutation might be exploited as a tool for adulterous intrigue. The diarist's description of his relationship with Betty Mitchell provides a particularly vivid example. Pepys had frequented the haberdasher's shop owned by Betty's parents and, as a result, had known her since she was a girl. He had long viewed her with affection, nicknaming her his 'wife' because of her resemblance to Elizabeth.[45] In the spring of 1666 she married Michael Mitchell, whose parents, booksellers in Westminster Hall, were also old friends of the diarist.[46] The young couple set up a tavern in Old Swan Lane and looked upon Pepys as a trusted source of advice and assistance in the world. On 13 May 1666, Pepys recalled meeting Betty Mitchell with her husband and his parents at St Margaret's Church, Westminster, where he 'had the opportunity to have salute[d] two or three times Betty and make an acquaintance; which they are pleased with, though not so much as I am or they think I am'.[47] While Michael Mitchell may have been flattered by the attentions of an older, influential man towards his wife, Pepys himself saw it as an opportunity of gaining Betty's trust to lay the basis for a future sexual relationship. As a civil servant in the Naval Office, Pepys knew that he was useful to the Mitchells, since he could cash the pay tickets that sailors used in exchange for drink in taverns, and he saw this as a perfect opportunity to become better acquainted with the young couple.[48]

Pepys visited the Mitchells' tavern two or three times a month during the following summer, and recorded with some relish the occasions when he had been able to 'steal a kiss or two from Betty'.[49] At this stage, Pepys described their kisses as being 'stolen', suggesting both their illicit and tentative nature and the thrill of a new amorous intrigue. By the autumn, Pepys's descriptions of their kisses had changed, relating how in spite of Betty remaining 'mighty modest' in her demeanour, he now 'had her lips as much as [he] would'. With this increased confidence about their relationship, Pepys finally took matters a stage further on 2 December when, sitting next to Betty in a coach returning from a christening, he placed her hands under his clothes and encouraged her to fondle him.[50]

While Pepys's intention may have been to use kissing to negotiate Betty's modesty with the ultimate aim of greater erotic arousal, it is also apparent from his description of his kisses, and the situations in which they occurred, that they offered distinctive pleasures of their own. Pepys took special delight in recording kisses that he had stolen from Betty while her husband was in close proximity. For instance, on 5 August 1666 Pepys recorded, in the idiosyncratic polyglot style he sometimes used in the diary's amorous passages, how he had visited Betty at the Old Swan and taken 'two or three long salutes from her out of sight of su marido, which pleased me mightily'.[51] Stolen kisses formed the pretext of an amorous game of concealment, which not only afforded Pepys the pleasure of Betty's embraces, but also contained the thrill of deceiving a younger, less experienced man. These kissing games contained the excitement of deception that came with cuckolding another man, but stopped short of the more complicated (and condemnable) business of intercourse.

This behaviour, together with other activities recorded in Pepys's diary and those of other men, gives support to Tim Hitchcock's argument that with regard to sexual relations in this period, we need to take a broad view that starts with the kiss.[52] The diarist's comments elsewhere suggest that this kind of activity did not trouble his conscience too greatly. Recalling a visit to the Dog Tavern with Doll Lane in October 1666, he remarked that he 'did nothing but salute and play with her, and talk'. Several weeks later, after a similar encounter with Doll at the Rose Tavern, he noted that 'there was no hurt in it, nor can be alleged from it' – a telling admission that suggests that Pepys believed that kissing and other forms of embracing and fondling were, legally speaking, relatively weak evidence of sexual impropriety.[53] These views were not held by all of Pepys's acquaintances. In October 1664, the wife of William Bagwell visited Pepys in his office in search of patronage for her husband. The diarist recalled that he 'kissed her only', but she gently rebuffed him, 'saying that I did [it] so much to many bodies' that 'it would be a stain to me'.[54] Pepys also recalled angrily that while embracing his regular mistress, Betty Lane, in a tavern in June 1663, a passer-by flung a stone at the window, crying 'Sir, why do you kiss the gentlewoman so?'[55] Whether this was a sign of violent disapproval or a practical joke is not recorded. However, the incident shows that some might consider public and indiscreet embracing as an offensive sign of sexual impropriety, in spite of the diarist's denials.

Power was at stake in these male accounts of kissing as much as sexual intimacy. The confidence with which Pepys approached women such as Betty Mitchell or Deb Willet derived from his higher social status and position of influence over them. What to Samuel Pepys seemed an amorous game might look more like sexual harassment to a less partial observer. Men such as Pepys could more easily hide behind codes of civility and sanctioned modes of salutation, in order to pursue their less honourable intentions, than either men of a lower status or, especially, women, for whom rules of modesty were stricter. However, it is possible that the women involved may have tolerated these advances, or used their kisses in order to cultivate the favour of a powerful patron. When the wife of Samuel Daniel visited Pepys in December 1665 to 'speak for her husband to be a Lieutenant', she gave him the opportunity of 'kissing her again and again', and came away with the assurance that he would 'be very willing to do [her spouse] any kindness'.[56] The commerce of kisses played an important role in the politics of influence and favour, and some women appeared highly adept at using their embraces for their family's gain.

In contrast, it was considered far more scandalous for a married woman to kiss a man much beneath her station. Among many allegations of sexual impropriety levelled against Dame Winifred Barlow of Slebech (Pembrokeshire) in a separation suit launched against her in the Court of Arches in 1705 was the claim that she had allowed William Rochford, the local ferryman, to kiss her at will. A witness told the court that Rochford had boasted to him that 'he could have a kiss of the s[ai]d Lady Barlow when he pleased and that he was used to put[ting] a silver penny in a little purse within her stayes and could look for [th]e same when he pleased and that when he could not find it he was to have twenty kisses'.[57] These kisses were all the more improper since they not only displayed a contempt for Winifred's husband, but also challenged the social hierarchy by allowing an inferior to take liberties above his station.

Most shocking of all were cases of mistress – servant adultery. Witnesses in such cases were highly attuned to any breach of household protocols that might imply sexual misconduct. Over 100 pages of evidence were brought against Diana Dormer in the London Consistory Court in 1715, recounting her scandalous familiarity with two of her footmen, Thomas Jones and Lawrence Burgess. The servant James Warham recalled that he had observed Diana 'sitting upon a blew and white velvet couch or squabb' in the dining room of the Dormers' house in Albemarle Street, London, with Thomas Jones 'standing by and close to her and stooping with his face toward hers as if it were to kisse her'.[58] Another servant recalled how she had once 'hastily' opened the parlour door and found Diana 'then sitting on a leather chaire before the fire with her arme leaning on a table', and Jones 'then standing by her and kissing her', upon which Jones, 'in a great surprize', ran out of the room.[59] If the very idea of a servant kissing his mistress was shocking enough to early modern sensibilities, the fact that Jones is described kissing his mistress's face is even more significant, since traditionally, the lower a person's status, the further from the face his or her kisses were supposed to be.[60] The scandalous nature of these kisses was also supported by the reactions of surprise exhibited by the lovers when caught. Sara Wilkinson, a former nurse to the Dormers' children, recalled how she had 'by accident' surprised the couple in the dining room, whereupon the footman ran out of the room 'as if he had been affrighted' while Diana seemed 'to be under a great surprise too, being very pale and as if shee were going to swoon'.[61]

Accounts of female seduction presented in marital separation suits present familiar anxieties about rituals of sociability being used by unfaithful wives to convey unlawful passions. Winifred Barlow's character was systematically blackened by a series of evidence designed to show her to be socially indiscreet and wholly lacking in modesty, someone who conducted herself in a 'very uncivill and scandalous manner', being too 'free and familiar' with others in her acquaintance. She was accused of greeting the gentlemen who visited her husband's house 'very indiscreetly', by giving them 'too great a freedome by kissing them after a wanton manner'.[62] Witnesses testifying on behalf of her husband, Sir George Barlow, had little doubt that Winifred used social greetings as a cover for communicating unlawful desires. Thus Thomas Davies observed that Hugh Philips was allowed to 'kiss . . . Lady Barlow very lovingly and otherwise than after [th]e usual way of saluting a woman.'[63] Kissing was one of several means by which she was alleged to turn virtuous social visits into occasions of seduction and vice. On another occasion,

Winifred's over-familiarity was noticed at a card game when the servant John Barden observed that one of the players, Captain Passinger, was permitted to 'sit with his arms about . . . Dame Winifred's waist as they and others sat playing'.[64] Henry Bowen, the Barlows' household chaplain, further recalled that when various neighbouring gentlemen were being entertained at the house during the evening time she would walk about the house in her night-clothes, which, as he informed her, was 'imbecomeing' [sic] a woman of her station.[65] It was implied that this indiscretion was also related to Winifred's habitual drunkenness, which led her to cast off normal constraints of bodily control and decorum. Walter Middleton, Sir George's grandfather, deposed that when 'merry' with drink Winifred 'was of a very free temper' and had 'kissed' him called him 'her little grandfather' and told him that 'he had been an old whoremonger'.[66]

Read against the grain and more sympathetically, this evidence might convey less the vicious conduct of a shameless adulteress than the frustra-tions of a young woman trapped in a loveless marriage, who saw in rituals of salutation a means of gaining the attention and affection from other men that may have been lacking from her husband. Court narratives of women's adultery reveal other ways in which kisses might display a rebellious side to female conduct. The kiss – or denial of a kiss – was a means of representing disrespect on the part of an adulterous wife towards her husband. Kissing was considered an important means of showing a wife's loyalty and affection towards her spouse – to deny a kiss was a gesture of domestic defiance. Hester Denton of Hillesden in Buckinghamshire, sued by her husband for separation in the Court of Arches in 1690 for her adultery with his friend Thomas Smith, was sometimes observed to 'carry herselfe very slightingly towards her husband', refusing 'to let him kisse her and to stay in the room where he was when he desired it'.[67] Martha Ryland, a servant called to testify to her mistress's misconduct, told the court that Hester 'behaved herself very slightingly and unkindly and not at all becoming a wife towards her . . . husband, and hath several times in [her] sight refused to let her . . . Husband kisse her when he has very earnestly desired it and turn'd away from him and flung up her head and made mouths at him'.[68] Replacing kisses with gestures of mockery, in full view of the servants, was an important means of building up the profile of Hester Denton as a bad wife and implied that her kisses were bestowed elsewhere. Indeed, when Thomas Smith came to the house, he was taken into a parlour where, as Martha Ryland observed through the keyhole, he would sit in Hester's lap, spending perhaps 'a quarter of an hour in that posture kissing and stroaking her upon the face and sometimes c[h]ucking her under the chin'.[69]

Saving her kisses for her lover in private, Hester Denton used kissing, in the words of Willem Frijhoff, as a 'rite of aggregation and of appropriation', separating her relationship with Thomas Smith from that which she shared with her husband.[70] Greeting her lover with 'great joy and satisfaction' and freely allowing him to 'kisse and embrace her' with 'his armes sometimes about her Neck and at other times about her Waist' were part of an elaborate ritual of seduction employed by Hester.[71] This also included the provision of 'extraordinary food' whenever Thomas came to visit, such as a 'Calves head hasht, sometimes fatt Chickens, Ducks, Turkeys, Fish, Cheesecakes, Tarts, Soups and other things w[hi]ch were not ordinary at other times'.[72] Women's seduction narratives present an intriguing connection between food, kissing and sex. Anthropologists have described kissing as 'eating without devouring', a ritual that establishes trust and physical compatibility between lovers.[73] Furthermore, the sharing of lascivious kisses and the provision of food were both representative of the sharing of the lovers' bodies during sex. This connection gave such evidence much symbolic importance in stories of illicit relationships presented to the courts.[74]

However, court records also show that the act of kissing was not just confined to the sphere of intimacy, nor did it serve simply as an expression of sexual passion. For a woman to kiss another man in the presence of her husband could be an aggressive or provocative gesture. The separation suit brought by William Hockmore of Newton Abbot in Devon against his wife, Mary, in 1698 is strikingly illustrative of the frustrations of a loveless marriage at its dysfunctional limits. Kissing was one of a series of gestures used by Mary as a means of humiliating her spouse in company – others included verbal abuse and physical violence. A particularly vivid example of this occurred at a social gathering hosted by Francis Risdon, one of the Hockmores' gentry neighbours, in October 1695. Mary was joined by two men, Edward Ford and Nicholas Cove, with whom she was widely rumoured to be having an affair. Seemingly quite oblivious to their fellow guests, and Mary's husband, the three of them were 'very familiar' together, 'kissing' and 'toying' with each other. Later on, the men took to 'jeering' William Hockmore about his wife, teasing him that he would soon be 'fitt[ed]' with cuckold's horns.[75] Allowing these men to kiss her before her husband and his closest friends was perhaps a means by which Mary Hockmore sought empowerment, as much a means of expressing her distaste for her husband and her marriage as an expression of passion for her lovers. For them too, the pleasure of kissing Mary seemed to be intimately linked with subordinating and humiliating her husband.

The history of gesture proceeds from the belief that even a relatively simple act may provide a key to unlocking the broader social and cultural system of which it is a part.[76] This chapter has attempted to show that instead of being a trivial (or straightforward) gesture, the kiss provides intriguing evidence of the complexity and contested nature of intimacy in early modern society. In spite of the perception, fostered in the accounts of foreign observers, that early modern England was remarkably free in its kissing habits, it is clear that practices of kissing were invested with danger and anxiety. The kiss provided a focus for tensions in rituals of visiting and greeting. Such anxieties were felt particularly keenly among the upper and increasingly wealthy middling ranks of society, for whom visits and favours were forms of 'social commerce' that bound families and individuals together.[77] Correct observation of rituals of salutation was supposed to offer reassurance; greetings signalled acceptance of the social order and the status quo.[78] Yet the erotic potential of kissing constantly threatened to invert these rituals, turning visits into adulterous intrigues. Such anxieties were already present in the early seventeenth century, when kissing was a widely accepted form of greeting, but became even more pronounced as the period progressed, dovetailing with enduring fears about dissimulation of manners and new concerns about men's sexually predatory nature that presented a constant threat to female chastity. Commentators of the late seventeenth and early eighteenth centuries used anxieties about the kiss of greeting to expose a darker side of the polite 'conversation' – virtuous social interaction between the sexes – that was valued so highly for inculcating good breeding and manners.[79]

The response to these anxieties among religious and social moralists was to urge greater caution in social relations and restraint. In this context, kissing became an exemplary gesture around which notions of proper and improper sociability were formed. Yet these new rules of engagement created their own anxieties. Periodicals highlighted cultural clashes between traditional and more modern, polite modes of sociability. That social civilities might act as a smokescreen, serving not as instruments of inhibition but as a means of deception that expressed illicit passions rather than held them at bay, is evident not only from the period's didactic literature and stage comedies, but also in the very practices of adulterous lovers. Within the context of illicit relationships, kissing rituals carried very diverse sets of meanings. Kissing developed an erotic language of its own in which 'stolen' embraces were invested with particular pleasure. It was a practice appropriated by different people for a variety of purposes. For philandering men, the kiss provided a means of breaking down women's modesty, with a view to more developed sexual relations. Bored wives of the social elite exploited rituals of salutation as a means of gaining the attention of other men that may have been lacking from their marriages or of humiliating their spouses. Furthermore, some poorer women may have used kisses in a ritual of exchange and barter, with a view to extracting favours from powerful men.

How, then, was kissing judged in the context of infidelity and marital breakdown? Though moralists condemned all 'wanton' and 'lascivious' embraces as synonymous with adulterous passions, it is apparent that outside the strictures of official morality kissing could be treated more ambivalently, as a form of intimacy that carried the capacity for emotional and sexual development, but fell short of actual infidelity. However, these understandings of kisses as playful gestures stood in sharp contrast to their powerful symbolic associations with betrayal. Seen from the perspective of the victims of adultery rather than its perpetrators, the kiss between an unfaithful partner and his or her lover might be even more painful than knowledge of their sexual relations. The kiss symbolised tenderness and equality between lovers that raised their relationship to a higher level than the mere satisfaction of base sexual urges. What accounts of seduction and betrayal reveal above all is the close relationship between intimacy and power in early modern Britain. If lawful kissing upheld the status quo, illicit embracing was closely linked with the abuse or exploitation of power relations. Within marriage too, the commerce of kisses held together a relationship, representing the spiritual equality of husband and wife. Embraces might settle marital disputes, but the withholding or wrongful bestowing of kisses was a source of particular pain and conflict within marriage. The records of marital breakdown reveal that what might serve as a means of securing love or establishing familiarity could equally act as a powerful symbol of contempt.

### NOTES

In addition to the organisers and participants at the conference 'The Kiss in History' held at the Institute of Historical Research (July 2000), I should like to thank members of the South Wales and West Women's History Network for their helpful comments on earlier versions of this chapter.

1  *The Spectator*, 527 (4 November 1712); ed. Donald F. Bond, 5 vols (Oxford, 1965), iv, pp. 378–9.
2  Norbert Elias, *The Civilizing Process, i: The History of Manners*, trans. Edmund Jephcott (1939; Oxford, 1978).
3  Paul Langford, *Englishness Identified: Manners and Character, 1650–1850* (Oxford, 2000), pp. 163–4. See also Adrianne Blue, *On Kissing: From the Metaphysical to the Erotic* (London, 1996), p. 157.
4  The literature on civility and politeness is voluminous. See, for example, Anna Bryson, *From Courtesy to Civility: Changing Codes of Conduct in Early Modern England* (Oxford, 1998); Philip Carter, *Men and the Emergence of Polite Society, Britain 1660–1800* (London and New York, 2000), chs 1–2; Michele Cohen, *Fashioning Masculinity: National Identity and Language in the Eighteenth Century* (London and New York, 1996); Fenela Childs, 'Prescriptions for Manners in English Courtesy Literature 1690–1760 and their Social Implications', DPhil dissertation, University of Oxford, 1984; Amanda Vickery, *The Gentleman's Daughter: Women's Lives in Georgian England* (New Haven, CT, and London, 1998); Lawrence Klein, 'Politeness for Plebes: Consumption and Social Identity in Early Eighteenth-Century England', in Ann Bermingham and John Brewer (eds), *The Consumption of Culture 1600–1800: Image, Object, Text* (London, 1995), pp. 362–82.

5 Langford, *Englishness Identified*, p. 163; *The Spectator*, 240 (4 November 1712); ed. Bond, ii, pp. 433–4; *Mundus Foppensis: or, The Fop Display'd* (London, 1691), pp. 12–13; *Satan's Harvest Home: or, The Present State of Whorecraft, Adultery, Fornication, Procuring, Pimping, and the Game at Flatts* (London, 1749), pp. 51–2.

6 *The Spectator*, 527 (4 November 1712); ed. Bond, iv, p. 379. The correspondent's concerns exemplify a growing gulf between rustic and urbane manners as well as the blurring of boundaries between social and sexual kissing, as Berry notes in Chapter 3 in this volume, and the ambiguity was compounded by changing perceptions of what constituted acceptable (polite) social conduct.

7 Anna Bryson, 'The Rhetoric of Status: Gesture, Demeanour and the Image of the Gentleman in Sixteenth- and Seventeenth-Century England', in Lucy Gent and Nigel Llewellyn (eds), *Renaissance Bodies: The Human Figure in English Culture* (London, 1990), p. 139.

8 This theme is developed further in David M. Turner, *Fashioning Adultery: Gender, Sex and Civility in England, 1660–1740* (Cambridge, 2002), ch. 2; Helen Berry, 'Rethinking Politeness in Eighteenth-Century England: Moll King's Coffee House and the Significance of "Flash Talk"', *Transactions of the Royal Historical Society*, 6th series, 11 (2001), 65–81.

9 William Brenchley Rye, *England as Seen by Foreigners in the Days of Elizabeth and James the First* (London, 1865), pp. 261, 90.

10 Ben Jonson, *Volpone* (1605), Act I, Scene iv, lines 100–2, in Ben Jonson, *Five Plays*, ed. G. A. Wilkes (Oxford, 1988), p. 252.

11 Rye (ed.), *England as Seen by Foreigners*, p. 261; see also Blue, *On Kissing*, p. 156.

12 Proverbs, 6:29, quoted in William Whateley, *A Bride-Bush, or A Wedding Sermon* (London, 1617), p. 3.

13 *Ibid.*

14 For this phrase see Jean-Frederic Ostervald, *The Nature of Uncleanness Consider'd* (London, 1708), p. 177.

15 J. S., *A Sermon against Adultery* (London, 1672), p. 18.

16 John Downame, *Foure Treatises, Tending to Diswade all Christians from Foure no Less Hainous then Common Sinnes; Namely the Abuses of Swearing, Drunkennesse, Whoredome and Briberie* (London, 1609), pp. 200–1. See also Martin Ingram, 'Sexual Manners: The Other Face of Civility in Early Modern England', in Peter Burke, Brian Harrison and Paul Slack (eds), *Civil Histories: Essays Presented to Sir Keith Thomas* (Oxford, 2000), p. 96.

17 William Gouge, *Of Domesticall Duties* (London, 1622), p. 221.

18 Martin Ingram, *Church Courts, Sex and Marriage in England, 1570–1640* (Cambridge, 1987), p. 239.

19 *Ibid.*, pp. 240–2.

20 John Ayliffe, *Parergon juris canonici Anglicani: or, A Commentary by Way of Supplement to the Canons and Constitutions of the Church of England* (London, 1726), p. 45.

21 Hereford Record Office, HD4/26, Office v. Foulkes, deposition of Elizabeth Atkinson, 18 September 1677.

22 Aspects of this case are discussed further in David M. Turner, ' "Nothing is so secret but shall be revealed": The Scandalous Life of Robert Foulkes', in Tim Hitchcock and Michèle Cohen (eds), *English Masculinities, 1660–1800* (London, 1999), pp. 169–92.

23 For example: London Metropolitan Archives (hereafter LMA), DL/C/255, Dormer v. Dormer, deposition of Francis Warrington, 17 May 1715, fol. 182$^v$.

24 N. H., *The Ladies Dictionary* (London, 1694), p. 155.

25  *The Spectator*, 430 (14 July 1712); ed. Bond, iv, p. 13; see also *ibid.*, 300 (13 February 1712); ed. Bond, iii, p. 72.

26  N. H., *Ladies Dictionary*, p. 70.

27  Childs, 'Prescriptions for Manners', p. 274.

28  [Edward Ward], *Female Grievances Debated, in Six Dialogues between Two Young Ladies Concerning Love and Marriage* (London, 1707), pp. 53–4.

29  Willem Frijhoff, 'The Kiss Sacred and Profane: Reflections on a Cross-Cultural Confrontation', in Jan Bremmer and Herman Roodenburg (eds), *A Cultural History of Gesture: From Antiquity to the Present Day* (London, 1991), pp. 201–36, at p. 212.

30  *Athenian Mercury*, 17: 7, question 5 (23 April 1695). See also *ibid*, 6:7, question 5 (23 February 1692). For more kissing dilemmas presented to this periodical see Berry in Chapter 3 above.

31  Charles Burnaby, *The Modish Husband* (London, 1702), Act I, p. 13.

32  *British Apollo*, supernumerary paper no. 7 (October 1708).

33  Laura Gowing, *Domestic Dangers: Women, Words and Sex in Early Modern London* (Oxford, 1996), p. 205. This theme is examined further in Turner, *Fashioning Adultery*, ch. 4.

34  *The True Narrative of the Execution of John Marketman, Chyrurgion, of West Ham in Essex, for Committing a Horrible and Bloody Murther upon the Body of his Wife* (n.p., n.d. [1680]), p. 3.

35  *The Pepys Ballads*, ed. Hyder Rollins, 8 vols (Cambridge, MA, 1931), iii, pp. 203–4.

36  Malcolm Gaskill, 'Reporting Murder: Fiction in the Archives in Early Modern England', *Social History*, 23 (1998), 23.

37  See, for instance, J. S., *Sermon against Adultery*, p. 7; Isaac Barrow, *The Theological Works of Isaac Barrow*, ed. Alexander Napier, 9 vols (Cambridge, 1859), vii, p. 491; William Fleetwood, *The Relative Duties of Parents and Children, Husbands and Wives, Masters and Servants, Consider'd in Sixteen Sermons* (London, 1705), p. 179.

38  For an account of this incident see Anthony Fletcher, *Gender, Sex and Subordination in England 1500–1800* (New Haven, CT, and London, 1995), pp. 170–1.

39  Samuel Pepys, *The Diary of Samuel Pepys*, ed. Robert Latham and William Matthews, 11 vols (London, 1970–83), ix, p. 339 (26 October 1668).

40  *Ibid.*, ix, p. 356 (10 November 1668).

41  *Ibid.*, viii, p. 585 (22 December 1667).

42  Whateley, *Bride-Bush*, p. 8; *British Apollo*, 2:28 (1 July 1709).

43  Diana O'Hara, 'The Language of Tokens and the Making of Marriage', *Rural History*, 3:1 (1992), 10; cf. Henry Swinburne, *A Treatise of Spousals, or Matrimonial Contracts* (London, 1686), pp. 41–2. See also Blue, *On Kissing*, p. 150.

44  Pepys, *Diary*, ix, p. 370 (20 November 1668).

45  *Ibid.*, iv, p. 234 (18 July 1663).

46  *Ibid.*, vii, p. 89 (2 April 1666).

47  *Ibid.*, vii, p. 123 (13 May 1666).

48  *Ibid.*, vii, p. 175 (21 June 1666).

49  *Ibid.*, vii, p. 196 (6 July 1666); see also vii, p. 207 (15 July 1666); vii, p. 230 (31 July 1666), vii, p. 234 (5 August 1666).

50  *Ibid.*, vii, p. 338 (23 October 1666); vii, p. 395 (2 December 1666).

51  *Ibid.*, vii, p. 234 (5 August 1666).

52  Tim Hitchcock, 'Sex and Gender: Redefining Sex in Eighteenth-Century England', *History Workshop Journal*, 41 (1996), 72–90, at 79. For evidence of a link between kissing and masturbation, see (for instance) William Byrd, *The London Diary (1717–1721)*

*and Other Writings*, ed. Louis B. Wright and Marion Trilling (New York, 1958), pp. 68, 71, 72, 77, 83, 85, 87.

53  Pepys, *Diary*, vii, p. 342 (26 October 1666); *ibid.*, p. 359 (7 November 1666).

54  *Ibid.*, v, p. 287 (3 October 1664)

55  *Ibid.*, iv, p. 203 (29 June 1663)

56  *Ibid.*, vi, p. 335 (20 December 1665).

57  Lambeth Palace Library, London (hereafter LPL), Bbb 903, Barlow v. Barlow, deposition of Thomas Davies, 18 October 1705.

58  LMA, DL/C/255, Dormer v. Dormer, deposition of James Warham, 16 February 1715, fol. 80$^v$.

59  *Ibid.*, deposition of Mary Jones, 4 March 1715, fol. 89$^v$.

60  Blue, *On Kissing*, p. 153.

61  LMA, DL/C/255, deposition of Sara Wilkinson, 15 March 1715, fol. 122$^v$.

62  LPL, E 15/37, Barlow v. Barlow, libel issued by Sir George Barlow, 1705.

63  LPL, Bbb 903, Barlow v. Barlow, deposition of Thomas Davies, 18 October 1705.

64  *Ibid.*, deposition of John Barden, 15 October 1705.

65  *Ibid.*, deposition of Henry Bowen, 13 October 1705.

66  *Ibid.*, deposition of Walter Middleton, 13 October 1705.

67  LPL, E9/38, libel issued by Alexander Denton, n.d. [*c*.1690].

68  LPL, Eee7, deposition of Martha Ryland, 8 February 1690, fol. 80$^v$.

69  *Ibid.*, fol. 81.

70  Frijhoff, 'The Kiss Sacred and Profane', p. 223.

71  LPL, E9/38, Denton v. Denton, allegation of Alexander Denton, n.d. [*c*.1690]; LPL, Eee 7, Denton v. Denton, deposition of Mary Blithman, 12 February 1690, foL. 92$^v$.

72  *Ibid.*, deposition of Martha Ryland, 8 February 1690, fol. 81.

73  Blue, *On Kissing*, p. 140.

74  For another example see Gowing, *Domestic Dangers*, p. 91.

75  LPL, Bbb 826/8, Hockmore v. Hockmore, deposition of Joanna Angell, 30 August 1698.

76  Keith Thomas, 'Introduction', in Bremmer and Roodenburg (eds), *A Cultural History of Gesture*, pp. 1–14.

77  Susan E. Whyman, *Sociability and Power in Late-Stuart England: The Cultural Worlds of the Verneys 1660–1720* (Oxford, 1999), p. 88.

78  Blue, *On Kissing*, p. 152.

79  See also Stephen Copley, 'Commerce, Conversation and Politeness in the Early Eighteenth-Century Periodical', *British Journal for Eighteenth-Century Studies*, 18 (1995), 63–77.

# 5

# The kiss of life in the eighteenth century: the fate of an ambiguous kiss

<>

## Luke Davidson

IN MEMORIAM ROY PORTER
(1946–2002)

> And if you'd see, what you so much desire,
> The object of your care again respire
> Let one the mouth and either nostril close,
> While th'inflating bellows up the other blows.
> The air with well-adjusted force convey,
> To put the flaccid lungs again in play
> Should bellows not be found, or found too late,
> Let some kind soul with willing mouth inflate.
> Then lightly squeeze – awhile compress the chest,
> That the excluded air may be exprest.
> (*William Hawes*, 1796)[1]

## INTRODUCTION

IF THEY had found themselves so inclined during the year 1745, members of the Royal Society of London could have attended a short lecture of considerable significance in the history of the kiss. Delivered by the eminent Quaker physician John Fothergill, the lecture served to reveal intelligence of an unusual practice that Fothergill felt sure could go on to produce large therapeutic benefits. His remarks were inspired by a small essay that he had recently read by an unknown Scottish physician named William Tossach. Tossach described how he had revived from apparent death a miner who had been overwhelmed by toxic fumes emanating from a mineshaft. Failing to find evidence of pulse or respiration, Tossach stopped the collier's nostrils and blew into his mouth 'as strong as I could', raising the chest fully. Within moments he identified six or seven 'very quick Beats of the Heart' and the pulse and the thorax thereafter continued to play.[2] Tossach was impressed and wondered whether this initiative might be of medical interest. Fothergill believed it was. It was the first time, Fothergill asserted, that the practice of inflating the lungs had been applied 'to the happy purpose of rescuing life from such imminent danger', and he was particularly enthusiastic about its possible use in recovering the drowned.[3]

Tossach's short piece is the first published medical account that describes what in the United Kingdom is called 'the kiss of life'[4] and what doctors call 'mouth-to-mouth ventilation'.[5] Like many treatments, the kiss of life is a very familiar procedure – most people have heard of it – but its history is little known. The American medical men responsible for the re-emergence of mouth-to-mouth ventilation in the 1950s, James Elam and Peter Safar, knew little of the pre-history of the practice.[6] Barring the occasional tiny reference in academic writing, it remains largely forgotten or ignored. However, as this chapter will show, the kiss of life enjoyed recognition as a life-saving treatment nearly 200 years before James Elam's initiatives. This volume offers a perfect opportunity to reveal what happened to the treatment and to tease out the reasons why it disappeared so thoroughly from medical practice that it had to be 'discovered' again many years later. After all, when we consider that the kiss of life is a treatment that enjoys support from the present medical and scientific community on the basis of its efficacy, its previous disappearance should strike us as decidedly odd.

The kiss of life is an unusual kiss.[7] It is performed following violent or sudden accidents in scenarios that are invariably unexpected and unceremonious. The recipient is expected to be unconscious and, at the same time, to be the only beneficiary. While there is no accounting for tastes, no-one is expected to take pleasure in it; unlike most kisses, it is supposed to be useful rather than gratifying or meaningful. In principle, cultural boundaries do not constitute proper grounds for not performing the kiss; it is valuable no matter the victim's race, sex or creed. Highly significant for our purposes is the fact that the practice's current reputation, at the turn of the twenty-first century, as a kiss is a historical accident. According to the *Oxford English Dictionary*, the phrase 'the kiss of life' was first coined in 1961 in the UK newspaper the *Daily Mail*.[8] In the 1770s, when mouth-to-mouth ventilation was first offered as a remedy for saving lives, contemporaries would refer to the procedure as 'blowing' into the mouth, or sometimes as 'blowing the breath'. Hence our preferred terms are anachronistic for the eighteenth century.

Is this a problem? Historians anxious to avoid 'presentist' or 'whig' distortions of the past may think so. I do not, provided we are aware of the discrepancy. There is no way in which there can be any ultimate decision on whether mouth-to-mouth ventilation is really a kiss or not. A kiss is not a timeless essence but a gestural motif capable of many historical variations. That eighteenth-century Britons were unaccustomed to thinking of mouth-to-mouth ventilation as a kiss does not mean we should avoid doing so from fears of being unhistorical. To compare mouth-to-mouth ventilation to a kiss is essential if we are to understand the treatment's bumpy ride through history.

Despite the differences in terminology, the instructions for the treatment in 1774 were essentially the same as today's. The life-saver was 'to blow with force into the lungs, by applying the mouth to that of the patient, closing the nostrils with one hand, and gently expelling the air again by pressing the chest with the other, imitating the strong breathing of a healthy person', to quote instructions published in 1774.[9] So, if the instructions were essentially the same, why do we now call the procedure the kiss of life?[10] Strangely, for something that has emerged comparatively recently, the answer to this is unclear.[11] The self-evident nature of the link between mouth-to-mouth vent-ilation and kissing as it appears to us today cannot be attributed to superior logic or observation skills. Rather, the link's intelligibility relies upon kissing's imaginative appeal. The reviving kiss is an emotionally charged moment celebrated in innumerable stories within Western European culture from the ancient Greeks to the present day. Just think of Sleeping Beauty.[12] Kissing has long been associated with animation, redemption and renewal. The visible likeness of the treatment to kissing has in a sense been made apparent by the slogan, and has been reinforced by a modern medical terminology that emphasises the centrality of the mouth in its definition of the procedure.

After John Fothergill's lecture to the Royal Society treatments for drown-ing remained as they had been for time immemorial: victims were hung by the heels to drain, or rolled over a barrel to have the water squeezed out from their cavities. There was no stampede to change emergency medical techniques. Yet in France a book had just been published that indirectly would bring techniques for restoring the apparently dead into the public eye. This was Jacques-Jean Bruhier's *Sur l'incertitude des signes de la mort* (1742), a translation of and commentary on a short Latin treatise by the famous Danish medical practitioner J.-B. Winslow.[13] Winslow and Bruhier argued – on the basis of somewhat lurid testimony concerning premature burials – that the signs of death were far more unreliable than had been popularly supposed, and that people who looked dead could still retain vestiges of life. Twenty-two years later, in 1767, a group of Dutch gentlemen in Amsterdam, impressed by Bruhier's advocacy, established a society designed to reduce the number of people who drowned in the city's many canals. This society offered Dutch citizens a reward if they co-operated with its members in restoring apparently drowned people hitherto considered dead or beyond help, using recommended techniques.

News of the society spread like wildfire throughout Europe. In the late 1760s and early 1770s similar initiatives were set up in St Petersburg, Milan, Venice and Hamburg, as well as other cities. Eventually, in 1774, the British Isles followed suit when two English medical men, William Hawes (1736–1808), an apothecary, and Thomas Cogan (1736–1818), a physician and man-midwife, set up their own society. Made up of friends and colleagues, it was dedicated to introducing similar measures across London. The society was particularly interested in using resuscitation techniques to revive persons drowned in the Thames. It came to be known as the Royal Humane Society (RHS),[14] and it was through its efforts that resuscitation techniques, including 'the kiss of life', were first introduced into Britain in 1774.

The RHS provides the historian of kisses with an opportunity to see what happens when a 'kiss' is introduced deliberately into a culture as part of a campaign to change people's behaviour.[15] Further, it allows us to answer an intriguing question: of the factors that we can ascertain in the treatment's demise in the eighteenth century, which of them was the most important – the arguments produced by experimental scientists, the numbers of people saved or reactions to the practice that can be attributed to its kiss-like nature?

### SCIENTIFIC ARGUMENTS

Was lung inflation via the mouth abandoned because the tide of scientific knowledge turned against it? The *prima facie* answer to this is yes, since it was proscribed on grounds provided by the latest experimental science. 'As the air expired by the most healthy is not pure air,' informed the RHS when it officially ditched mouth-to-mouth ventilation in 1812, 'but chiefly carbonic, or what arises from burning charcoal, it is more likely to destroy than to promote the action of the lungs, and hence should be avoided'.[16] In fact, the role of physiological and pathological arguments in the decline of the treatment is less dramatic than this decisive proclamation suggests. After all, when mouth-to-mouth ventilation was first presented to unsuspecting Britons in 1774, it did not have a theoretical underpinning. In 1774, mouth-to-mouth ventilation was an untried experimental entity still to prove itself.

As mouth-to-mouth ventilation was recommended by the Dutch society in its course of treatment, the RHS included the procedure as a matter of course.[17] Further back in time, the origins of the treatment become obscure. Elijah's miraculous revival of a dead boy upon whom he 'put his mouth upon his mouth, and his eyes upon his eyes, and his hands upon his hands' (2 Kings 4:34) offers a biblical precedent of dubious historical pedigree. Shakespeare's characters offer kisses to the dying in the hope of reviving them, while blowing into the mouth of still-born infants was recommended as far back as the fifteenth century.[18] Independently of the Dutch, experiments by

British man-midwives in the 1760s probably suggested to the RHS co-founder Thomas Cogan that lung inflation was useful in reviving still-born infants and thus might very well work on adults too.[19]

Insofar as there was a theory behind mouth-to-mouth ventilation, it was one shared with the other remedies for resuscitation. It had absolutely nothing to do with our post-Lavoisieran view on respiration that sees breathing as an exchange of gases designed to maintain oxygen levels in the body. Instead, it was thought that once respiration and circulation had ceased, only a latent capacity for muscle expansion and contraction remained. This capacity was called 'irritability'. The purpose of all remedies was to provoke the irritability of the muscles into kick-starting the animal functions again. Hence, mouth-to-mouth ventilation's purpose was to stimulate a property located in the muscles of the lungs, and not to provide chemical support for the blood.

This fact presents an historical irony because in 1772 – two years before the foundation of the RHS – the radical experimentalist Joseph Priestley published a paper in which he identified the gas we call oxygen, or what he called 'dephlogisticated air'. Yet Priestley's paper had no influence upon the RHS's support for mouth-to-mouth ventilation. In fact, the procedure failed to benefit from the interest taken in the chemistry of the atmosphere, or 'pneumatic chemistry' as it was called in the eighteenth century. This is not because those interested in resuscitation were not fascinated by pneumatic chemistry. In fact, the medical men who contributed to theories of resuscitation in the 1780s and 1790s made lung inflation with dephlogisticated air an objective of great importance. Their preference, however, was for an alternative means of artificial respiration: the use of bellows attached to a flexible pipe that was introduced into the mouth or nose of the victim.[20] Their support for bellows may partly have been the consequence of their use of puppies and kittens as experimental subjects, which did not encourage the performance of mouth-to-mouth ventilation under laboratory conditions!

But if mouth-to-mouth ventilation did not benefit from the new ideas of pneumatic chemistry, it was not immediately damaged by the support the scientists had for the bellows. This is for three main reasons. First, despite the scientists' interest in a new gas-based physiology, the older notion of irritability upon which mouth-to-mouth ventilation depended remained central to their analyses of vitality. Second, mouth-to-mouth ventilation enjoyed support – if only tacitly – from those practitioners, such as Charles Kite, who believed that lung inflation worked primarily mechanically and not chemically.[21] The kind of air that was put into the lungs was for such practitioners rather less important than the fact that the lungs were actively inflated. Hence the views of pneumatic chemistry's supporters, such as Edmund Coleman or Anthony Fothergill, that saw respired air as depleted of vital goodness, did not immediately hold sway. Finally, the scientists did not automatically get their own way. The co-founder of the RHS William Hawes, while excited by experimental knowledge, set large store by the accumulation of evidence in the field. He was quite prepared to ignore scientific arguments if they contrasted with his own experience. Mouth-to-mouth ventilation benefited, I am sure, from Hawes's protection; it was not abandoned by the RHS until four years after his death, a full fifteen years after the last major work on resuscitation was published.

### EFFICACY AND RESULTS IN THE FIELD

Empiricists and practitioners among the readers of this book may well be becoming impatient and asking themelves the following question: did the treatment bring about recoveries? The answer has to be no. Out of the 600 or so cases published by the RHS that present a successful recovery from drowning, there is not a single resuscitation that unambiguously makes the case for the efficacy of 'blowing breath'. In 1792, Charles Kite, who was at the forefront of medical thinking on resuscitation, observed how of the great number of recoveries mentioned in the reports, 'very few are the cases where artificial respiration was used at all'.[22] This clearly must constitute a central reason for mouth-to-mouth ventilation's demise. Yet this should be puzzling to us because the practice is promoted today on the assumption that it can and does save lives by maintaining oxygen levels in the blood.

What went wrong? The first problem was that many of the victims of drowning did not need oxygenation. The majority of people dragged out of the River Thames were suffering from hypothermia. Their respiration was almost at a standstill but, as is well known, a body that is very cold will almost cease to respire in order to minimise energy consumption. To witnesses of this kind of apparent death, it might well have appeared that the body had given up respiring altogether. The RHS's advice to dry and gently warm the body would have been sufficient to precipitate the gradual recovery of normal breathing. The practitioner Alexander Johnson observed that the impact of frictions (intensive rubbing of the body) caused the lungs to move 'as soon as any other part of the body'. Only if frictions did not work was there any attempt to 'blow air into the lungs'.[23] So in the majority of cases of apparent death by drowning, victims recovered their breathing without recourse to ventilation of the lungs.

There was also very little instruction in the right technique, or consensus among medical men about the best time to commence artificial respiration. Judging by twenty-first-century standards, the RHS failed to publicise the importance of tilting the head back to free the airway before beginning artificial respiration, which is not to say that some individuals were ignorant of this manoeuvre.[24] So it is likely that some attempts were doomed from the start. In addition, mouth-to-mouth ventilation suffered from a fundamental vagueness about the best time to inflate the lungs: was it before the patient began to breathe, or after? William Cullen suggested it was afterwards, and he was probably the most prestigious physician of the day.[25] If treatment was begun after breathing had been identified, then the conditions were hardly propitious for a display of mouth-to-mouth ventilation's efficacy.

Further, as the RHS was pluralist about the techniques to be used for resuscitation, individual remedies were not deliberately isolated in the field. In principle, mouth-to-mouth ventilation may have been used alongside all the other initiatives, which, as well as drying, warming and rubbing the body, included applying brandy to the skin, taking blood from the patient, using smelling salts, introducing tobacco smoke into the rectum and very occasionally using electric shock. Since there was little consensus of either an educated or a popular nature on what precisely was happening under the skin during a recovery from apparent death, it was particularly hard to identify among all these competing therapies one with a clearly recognisable agency in a recovery.[26] This, I suspect, was true of artficial respiration; because people had no experience of it, they were not skilled in identifying and isolating its effects.

The cases that the RHS published were sent in by the medical practitioners who had orchestrated the recoveries. The RHS reproduced only the successful ones, reducing the presentation of the unsuccessful ones to a small table. This is questionable science and very inconvenient for the historian. Who knows how many attempted mouth-to-mouth ventilations were performed on those who did not recover? Yet this lopsided presentation cannot ultimately disguise the sheer absence of explicit mention of mouth-to-mouth ventilation in the successful cases, unless one suspects that the medical men deliberately suppressed any mention of the practice for fear of bad publicity it might bring. What this indicates is not only that there is little evidence of the treatment bringing about recoveries, but that there is little direct evidence to confirm that it was ever performed. This last factor is of the utmost significance.

It is also surprising. In principle mouth-to-mouth ventilation stole a march on almost all its competitors when it came to ease of implementation. John Fothergill in his lecture to the Royal Society asserted that the new treatment was 'practicable by every one who happens to be present at the accident, without loss of time, without expence [sic], with little trouble, and less skill; and it is, perhaps, the only expedient of which it can be justly said, that it may possibly do great good, but cannot do harm'.[27] By contrast, both the tobacco-smoke enema and artificial respiration via the bellows required the skills of a practitioner, which was conceivably a reason why the bellows were popular, since they were embodiments of expertise and hence displays of the power of Enlightened medicine. The remaining remedies also required additional tools and ingredients, such as a lancet, blankets, brandy and salt.

Indeed, even though 'blowing the breath' was officially demoted in 1788 to become a back-up remedy to artificial respiration by bellows, it stood to benefit from the problems practitioners had in obtaining and using the new bellows. Practitioners remarked upon how hard it was to mimic natural breathing with the bellows, and to obtain a set of bellows when they needed one.[28] So, ironically, the cause of direct lung inflation was in fact not progressed by the bellows in practice. Presumably, mouth-to-mouth ventilation was diminished by association.[29]

Yet there was a condition for which mouth-to-mouth ventilation seemed to work: the recovery of the still-born. Cases of the still-born were very rarely recorded in the RHS's reports. The surgeon John Grigg, writing in the RHS's reports of 1792, was astonished by the continued neglect of lung inflation, both on children and adults, despite the 'immense numbers' of infants he reported had been restored by the practice since the inauguration of the RHS.[30] One midwife received a gold medal in 1802 from the RHS for performing mouth-to-mouth ventilation upon infants 500 times.[31] The author of the first English pamphlet on the Dutch society for the recovery of the drowned, Alexander Johnson, maintained in 1785 that most nurses believed of the still-born that, 'by blowing breath into them, they may be brought to life again'.[32] The accoucheur William Hunter remarked in his essay on infanticide (1784) that, 'It is . . . generally known that a child, born apparently dead, may be brought to life by inflating the lungs'.[33] As late as 1809, the accoucheur John Burns made it the most important remedy for babies in critical conditions.[34] A curious discrepancy is beginning to emerge.

## THE SIGNIFICANCE OF THE KISS

We have ascertained that mouth-to-mouth ventilation did not enjoy the support of advanced scientific opinion, and that for various reasons it was not seen to bring about recoveries in adults, a feature which compromised claims for its efficacy. Yet these reasons, while crucial to understanding why mouth-to-mouth ventilation fell into disrepute, do not amount to a complete explanation for the demise of the procedure. They do not – indeed cannot – explain how blowing into the lungs could succeed as a treatment for infants, but not succeed as a treatment for adults. To find an explanation, we must move from discussions of scientific knowledge, efficacy and therapeutic technique to the topic of kissing.

We have observed how infrequently mouth-to-mouth ventilation is mentioned in the case reports of the RHS. However, it is not true that there were no attempts to perform mouth-to-mouth ventilation; the practitioner Charles

Kite suggests that medical men made 'frequent', if unsuccessful, attempts to initiate the practice.[35] However, these attempts did not result in actual performances of the technique. Clearly, people were not prepared to implement the treatment. Why?

Today the fear of contracting HIV discourages direct contact with the lips of unknown patients. Did similar fears hold sway in the eighteenth century? Without offering evidence to support the view, a couple of historians have suggested that assumptions about contagion may have put paid to mouth-to-mouth ventilation.[36] This is yet to be proved. It was known, however, that venereal disease was passed through intimate contact. One practitioner, when discussing the causes of venereal disease, advised that chaste kissing was safe while lascivious kissing was not, a view that may have been commonplace.[37] Since the new resuscitation technique involved the meeting of lips and open mouths in the manner of 'lascivious' kissing, perhaps people saw the treatment as posing a risk of venereal disease.

Second, the state of the victim's mouth would have been off-putting. After drowning, mouths could be filled with froth brought up from the lungs, or with detritus from the surrounding water. Practitioners asked those attending the body to clear such obstructions before embarking on artificial respiration. Of course, the state of a drowned person's mouth is not pleasant today, but eighteenth-century mouths were unpleasant in eighteenth-century ways. The radical increase in sugar and chocolate consumption during the period led to predictable effects on teeth. Substances that produce halitosis, such as coffee, tobacco and gin, were consumed heavily during this period. The use of mercury as a specific for syphilis led to stained and lost teeth, stinking breath and twice the normal levels of salivation (three to four pints a day).[38] In 1787, in a self-portrait, the artist Madame Vigée-Lebrun plucked up the courage to depart from the millennia-old tradition of keeping the sitter's mouth firmly closed. Hitherto, mouths in portraits had stayed shut for a reason: foul and missing teeth.[39] This may explain why two Danish practitioners observed how 'People of Propriety' disliked the idea of performing mouth-to-mouth ventilation on 'People of advanced years';[40] members of this constituency were unlikely to have possessed pleasant teeth, if they had teeth at all.

The death-like appearance of the body was another source of unease. The RHS was keen that recoveries be attempted on those that looked dead but were not. This brought criticisms from some quarters that the RHS was trying to attempt to raise the dead, which was considered an impossibility and a blasphemous impossibility at that. Yet these criticisms, which were hostile to resuscitation (as the critics understood it) in principle, did not threaten any treatment in particular. However, those treating a body may very well have objected to pressing their mouths to the mouth of what they thought was a dead body, over and above bleeding it or rubbing it down. In Germany during this period there still existed taboos about touching drowned persons, and these may have existed in Britain, too.[41] If the victim was a suicide, reluctance to touch the body is likely to have been greater.[42] In one case involving the recovery of a female suicide, the girls attending the body refused to perform mouth-to-mouth ventilation until the medium of a hand-kerchief was made available. Although we are not told precisely why the girls made their objections, we do know that they had believed at first the suicide to be dead and that they knew she was a suicide.[43]

This is a point of such emotional intelligibility that we can easily overstate its relevance. After all, already mentioned, blowing into the lungs was recom-mended by some practitioners to be undertaken once the first signs of respira-tion had been identified: that is, once it was clear that the body was alive. These practitioners were perhaps convinced of the futility or impropriety of encouraging people to kiss apparently dead bodies. Whatever their rationale, this advice, if followed, radically reduced the likelihood of anyone kissing recently dead people. In fact, the number of drowned persons treated for apparent death was far smaller than that of those treated for states that were critical but still evidently vital. We should not imagine therefore that the only bodies that people had to confront were apparently dead. It was the job of the practitioners orchestrating the treatment to persuade people that the body was alive and hence that fears of kissing the dead had little foundation.

Kissing a recovering person was disagreeable too. Because the tobacco-smoke enema was the first remedy of choice for many practitioners, the recovering patient was likely already to be showing disagreeable symptoms of tobacco poisoning – profuse sweating, vomiting, defecation and so on – that made mouth-to-mouth ventilation even less attractive. Although detritus in and around the mouth was unpleasant enough, fluids such as ammonia salts that were placed on the mouth and nose as stimulants would have made the mouth area smell and taste repugnant. We may now understand why Charles Kite observed that 'The blowing into the mouth may, upon an emergency, answer for a few times; but the difficulty of getting people to continue it will be easily conceived, on account of the operation being so extremely disagree-able and troublesome'.[44]

My interest so far in the possible anxieties generated by the act of kissing has perhaps caused me to overemphasise the significance of the meeting of lips. Kissing corpses was not taboo in itself; kissing a deceased person while he or she was laid out before burial was a familiar ritual.[45] Kissing dying loved ones on the lips was a common literary figure of love and intimacy. Ann Pasternak Slater has noted how Shakespeare's characters kiss the dying on the mouth for three reasons: to revive them, to conclude the relationship in a final mingling and to help transport the soul to a better hereafter.[46]

Shakespeare never portrays the act as disgusting. Current historical knowledge does not allow me to assert that Shakespeare was representing dominant attitudes to kissing during his own lifetime, let alone during the late eighteenth century. Yet the existence of such scenes should remind us that we must not overstate the importance of the kiss-like nature of the treatment. It was, after all, 'blowing' rather than kissing that was the action most readily associated with it.

The view that the soul of the dying could be caught in a final embrace owed some of its appeal to Neo-Platonic, pre-Christian beliefs in which kissing was seen as the mutual exchange of soul through breath. The concept of breath was fundamental to the Christian story, too. Adam was created when 'the Lord God formed man of the dust of the ground, and breathed into his nostrils the breath of life; and man became a living soul' (Genesis 2:7). Breath was a vessel of spirit, perhaps spirit itself. More prosaically in the eighteenth century, breath was an index of health and sickness; bad breath was considered not only a symptom of malady, but also a cause of illness in others. This view was intelligible because it dovetailed with identical assumptions about the nature of smell. As the historian Alain Corbin has so beautifully shown in his *The Foul and the Fragrant*, in the eighteenth century a direct correlation was made between pleasant smell and good health.[47] Such assumptions continued to be active in the new pneumatic chemistry. William Buchan, the author of the best-selling *Domestic Medicine* (1769), advised readers that 'unwholesome air is a very common cause of diseases', while the RHS supporter Anthony Fothergill wanted to dispense oxygen in crowded public places to prevent ill health.[48]

Noxious smells generated by putresence or by natural fermentations common to bodies were deemed particularly bad, to be countered by sweeter fragrances. The foul-smelling exhalations from rotting corpses piled one on top of the other in burial vaults across the country horrified medical men, particularly from the 1770s onwards.[49] The RHS used smell therapeutically; the stench of ammonia or burning feathers was used to access the senses of apparently dead people. Unpleasant though these smells may have been, they were not bad, for they did not originate in rotting or decomposing matter. Disagreeable stenches were likely to carry or cause disease, and bad breath was a case in point. This view had an old pedigree. Galen had observed that it was especially dangerous to associate with the sick when their breath was so putrid that it stank out houses.[50]

Breath was considered the waste product of respiration, whether expiration was understood to manage the balance of the humours or discharge phlogiston from the blood.[51] It is this belief that informs the work of writers on resuscitation during this period. In 1792, Edmund Coleman dismissed mouth-to-mouth ventilation on the grounds that 'air blown from the mouth of another must be highly improper, as being robbed in some measure of its purity'.[52] The bellows were considered by Alexander Johnson to be 'preferable to the intrusion of nauseous breath' (i.e. the breath of the life-saver).[53]

Despite the acceptability of kissing a dead loved one, and the fact that dying kisses appear not to have given Shakespeare's characters anxieties about health, for some eighteenth-century doctors the breath of mortally ill people was considered dangerous. Alain Corbin tells the story of one doctor who, in 1790, administered mouth-to-mouth ventilation to a cesspool cleaner who had been dragged out of a cesspool asphyxiated by the overwhelming stench. The doctor, Monsieur Verville, 'had scarcely inhaled the air that was coming from the mouth of the mortally ill man', an onlooker reported, 'when he shouted "I am a dead man!" and fell down unconscious'. Verville proceeded to have a fit. Why? According to Verville, he had inhaled the breath of a mortally ill person that had been rendered hyper-toxic by the transmission of the smells of the cesspool.[54] When we consider that a foul stench emanated from sections of the River Thames during this period, we can see that such assumptions were likely to be detrimental to mouth-to-mouth ventilation as a treatment for the drowned.

Disgust is a universal human response, but it takes historically specific forms.[55] In the eighteenth century, social disgust was created out of ideals of decorum.[56] Peddled endlessly in popular conduct literature of the period, decorum represented the ideal of gentlemanly behaviour. Resuscitations were not obviously compatible with the ideal of decorum. After all, accidents were hurried, frantic, distressing occasions. Conduct books for gentlemen, by contrast, stressed the virtues of equanimity and dignity, a mildness of manner and stateliness quite at odds with a resuscitation. Further, the ideal beau was supposed to smile rather than laugh, and was to take care 'to confine his mouth within the rules of good breeding', according to an author in the *Guardian*.[57] As an open mouth was considered gauche by the decorous, mouth-to-mouth ventilation would surely have been considered particularly unseemly.

Moreover, decorum involved a behaviour tuned carefully to the dynamics of rank; one behaved different ways to one's superiors and one's inferiors. Over-familiarity with either rank was considered gross. Mouth-to-mouth ventilation must have been appalling from this point of view, since an accident could bring together all ranks in positions of victims and life-savers, and kissing on the lips was almost certainly the behaviour of intimates of equal rank only. After all, physicians – who in this period still identified strongly with the aristocracy – did not even touch their patients, save perhaps to take the pulse.[58] The medical men associated with the RHS were characterised as gentlemen and would have been expected to identify with behaviour appropriate to a gentleman. Significantly, for the most part they orchestrated resuscitations but did not always participate. Since resuscitations took place on river banks and in public houses, in full view of gawping spectators, the likelihood of compromising one's dignity before less exalted ranks was increased.

Decorous behaviour sought to conform to an ideal. It eschewed eccentricity, self-conscious idiosyncrasy or what conduct book authors called 'singularity'. Some medical practitioners fought shy of resuscitation precisely because they dreaded attracting the criticism of singularity.[59] Mouth-to-mouth ventilation was not highlighted as being any more singular than the rest of the remedies, but it cannot have benefited from the general horror of social nonconformity. It is interesting that in selling the treatment to potential subscribers, the RHS emphasised the overwhelming, positive feelings associated with participating in a recovery, but never focused on the process of the treatment itself.[60]

In an address delivered to the Massachusetts Humane Society in 1790, the American medical practitioner Benjamin Waterhouse dismissed mouth-to-mouth ventilation by saying that 'To blow one's own breath into the lungs of another, is an absurd and pernicious practice'.[61] He offered no recognisably medical reasons for this opinion, nor did he expand on his view. We should at least suspect that his indignation was provoked by the perceived indignity of the practice, rather than its therapeutic limitations. Of the other words used to describe 'blowing the breath' the most common was 'indelicate'. Both Charles Kite and Anthony Fothergill, medical men close to the RHS, accused mouth-to-mouth ventilation of 'indelicacy'.[62] They did not reveal their precise reasons for choosing this word; presumably they wrote for an audience who knew well enough what indelicacy was. 'Indelicacy' carried overtones of 'immodesty' and 'indecency', implying shameful sexual impropriety, as well as suggesting a crude and excessive forcefulness. Certainly, mouth-to-mouth ventilation was accused of requiring too much effort, of being 'Toilsome'. The practitioner John Franks was adamant that humans simply did not have the puff to fill all the remote cells of the lungs and bring about changes in the blood.[63]

But what about sex? Even if mouth-to-mouth ventilation was not explicitly associated with kissing, sex, surely, had something to do with it. Here was a remedy in which a man and a woman, strangers to one another, might be invited to adopt attitudes of familiarity appropriate only to intimates and equals. In a period obsessed with chastity, did the RHS not attract criticism for encouraging vice? Surprisingly, it did not. It is significant that the RHS never described mouth-to-mouth ventilation in detail, never formally acknowledged that it was a provocative behaviour, even if it did suggest that the use of a handkerchief 'might render the operation less indelicate'.[64] Did this constitute active denial or a genuine lack of concern?

There was certainly every good reason to downplay any erotic similarity; as Roy Porter revealed, medical men were widely lampooned for their lechery and prurience during this period.[65] It was precisely from the disreputable associations of the medical profession that the RHS sought to distance itself. At the same time, we may infer that the RHS said little about the procedure because it did not see much to write about. The existing cases do not provide anything upon which to generalise about the sexes of the treated and those treating the body. The RHS saw no need to raise publicly the issue of whether men should treat drowned women, or women should treat drowned men. Except for one medical practitioner, the medical assistants who wrote up the cases never mentioned whether people on the scene had found the admixture of the sexes distressing. Medical practitioners had every reason to present the treatments they orchestrated as seamless and uncontroversial, however.

Our suspicions of erotic denial are a consequence of the way in which the 'kiss of life' has become naturalised; the erotic frisson of mouth-to-mouth ventilation has become a common figure of fun. Benny Hill skits, Disney cartoons and Hollywood blockbusters have all played on the implied sexual awkwardness of the practice, and perhaps this makes it particularly hard for us to imagine a world where that connection could not be perceived. Of course, cartoons and movies are in a sense fantasies, and rarely constitute deliberate attempts at realist descriptions of practice suitable for educational purposes. Fantasies are important, however. Do eighteenth-century fantasies as expressed in the period's literature and art suggest that the circumstances of apparent death could be erotically construed?

They do. In eighteenth-century Europe, eroticised fantasies of unconscious and apparently dead women existed in folk-tales, such as *Sleeping Beauty* (published for the first time in English by Robert Samber in 1729), or classical myths. Jacques-Jean Bruhier supplied as part of his evidence for the reality of apparent death a story of an aristocrat posing as a monk who impregnated a beautiful woman who he thought to be dead but found too desirable to resist.[66] In Samuel Richardson's *Clarissa*, the heroine's virtue is finally taken by the determined Lovelace after he drugs her unconscious. In the early nineteenth century, Heinrich von Kleist's 'Die Marquise von O' ('The Marquise of O') and James Hogg's *The Perils of Three Women* (1823) play on the theme of erotic desire stimulated by apparently dead and completely unconscious women.[67] In the area of painting, Henry Fuseli's *The Nightmare* of 1781, which represents a sleeping woman in an erotic pose, is perhaps the most dramatic and explicit image in this tradition.

As we have observed, the Danish practitioners J. D. Herholdt and C. G. Rafn, writing in 1796, specified that 'People of Propriety' disliked mouth-to-mouth ventilation, and this was true 'especially in adults'.[68] Whether erotic awkwardness was the reason for this can only be a matter for speculation.[69]

It is worth taking seriously as an idea, however, since if anything distinguishes the experience of kissing adults from that of kissing infants, then it is the presence of sexual desire. My allusion to the figure of the desirable unconscious woman is designed to persuade you that the presence of such associations, and therefore feelings, was at least conceivable during this period. Consider, too, that the tobacco-smoke enema and frictions involved a degree of nakedness that might involve the exposure of genitalia or buttocks, and that not all resuscitations were supervised, or indeed could be supervised. And lest one dismiss the desirability of the apparently dead body as impossible whimsy, consider the observation of the RHS prize-winner Charles Kite, who observed in his *Essay on the Recovery of the Apparently Dead* (1788) that 'it is no uncommon remark, that the countenances of some people look much better, and more natural, when dead than while alive'.[70]

## CONCLUSION

We have considered three main answers to the question of why, having introduced in 1774 a treatment that we now call 'the kiss of life', the RHS came to condemn it almost forty years later. We have observed, firstly, that the treatment did not enjoy the support of scientific opinion, and secondly, that it failed to exhibit clearly and unambiguously its efficacy to contemporaries. Yet we have argued that scientific argument of a physiological or pathological nature was not the most important contributor to the treatment's desultory public profile. While the medical value of 'blowing the breath' remained uncertain, it survived as a recommended treatment, surprisingly neither helped, nor especially hindered, by the enthusiasm among the more scientifically minded medical men for the use of bellows. That the treatment did not 'work' was predetermined by unresolved disagreements about the nature of recovery, the absence of a clear ventilation technique and the therapeutic pluralism characteristic of resuscitation and eighteenth-century medical treatment generally. These factors made a clear display of lung inflation's efficacy almost completely impossible.

Yet more significant than either of these critical factors was the fact that few people were sufficiently willing to perform the procedure. The situation was akin to an experimental scientist finding laboratory mice staging a rebellion. The lack of public compliance undermined the endeavour completely. Late eighteenth-century society did not provide the experimental conditions for the reliable implementation of a treatment that involved the meeting of lips and the passing of breath between strangers. The populace did not take to it; the medical men were not powerful enough, or dedicated enough, to make people do it. The financial rewards the RHS gave to those who aided the medical men in a resuscitation did not persuade people in significant numbers to overcome their scruples, nor was the RHS's advice to use a handkerchief any more successful. Despite the RHS's high-profile marketing campaign that linked the spread of resuscitation to the triumphant march of humanity, the RHS did not, and almost certainly could not, mobilise eighteenth-century Britons' support for the treatment.

The kiss-like nature of the procedure helps us understand this reluctance and this failure. Mouth-to-mouth ventilation presented an emotional challenge to adults who, either in practice or in their imaginations, saw it provoke an improper or troubling physical proximity with another adult, apparently dead or alive. I have suggested that among upper-class males it may have constituted a shameful abandon of the body's dignity. The responses among working people, such as boatmen and sailors, might have ignored issues of decorum, but the resulting avoidance of mouth-to-mouth ventilation was the same. The kiss-like action, either through the exchange of breath or through the meeting of lips, was probably suspected of spreading disease. Marks of ill health, old age or death itself were repellent to the life-saver, while the notion of a kiss given regardless of the ordinary social buffers that kept men and women apart was criticised as 'indelicate'.

Consequently, during the period when it remained an officially recognised treatment, mouth-to-mouth ventilation never really competed with the other remedies, nor did it ever achieve a distinctive identity of its own. Although practitioners referred to it occasionally as 'blowing the breath', this was neither a slogan – such as 'the kiss of life' – nor yet an example of technical nomenclature – such as 'mouth-to-mouth ventilation' – but a provisional description. The phrase 'kiss of life', by contrast, has caught our imagination and reified the practice, conferring upon mouth-to-mouth ventilation a public profile and therapeutic approval which today, intriguingly, is beginning to unravel.[71]

In the eighteenth century, mouth-to-mouth ventilation was seen as an act of breathing rather than an act involving mouths and lips that the expressions 'mouth-to-mouth ventilation' and 'mouth-to-mouth resuscitation' highlight for us today. There are good eighteenth-century reasons why eighteenth-century doctors did not see the treatment as a kiss, let alone market it as 'the kiss of life'. In the first instance, the RHS would have had every interest in disassociating the treatment from an action that could link the RHS to common medical lechery. Secondly, resuscitation troubled contemporaries because it appeared to mimic hubristically the unique capacity of God to create life and dispense with it. If the notion 'the kiss of life' had been presented to them, it would have been seen by these religious people as arrogant. What makes the present phrase 'kiss of life' acceptable is not only a widespread eroticisation of the market place unthinkable in the eighteenth century, but a subsequent process of secularisation that resuscitation has in fact facilitated.

Mouth-to-mouth ventilation was unpleasant to perform and challenged propriety, and propriety was a social value shared by medical men and the RHS's subscribers and supporters alike. It was medical men who, in the nineteenth century, discouraged giving infants mouth-to-mouth or mouth-to-nose ventilation on the grounds that it was 'a vulgar act'.[72] As Thévenot observed in his *L'Art de nager* (1786), 'il faut avoir beaucoup de zèle et de courage pour surmonter la répugnance qu'inspire une aussi dégoûtante opération'.[73]

In a sense, the history of the kiss of life is a gross parody of the history of the kiss of desire. While it mimics the kiss of desire, it is performed only in situations that repel desire, that elicit anxiety and disgust. Perhaps therein lies the reason why hitherto historians of medicine have not addressed the topic. It is of course correct to assert that in the late eighteenth century mouth-to-mouth ventilation did not satisfy the medical and scientific community of its utility, and this factor is crucial to understanding why it was not performed. We must also assert, however, that the RHS's willingness to support the treatment could not overcome a deep-seated, culturally specific resistance to the practice that was expressed by medical men and non-medical persons alike. This resistance was organised around aspects of the procedure's kiss-like nature. In eighteenth-century Britain, a culture which thrilled to the humanitarian cause of resuscitation, mouth-to-mouth ventilation was condemned to living the life of a stranger and imposter. Unwelcome from the start, it remained almost entirely friendless. It clung to a second-class status for forty years, only to be exposed finally as false and banished from official favour. It would take another hundred and fifty years for the treatment to be rehabilitated as an unprecedented example of the power of medical therapeutics. Only this time it had metamorphosed into something rather more seductive. It had returned as a kiss.

### NOTES

Earlier versions of this chapter were delivered to the conference 'The Kiss in History' and to the Department of the History and Philosophy of Science, Cambridge. Comments at both meetings proved most stimulating. I should also like to thank Julian de Bono for his excellent copy-editing and Dr Mark Jenner and Dr John Tercier for their comments and support.

1 *The Royal Humane Society, Instituted 1774: The Annual Report 1796, by William Hawes M. D.* (n.p., n.d.), p. 9.

2 William Tossach, 'A Man Dead in Appearance, Recover'd by Distending the Lungs with Air', *Medical Essays and Observations*, 5 (1744), 607.

3 John Fothergill, *The Works of John Fothergill*, ed. J. C. Lettsom (London, 1784), i, p. 148.

4 The phrase 'kiss of life' emerged in the UK during the late 1960s and remains most common there; it is used far less in the United States and Canada, according to

Dr John Tercier, an emergency room specialist and author of a forthcoming PhD dissertation on representations of resuscitation in contemporary media.

5 Mouth-to-mouth ventilation is also known as 'mouth-to-mouth resuscitation' or 'mouth-to-mouth respiration'. It is common to refer to it simply as 'mouth to mouth'.

6 Mickey S. Eisenberg, *Life in the Balance: Emergency Medicine and the Quest to Reverse Sudden Death* (Oxford, 1997), p. 86.

7 For an excellent introduction to the history of the kiss, see Willem Frijhoff, 'The Kiss Sacred and Profane: Reflections on a Cross-Cultural Confrontation', in Jan Bremmer and Herman Roodenburg (eds), *A Cultural History of Gesture: From Antiquity to the Present Day* (London, 1991), pp. 210–36.

8 *Oxford English Dictionary*, 2nd edn (Oxford, 1989), viii, p. 462.

9 *Society for the Recovery of Persons Apparently Drowned: Instituted MDCCLXXIV* (London, 1774), p. 8.

10 I suspect the phrase was first used in promotional literature and was taken up in the UK media because it is a dramatic catchphrase. A sign of its rude health as an idea is that the kiss of life remains a source of humour to this day.

11 When, at my behest, Professor Chamberlain of the Resuscitation Council of the UK kindly asked colleagues at the forefront of resuscitation studies around the world if they knew the origins of the slogan, he found that not one of them did.

12 Christopher Nyrop observed over a century ago in his philological study of the kiss that '[the kiss] carries life with it': Christopher Nyrop, *The Kiss and its History*, trans. William Frederick Harvey (1901; London, 1968), p. 37.

13 J.-B. Winslow, *Dissertation sur l'incertitude des signes de la mort, et l'abus des enterremens, et embaumemens précipités*, trans. and commentary by J.-J. Bruhier (Paris, 1742).

14 The RHS still exists in a small office near Lancaster Gate in London and promotes bravery in life-saving.

15 For a full history and bibliography on resuscitation in the eighteenth century please consult Luke Davidson, 'Raising up Humanity: A Cultural History of Resuscitation and the Royal Humane Society of London, 1774–1808', DPhil dissertation, University of York, 2001.

16 *Annual Report of the Royal Humane Society for the Recovery of the Apparently Drowned 1812* (London, 1812), p. 27.

17 Thomas Cogan, *Memoirs of the Society Instituted at Amsterdam in Favour of Drowned Persons* (London, 1773).

18 A. Barrington Baker, 'Artificial Respiration: The History of an Idea', *Medical History*, 15 (1971), 337.

19 See Davidson, 'Raising up Humanity', pp. 42–8 for a detailed discussion of the origins of the practice.

20 e.g. Edward Coleman, *A Dissertation on Suspended Respiration, from Drowning, Hanging, and Suffocation* (London, 1791); Edmund Goodwyn, *The Connexion of Life with Respiration* (London, 1788); Charles Kite, *An Essay on the Recovery of the Apparently Dead* (London, 1788); A. Fothergill, *A New Inquiry into the Suspension of Vital Action, in Cases of Drowning and Suffocation* (Bath, 1795).

21 'It appears to me as of little consequence, or at least as a secondary consideration, whether the lungs are inflated with dephlogisticated or atmospheric air, or whether the air be blown from the lungs of a healthy person: it is their expansion and contraction we are to endeavour to promote, in order to force the blood from the right to the left ventricle of the heart': Kite, *An Essay*, p. 152; see also Fothergill, *A New Inquiry*, p. 112.

22  Charles Kite, 'On the Submersion of Animals', *Memoirs of the Medical Society of London*, 3 (1792), 246. 'Artificial respiration' here referred to mouth-to-mouth ventilation and respiration by bellows.

23  Alexander Johnson, *Directions for an Extension of the Practice of Recovering Persons Apparently Dead* (London, 1785), p. 3.

24  William Cullen, *A Letter to Lord Cathcart* (London, 1776), p. 18; Kite, *An Essay*, p. 148; *Royal Humane Society, 1774 . . . Annual Report Published for the Anniversary Festival 1798 by W. Hawes M.D.* (London, [1798]), p. 63.

25  Cullen, *A Letter to Lord Cathcart*, p. 16.

26  The tobacco-smoke enema was an exception to this since it provoked a range of obvious symptoms that some practitioners attributed to the process of recovery, and others to the symptoms of poisoning.

27  Fothergill, *The Works of John Fothergill*, i, p. 151.

28  e.g. Kite, *An Essay*, pp. 140–7; Christian August Struve, *A Practical Essay on the Art of Recovering Suspended Animation* (1801; London, 1803), pp. 88–9. It took time for the RHS to provide officially recognised medical assistants with the requisite equipment.

29  In 1835, the editor of the RHS's reports, John Dalrymple, observed a 'singular fact' that one of the 'most active and useful medical assistants', one Mr. Woolley, had never restored life through inflation of the lungs. See Arthur Keith, 'Three Hunterian Lectures on the Mechanism underlying the Various Methods of Artificial Respiration Practised since the Foundation of the Royal Humane Society in 1774', *The Lancet* (1909), 748.

30  *Royal Humane Society, Instituted 1774, Published for the Anniversary Festival 1792* ([London], [1792]), p. 9. These 'immense numbers' were neither written up by medical men as cases, nor especially celebrated within the pages of the reports. The reason for this is obscure.

31  L. H. Hawkins, 'The History of Resuscitation', *British Journal of Hospital Medicine*, 4 (1970), 497.

32  This sentence may be taken as evidence of the use of mouth-to-mouth ventilation among midwives before the RHS, since the provenance of the nurses' beliefs mentioned by Johnson is vague. See Johnson, *Directions*, p. 3.

33  William Hunter, 'On the Uncertainty of the Signs of Murder in the Case of Bastard Children', *Medical Observations and Inquiries*, 6 vols (London, 1757–84), vi (1784), p. 285. Its points were reproduced in William Hawes, *Transactions of the Royal Humane Society* (London, 1795), 423–29. The German physician Struve, writing in 1803 and an opponent of artificial respiration, conceded that artificial respiration was known to work in still-born children. See Struve, *Practical Essay*, p. 89.

34  John Burns, *The Principles of Midwifery; Including the Diseases of Women and Children* (London, 1809).

35  Kite, *An Essay*, p. 265.

36  The theory that fear of contagion caused mouth-to-mouth ventilation's demise has been put forward by Richard Lee in an article published in 1972, but only as an intriguing conjecture with no evidence marshalled to support it. See Richard V. Lee, 'Cardiopulmonary Resuscitation in the Eighteenth Century: A Historical Perspective on Present Practice', *Journal for the History of Medicine and Allied Sciences*, 27 (1972), 419. James Elam, who helped reintroduce mouth-to-mouth ventilation, said of his interest in the remedy that 'It was fresh in my mind that midwives had never abandoned the method in Europe, that it had fallen into disrepute with the advent of the germ theory, and that there were religious, cultural and all kinds of objections of which the medical profession had virtually been unaware': Eisenberg, *Life in the Balance*, p. 87.

Elam's emphasis on the germ theory is wrong, however; the theory had still to be conceived by the time when the RHS put mouth-to-mouth ventilation on its black list. The whole idea of direct ventilation of the lungs had fallen into disrepute by the mid-1830s, some time before the germ theory became established. It should be observed that, to date, there has not been a single case that proves that mouth-to-mouth ventilation has transmitted HIV. I would like to thank Dr John Tercier for this information.

37 See John Atkins, *The Navy-Surgeon* (London, 1734), pp. 209 ff., quoted in W. F. Bynum, 'Treating the Wages of Sin: Venereal Disease and Specialism in Eighteenth-Century Britain', in W. F. Bynum and Roy Porter (eds), *Medical Fringe and Medical Orthodoxy 1750–1850* (London, 1987), p. 13.

38 *Ibid.*, p. 16.

39 The history of halitosis remains unexplored. For the effects of mercury on the mouth, see *ibid.*, p. 16. For the changing nature of dental practice in eighteenth-century France and attitudes to the mouth, see Colin Jones, 'Pulling Teeth in Eighteenth-Century Paris', *Past & Present*, 166 (2000), 101–45. I am grateful to Professor Jones for kindly sending me a copy of this paper.

40 J. D. Herholdt and C. G. Rafn, *An Attempt at an Historical Survey of Life-Saving Measures for Drowning Persons and Information of the Best Means by which they can Again be Brought back to Life* (1796), trans. Donald W. Hannah and A. Rousing, with introauction by Henning Poulsen (Copenhagen, 1960), unpaginated.

41 For discussion of the folklore of the corpse, see Davidson, 'Raising up Humanity', p. 269 ff.

42 Michael MacDonald and Terence R. Murphy, *Sleepless Souls: Suicide in Early Modern England* (Oxford, 1990).

43 *Reports of the Humane Society Instituted in the year 1774, for the Recovery of Persons Apparently Drowned: For the Year MDCCLXXVII* ([London], [1777]), p. 11.

44 Kite, *An Essay*, pp. 139–40.

45 Christopher Nyrop, while no anthropologist, and moreover not familiar with Britain, nevertheless observed in 1901 that 'The death-kiss is something so natural that it is superfluous to point out its existence amongst different nations. It was not only a mark of love, but it was also an article of belief that the soul may be detained for a brief while by such a kiss. Even in our own days, popular belief in many places demands that the nearest relative shall kiss the corpse's forehead ere the coffin is screwed on, in certain parts, indeed, it is incumbent on every one who sees a dead body to kiss it, otherwise he'll get no peace from the dead.' See Nyrop, *The Kiss*, p. 98.

46 Ann Pasternak Slater, *Shakespeare the Director* (Brighton and Totawa, NJ, 1982), pp. 79–100.

47 Alain Corbin, *The Foul and the Fragrant: Odour and the Social Imagination* (London, 1994).

48 William Buchan, *Domestic Medicine* (1769; London, 1772), p. 92, cited in Mark S. R. Jenner, 'Civilization and Deodorization? Smell in Early Modern English Culture', in Peter Burke, Brian Harrison and Paul Slack (eds), *Civil Histories: Essays Presented to Sir Keith Thomas* (Oxford, 2000), p. 134.

49 The concern over the unwholesome properties of corpses went back further. See Corbin, *The Foul and the Fragrant*; Philippe Ariès, *The Hour of our Death* (Harmondsworth, 1981).

50 Richard Palmer, 'In Bad Odour: Smell and its Significance in Medicine from Antiquity to the Seventeenth Century', in W. Bynum and Roy Porter (eds), *Medicine and the Five Senses* (Cambridge, 1993), p. 64.

51  Everett Mendelsohn, *Heat and Life: The Development of the Theory of Animal Heat* (Cambridge, MA, 1964).

52  Coleman, *A Dissertation*, p. 190.

53  Johnson, *Directions*, p. 3.

54  Corbin, *The Foul and the Fragrant*, p. 3.

55  William Ian Miller, *The Anatomy of Disgust* (Harvard, 1998).

56  Fenela Ann Childs, 'Prescriptions for Manners in English Courtesy Literature, 1690–1760, and their Social Implications', DPhil dissertation, University of Oxford, 1984.

57  *Ibid.*, p. 183.

58  Mary E. Fissell, 'Innocent and Honourable Bribes: Medical Manners in Eighteenth-Century Britain', in Robert Baker, Dorothy Porter and Roy Porter (eds), *The Codification of Medical Morality: Historical and Philosophical Studies of the Formalization of Western Medical Morality in the Eighteenth and Nineteenth Centuries* (Dordrecht, 1993), pp. 15–45.

59  Davidson, 'Raising up Humanity', pp. 288–9.

60  *Ibid.*, ch. 5.

61  B. Waterhouse, *On the Principle of Vitality* (Boston, 1790), p. 17.

62  Kite, *An Essay*, p. 265; Fothergill, *A New Inquiry*, p. 112.

63  John Franks, *Observations on Animal Life, and Apparent Death* (London, 1790), p. 91.

64  *Society for the Recovery of Persons Apparently Drowned*, p. 12.

65  Roy Porter, 'A Touch of Danger: The Man-Midwife as Sexual Predator', in G. Rousseau and R. Porter (eds), *Sexual Underworlds of the Enlightenment* (Manchester, 1987), pp. 206–32.

66  J.-J Bruhier, *Dissertation sur l'incertitude des signes de la mort, et l'abus des enterremens, et embaumemens précipités*, 2nd edn, 2 vols (Paris, 1749).

67  Heinrich von Kleist, *The Marquise of O—and Other Stories* (Harmondsworth, 1978); for Hogg, see John Barrell, 'Putting Down the Rising', *London Review of Books*, 18 (1996), 14–15.

68  Herholdt and Rafn, *An Attempt at an Historical Survey of Life-Saving Measures*, unpaginated.

69  The case histories do not provide sufficient evidence for us to theorise about the relevance of the sexes of the victim and carer in the choice of treatments during life-saving. It is impossible to know for sure who was watching the body. Given that the RHS left the decision of who performed the treatment up to the medical practitioner and his assistants, we may infer they felt that it was something they did not need to worry about unduly. By contrast, we may imagine that the proximity of the sexes during resuscitation was something the RHS felt unable to worry about publicly.

70  Kite, *An Essay*, p. 99.

71  The kiss of life is on the verge of being downgraded in favour of simple chest compressions. The growth in the number of middle-aged heart attack victims has precipitated this alteration in mouth-to-mouth ventilation's status, as such sufferers have plenty of oxygenated blood in the system, but cannot keep the heart pumping. Chest compressions are going to be promoted as the first aid treatment of preference. People are also much happier to give strangers chest compressions than mouth-to-mouth ventilation. Mouth-to-mouth ventilation still 'works' but is being left behind by the changing disease profile of Western nations.

72  Hart Ellis Fisher, 'Resuscitation', in Otto Glasser (ed.), *Medical Physics* (Chicago, 1944), 1241–54, quoted in Eisenberg, *Life in the Balance*, p. 86.

73  'It is necessary to have much zeal and courage to overcome the repugnance that such a disgusting operation inspires': in Joseph Rechtman, 'William Buchan (1729–1805):

Le bouche à bouche et le massage cardiaque externe', *Histoire des Sciences Médicales*, 13 (1979), 292. Interestingly, twelve years after the RHS officially prohibited 'blowing the breath', it observed that it frequently happened that unnamed 'persons' (probably medical practitioners) were 'forcibly breathing into the mouth' when bellows could not be found. Had the stigma begun to disappear? See Hawkins, 'The History of Resuscitation', 497.

# PART III

# Power
# and
# intimacy

# 6

# Kisses for votes: the kiss and corruption in eighteenth-century English elections

<>

Elaine Chalus

> The ladies may think it a hardship that they are neither allowed a place in the Senate nor a voice in the choice of what is called the representative of the nation. However their influence appears to be such in many instances that they have no reason to complain. In boroughs the candidates are so wise as to apply chiefly to the wife. A certain candidate for a Norfolk borough kissed the voters' wives with guineas in his mouth for which he was expelled the House; and for this reason others, I suppose, will be more private in their addresses to the ladies.[1]

WHILE THIS incident, described in a 1758 publication, does not find its way into the Commons journals and may be apocryphal, personal notes which survive from MPs who sat on controverted election cases reveal just how little of the information given in the depositions was included in the official record.[2] Certainly, the sum is not unusual, nor is it unusual to find politicians seeking female influence. It was a commonplace among eighteenth-century politicians, canvassers and satirists that voters' wives had influence over, and at times even controlled, their husbands' votes. Political correspondences, election ephemera and satirical publications all attest to this and, while many eighteenth-century men would have been only too happy to see the end of such petticoat government,[3] as practical politicians they recognised the power of influence and knew that they ignored voters' womenfolk at their peril. Thus, kissing voters' wives was customary practice for candidates; so too was providing them with gifts of various sorts, including small amounts of money.[4] Moreover, electoral myth or not, the tale had currency, as this particular combination of kiss and coin reappears in a strikingly similar form in John Trusler's farce *The Country Election* (first published in 1768 to accompany Hogarth's series of election prints).[5]

In Trusler's version, the kiss is employed by Artful, the opposition candidate for the county. Under the cover of greeting Mrs Blunt, an independent freeholder's wife, he kisses her and transfers a guinea from his mouth into hers. The money and some astute flattery of her children 'buys' her support and, by implication, her influence over her husband's vote. In this instance, however, Artful's efforts are doomed to failure. He receives his comeuppance from Blunt himself soon afterwards at the local tavern. After demanding from Artful the same sort of salutation as his wife received and consequently securing his guinea, he then informs Artful that his vote is promised to the rival candidate. The interchange ends with Blunt contemptuously dismissing Artful's attempted bribery: 'Now testify your joy to [i.e., kiss] my *Breech*'.[6]

Trusler clearly intended his audience to see this combination of kiss and coin as corrupt and potentially corrupting. They would have recognised in Mrs Blunt stereotypical female malleability and a predisposition to corruption, stemming from traditional assumptions about women's 'natural' lustfulness, their avariciousness and their weakness for flattery. They would also have been expected to cheer for Blunt, who typified sturdy honest independence and not only turned the tables on his 'betters' but also used the system to his advantage. In another scene Trusler returns to the kiss as an electioneering technique to reveal its influence on an overly deferential and politically naive electorate, even when no money was involved. Here, a small group of yokels have gathered to discuss the relative merits of the candidates. Two have been swayed in Artful's favour by his willingness to cross class boundaries (thus proving himself to be a real gentleman and a worthy candidate), as demonstrated by his kissing their wives as if they had been his equals. Only one of the group questions the political value of the kiss, but even his concerns are as mercenary as ideological:

Artful 2nd mob: He went to see my dame, and was so lovingly fond of her, as thoff she'd been madam: he squeezed her so close, and hugged her and kissed her, as thoff he would have eat her up. Sue was ready to die away in his arms for joy.

Simple 2nd mob: If that's the case, the Squire is a good gentleman.

Simple 3rd mob: Zounds, what argufies all this kissing and slobbering, will he take off the militia bill? Has he gee you nay of his money?[7]

While Trusler focused on kissing by candidates, the kiss was actually one of a repertoire of customary electioneering behaviours employed knowingly, if not always eagerly, by men and women alike in eighteenth-century elections. Although the practice of elite female canvassers kissing voters appears to have largely disappeared by the beginning of the nineteenth century, the practice continued for men: Victorian candidates and canvassers were still regularly expected to kiss voters' wives. As Justin McCarthy astutely pointed out in 'The Petticoat in the Politics of England' in 1870, a 'smiling salutation' was assumed to be an effective means of securing the influence of 'that class of wives who are above the money bribe'.[8] Thus, a kiss from a candidate was a social signifier as well as a token of paternalistic condescension. In either case, by the nineteenth century it was unlikely to spawn accusations of corruption.

The gradual desexualisation of the electioneering kiss over time, even for men, is perhaps best exemplified in the 'safe' kissing of the very old and the very young. While eighteenth-century candidates regularly made a fuss over individual voters' children and might even agree to standing as godparent to a privileged child, there is no indication in eighteenth-century sources – serious or satirical – that kissing children was part of an overarching canvassing strategy. It was not until the nineteenth century that the actuality was well enough established to be satirised by Charles Dickens in his famous depiction of the Eatanswill election in *The Pickwick Papers* (1836).

Like Trusler, Dickens took women's influence over men's votes for granted and assumed that it was crucial to the outcome of elections; similarly, he portrayed it as being readily 'bought' by candidates and their agents. In Eatanswill, it is not purchased 'corruptly' by coins and kisses, but 'respectably', by flattering the women's sense of social importance and appealing to their vanity and love of luxury. The election agent holds a special tea party for the women, and the parting gift of a parasol each in the candidate's colours secures their support. As he proudly explains to Mr Pickwick, it may have been expensive, but it was worth it:

> 'A parasol!' said Mr. Pickwick.
> 'Fact, my dear Sir, fact. Five-and-forty green parasols, at seven and sixpence a-piece. All women like finery, – extraordinary the effect of those parasols. Secured all their husbands, and half their brothers – beats stockings, and flannel, and all that sort of thing hollow. My idea, my dear Sir, entirely. Hail, rain, or sunshine, you can't walk half a dozen yards up the street, without encountering half a dozen green parasols.'[9]

In Eatanswill, the electioneering kiss makes its appearance only in conjunction with children, but in so doing, it provides the crowning touch to the formal canvass. The candidate, Sir Samuel Slumkey, shows very typical elite reluctance to kiss at the outset and has to be chivvied into it by his agent, but once he recognises its efficacy, he proceeds with enthusiasm:

> 'Nothing has been left undone, my dear sir – nothing whatever. There are twenty washed men at the street door for you to shake hands with; and six children in arms that you're to pat on the head, and inquire the age of; be particular about the children, my dear sir – it has always a great effect, that sort of thing.'
> 'I'll take care,' said the Honourable Samuel Slumkey.

'And, perhaps, my dear Sir – 'said the cautious little man, 'perhaps if you *could* – I don't mean to say it's indispensable – but if you *could* manage to kiss one of 'em, it would produce a very great impression on the crowd.'

'Wouldn't it have as good an effect if the proposer or seconder did that?' said the honourable Samuel Slumkey.

'Why, I am afraid it wouldn't,' replied the agent; 'if it were done by yourself, my dear Sir, I think it would make you very popular.'

'Very well,' said the honourable Samuel Slumkey, with a resigned air, 'then it must be done. That's all.'

[ . . . . the procession begins; he shakes the men's hands . . . ]

'He has patted the babes on the head,' said Mr. Perker, trembling with anxiety.

A roar of applause that rent the air.

'He has kissed one of 'em!' exclaimed the delighted little man.

A second roar.

'He has kissed another,' gasped the excited manager.

A third roar.

'He's kissing 'em all!' screamed the enthusiastic little gentleman, and hailed by the deafening shouts of the multitude, the procession moved on.[10]

The modern stereotype of the politician kissing babies to win votes had been born.

If, as Sean Wilentz has argued, politics is a 'realm of social experience and action in its own right – a realm partly (but never entirely) independent of other social realms . . . a form of cultural interaction, a relationship (or a set of relationships) tied to broader moral and social systems', then political symbols and customs, including symbolic acts of persuasion and/or contract such as the electioneering kiss, must inevitably reflect to some degree the conventions, hopes and fears of the society from which they emerge.[11] They cannot be seen as separate, nor should they be dismissed out of hand as too trivial to be worthy of study. Indeed, they reflect and are shaped by pervasive societal beliefs, be they notions of gender or class, or hierarchy or authority. They provide yet another avenue for exploring the ways in which power, politics and culture were intertwined in a particular polity at a specific point in time. They inform us not only of particular practices, but also, in the case of the kiss, about notions of power and corruption in eighteenth-century England and the ways in which these were gendered.

Indeed, studying such symbolic political customs may well throw new light upon the 'master fictions' which ordered and governed the eighteenth-century English polity. If, as Wilentz has suggested, drawing upon the work of Clifford Geertz, all polities are ordered and governed by a number of master fictions – peculiar combinations of 'fact, myth, and wishful thinking', which serve as 'the unchallenged first principles of a political order, making any given hierarchy appear natural and just to rulers and ruled'[12] – then one of the leading fictions which underpinned the English polity in the eighteenth-century was that it was *male* and that politics was *men's* business. Traditional beliefs about women's inferior status due to their sexuality and emotionality, their 'natural' passivity and dependence and their intellectual as well as physical inferiority to men in all ways were used to bar them from full citizenship.[13]

Thus, although women were often extensively involved in politics in actuality and might well be political figures in their own localities or even recognised as important political figures by the administration in London, they remained outside the imagined political order. Including them would have meant challenging the nature of the polity itself. Arguably, the time that it took to re-envision the polity is reflected in the complexities and delays of the suffrage movement of the nineteenth and twentieth centuries, as women had to be re-imagined as citizens and the definitions of the polity reshaped to include them, albeit grudgingly. Indeed, it is a testimony to the persistence and power of this fiction that the official political arena today is still primarily male in composition and mindset. In the eighteenth century, however, the gap between societal rhetoric about women and the reality of their political involvement was made easier to bridge by the familial nature of politics at the time: even extensive female participation could be rationalised as non-threatening if it could be interpreted as supportive of (and/or subordinate to) a man, preferably a family member, or carried out in the line of duty to the family interest. As such, it could be fitted quite neatly into contemporary beliefs about the importance for women of attention to family and duty.

When, however, a woman stepped outside this familial framework and entered the political arena in her own right, and especially when she proved herself to be at least as capable a politician as any man, as the Duchess of Devonshire did in the 1784 Westminster election, she posed a dual threat – a threat to the fundamental balance of power between men and women, and, linked to that, a threat to the continued existence of a solely male political order. In order to preserve the status quo, her political activities had to be devalued and dismissed. The best way to do this at the time was to label them unnatural and/or corrupt, and, given the importance placed on female reputation, to designate them immodest, unladylike and, even worse, sexually questionable. Since eighteenth-century understandings of political corruption centred on notions of secret and undue influence, and women's political power often, although not always, involved influence, which by its very nature was politically unaccountable and unchallengeable, their political involvement could readily be as portrayed as corrupt and corrupting. Furthermore, the assumption that women's influence stemmed primarily from their sexuality and men's inability to withstand it only served to strengthen the connection between women and corruption:

> Which is the most genuine description of *Secret Influence*? A Peer of the realm advising his Sovereign in great national concerns, and avowing it openly in the great national assembly, or a P—e [Prince] obliging his tradesmen by the terrors of dismission, and D—sses [Duchesses] employing all the fascinating attractions of female beauty, to cause them to vote contrary to their judgement, and in opposition to what they conceive to be for the public welfare?[14]

Reformers from the 1760s on thus saw the removal of female influence and involvement in politics, especially as wielded by aristocratic women – the aristocracy itself being increasingly depicted as corrupt and effeminate by middling-sort reformers – as essential to reforming the political order and making it more 'manly' and pure.[15]

As an electioneering behaviour, the kiss was always problematic, and particularly so when used by elite women. It was never very popular, however, even with elite men. It was not until the Duchess of Devonshire canvassed so successfully for Charles James Fox in the 1784 Westminster election that she was deemed to have secured the election for him, and in many ways became more the candidate than he was in the eyes of the press and public, that the kiss came to be depicted as a danger to the political order itself. In order to counter the duchess's influence, the Pittite press (promoted by the Whigs who supported William Pitt the younger's administration and by extension the King) ran the notorious kisses-for-votes campaign against her, exploiting to the full various negative stereotypes about women, women's sexuality and women and politics. That the duchess already had a high public profile as a leader of the *bon ton*, a known gambler and a close (perhaps too close) friend of the notoriously rakish and impecunious Fox only played into the hands of the press. The campaign also coincided with and drew unashamedly and self-interestedly upon wider and increasingly vocal concerns about sexual and political corruption expressed by reformers and moralists alike. Socially, their concerns translated into a desire for ever tighter controls over female sexuality and a more domestic role for women; politically, they emerged as demands for a more accountable, respectable form of politics.[16]

The press campaign did not stop women from being involved in electoral politics thereafter, but it does appears to have rung the deathknell for the kiss as a female electioneering strategy. After 1784, any elite woman whose canvassing included kissing men of the lower sort would have risked attracting press commentary and having her respectability called into question. This is not to say that the practice vanished immediately. Hardy elite women existed, and it would not have been out of character for a vivacious and unconventional woman like Pitt's own leading political hostess, the Duchess of Gordon, to have continued the practice. She did, after all, recruit soldiers for the Gordon Highlanders during the French Revolutionary Wars by having them take the king's shilling from her lips.[17]

The tension around the electioneering kiss stemmed from its conflation of two radically different kinds of kisses: the kiss as a time-honoured public and symbolic, non-sexual gesture marking the sealing of a compact; and the kiss as a private, socially levelling and implicitly sexual interchange between two individuals.[18] The connection with corruption arose from fear of the undue, unaccountable and incontestable influence that the latter could have if turned to political ends, particularly if used by politically unaccountable elite women on men of the lower sort. Not only was this combination of sex and class deemed particularly potent, especially if augmented by youth and beauty on the woman's side, but it also triggered deep concerns about the maintenance of conventional social hierarchies through the control of elite female sexuality. Elite men kissing women of the lower sort raised few eyebrows: even if one thing led to another and the woman fell pregnant it would pose no threat to a propertied family's bloodline or inheritance. The same situation did not obtain for elite women: if a kiss led on to more directly sexual encounters and a pregnancy resulted, it would have been a challenge to property and patriarchy, and thus to the very fabric of eighteenth-century society.

Eighteenth-century elections were rumbustious affairs that revolved almost exclusively around local issues and local personalities. Despite the fact that many contests never went all the way to a poll, there were few seats that were totally secure. While the number of recorded contests rose in the second half of the eighteenth century, there were also many campaigns which were settled well before the poll but consumed copious amounts of time, energy, money and ale along the way. Frank O'Gorman has argued convincingly that 75 per cent of all eighteenth-century elections experienced some degree of contest.[19] These contests were inclusive affairs that frequently involved entire communities, voters and non-voters alike. As has frequently been remarked, by the middle of the eighteenth century they had become carnivalesque episodes of self-conscious political theatre characterised by rituals of social inversion.[20] During election campaigns patrons and candidates, their families and their elite supporters temporarily stepped out of their social spheres and roles to mix willingly or unwillingly with their social inferiors. Public houses and great houses were opened; hogsheads of ale were broached; punch was brewed; long-standing debts to tradesmen were paid; local artisans' wares were purchased (frequently in larger numbers and for higher prices than usual); tenants' debts were paid or forgiven; leases were extended or renegotiated; and patronage was promised. Voters and their womenfolk were flattered, visited, wined, dined and whirled about dance floors; *douceurs* of all sorts were dispensed. Most of the latter were too small to be considered bribes: a few shillings here, a guinea somewhere else; a new dress for a voter's wife, a bit of lace for a voter's daughter, the gift of some game or a pineapple or two.[21] They were meant to flatter voters' self-importance and/or secure the influence of their womenfolk.

The kiss needs to be seen in this context: as one of a number of symbolic behaviours in a culture of influence. For men, it was almost always assumed to involve women of the lower sort. One of the few exceptions to this can be found in a poem published during the fierce contest for the city of Durham in 1813, where a battle ensued as two candidates, one young and the other significantly older, vied for the support and political interest of the recently widowed Lady Antrim. The situation was ripe for sexual innuendo, and the political hacks made much of the appeal that a young man was assumed to have to a lusty widow. 'The Struggle' depicts a pointedly similar situation, albeit cast in the light of a courtship. The poem implies that the candidate who won Lady Antrim's political support would have to be prepared, like the suitor in the poem, to supply what the widow was missing:

> The Captain was modest; he made a low bow,
>  Saluted and thought all was right
> The General succeeded; – pray what did he do?
> He staid with the widow all night![22]

The purpose of the electioneering kiss was symbolic: to demonstrate the worthiness of the candidate through his approachability and genuine polite-ness (or indirectly through that of whoever was canvassing for him), to flatter the voters' sense of self-importance and to create a sense of obligation or seal a compact. Among elite men and women it was usually depicted as one of the distasteful but necessary duties that came with being politically active and maintaining a political interest. Thus, Lord Dartford saw it as a suitable penance for Lord North when North went dutifully to his borough of Banbury in August 1766 instead paying him a visit: 'I hope for his punishment he will spend all this delightful weather in eating Venison in Banbury, and kissing the Aldermen's Ladies'.[23] Aldermen's ladies were conventionally described as vulgar and unappealing, but they were at least higher on the social ladder than freeholders' wives, who were often depicted as loathsome. The idea of candidates having to kiss either group provided both satirists and reformers with copy. In *The Humours of a Country Election* (1734), the Mayoress and aldermen's wives are portrayed as lustful, foul-mouthed, violent harridans whose control over their husbands' votes is complete. The two young can-didates secure their support sexually, through a combination of kisses and sexual favours.[24] For William Godwin, complaining about elections half a century later, the practice of kissing freeholders' wives inspired anything but lasciviousness. It was one of the things that made elections 'disgustful' to gentlemen: 'He must kiss the frost-bitten lips of the green-grocers. He must smooth the frowzy cheeks of chandlers-shop women. He must stroke down the infinite belly of a Wapping landlady'.[25] Robert Burns, writing about the contest for Dumfries in 1790, included the women of the lowest sort in his summary of the canvassing necessary to 'buy' a borough: 'shaking hands wi' wabster-loons / And kissing barefit bunters'.[26]

Although contemporary writers tended to assume that the women who were being kissed welcomed the men's attentions socially or sexually, or both, there is little in the sources to reveal whether this was so. Some customary practices might well have been more off-putting than appealing. In Okehampton – a freeman borough where women who were the daughters of freemen had the right to make their husbands into voters – it is questionable whether they felt a great deal of enthusiasm for the practice that obtained at mid-century. After a long and very alcoholic election dinner given by the mayor and magistrates, the men would adjourn drunkenly at about 2 a.m. in order to go 'from house to house to kiss the ladies, as was customary, and ask for the votes of their husbands.'[27]

Elite women were also expected to kiss and be kissed during election campaigns, usually as part of their duty to their husbands' political interests. The social inversion of eighteenth-century elections gave voters the opportunity to make demands on elite women that they might never have made otherwise – and given that it was fashionable for elite women to express dislike at even having to mix socially with the voters and their womenfolk,[28] it would have been surprising if they had eagerly embraced the practice of voters claiming kisses for promises of support. Refusing to kiss or be kissed was equated with arrogance and a lack of genuine politeness, however, and could mean risking a vote: in a heated contest, this was not a risk worth taking (which may explain why the criticism of women for kissing came from moralists and reformers – or adherents of the opposing candidate(s)).

Just how frequently these sorts of demands were made is difficult to ascertain. They may well have contributed to the unwillingness of women who were retiring, such as Mrs Shore, or haughty, such as Lavinia, Lady Spencer, to canvass for their husbands.[29] Nor is it always clear what kinds of kisses were expected. As a writer in the *Edinburgh Evening Courant* remarked acidly during the 1784 election, the canvassing lady might well bring gifts for the voter's wife and children, and even send for her own physician if someone in the voter's family was ill, but securing the vote might well demand more direct involvement: 'She goes still further – the young farms [*sic*] looking sulky – they talk of liberty and property – her ladyship salutes them, must not turn her cheek, for that is the French fashion – they abhor everything French – so her ladyship must kiss in the old English way; and this has considerably increased the price of *lip salve*.'[30]

Similarly, it is impossible to determine just how many elite women included kissing in their repertoire of electioneering tactics. Not all such women canvassed, even for contested elections, and of those who did there would have always been some who refused to kiss or be kissed. Still, the practice was common enough to find its way into election poetry and other pieces of contemporary writing. Indeed, women's dislike of it was exploited by contemporary writers. The long-suffering political wife in George Colman's and Bonnell Thornton's *The Connoisseur* provides an amusing and representative sketch of a situation that might force an unwilling wife to allow herself to be kissed during a contested county election:

> We never sit down to table without a dozen or more of boisterous two-legged creatures as rude as bears; and I have nothing to do but to heap up their plates, and drink to each of their healths: what is worse than all, one of the beasts got tipsy, and nothing would serve him but he must kiss me, which I was obliged to submit to for fear of losing his vote and interest . . . All this and more I have been obliged to comply with, that the country fellows might not say my lady is proud and above them.[31]

In *The Clandestine Marriage* (1768), Colman, this time writing with David Garrick, used the custom as a way to satirise the vulgar *nouveaux riches*, who entered the political game but did not know the rules (as the elite did) and were unwilling to sacrifice their assumed delicacy and self-importance in order to attain their goals. Thus, when the coarse Mrs Heidelberg, a citizen's widow, speaks with pride of her unwillingness to be kissed by the voters, despite the consequences to her husband's cause, it is symbolic of her lack of *ton* and political understanding: 'My dear child . . . Mr. Heidelberg lost his election for member of parliament, because I would not demean myself to be slobbered about by drunken shoemakers, beastly cheesemongers and greasy butchers and tallow-chandlers.'[32] The image of the passive woman being 'slobbered about' by voters in order to fulfil her duty to her husband may not at first glance appear to coincide with conduct-book examples of wifely behaviour, but wives were frequently admonished to accommodate themselves to the needs of their husband and to put his interests and those of his family above their own.[33] Political involvement when interpreted as a manifestation of duty to husband and family thus becomes understandable and acceptable. When women were presented in this way, as dutiful wives playing a recognised and subordinate role, either the electioneering kiss was depicted as non-sexual or any advances are presented as unwelcome – that is, coming from the voter and thus deemed 'liberties' or affronts. To what extent voters did try to take 'liberties' is difficult to determine. The deeply ingrained deference of the period may well have militated against it, but writers certainly suggested that it occurred. One of the many poems published about the Duchess of Devonshire's experiences in 1784 summed it up neatly: 'For ev'ry man salutes your Grace, / Some kiss your hand, and some your face, / And some are rather rude'. Other writers echoed the same theme: 'A certain lady of great beauty and high rank, requests that in future when she condescends to favour any shoemaker, or other mechanic, with a salute, that he will *kiss fair*, and not take improper liberties'.[34]

It was when women were assumed to be the providers rather than the recipients of electioneering kisses – specifically, when they were so politically active and successful in their own right that they usurped the candidate in the eyes of the public and/or the press – that their actions not only challenged the established patriarchal order, but also called into question the deeply embedded beliefs about the 'naturalness' of women's exclusion from the polity and, by extension, the assumptions upon which the polity itself was based. It was then that their actions and the kiss itself were most likely to be depicted as sexually and politically corrupt and corrupting. The best example of this can be found in the infamous kisses-for-votes campaign waged against the Duchess of Devonshire during the 1784 Westminster election.

Much has been written about this election and the activities of the charismatic Georgiana, Duchess of Devonshire, whose canvassing for the leader of the Foxite Whigs, Charles James Fox, turned the election in his favour.[35] Westminster was a scot-and-lot borough with an electorate of 12,000, the largest urban borough electorate in the country; moreover, because of the nature of its franchise, many of the lower ranks of tradesmen and retailers were freeholders, which made it more than usually democratic.[36] Its size made it simply too large to be 'bought' by any candidate using conventional eighteenth-century means: instead, its electorate had to be wooed and won over through effective and insistent canvassing. In addition, it was the most undeniably prestigious and highly politicised borough in the country. Not only did Westminster contain both houses of Parliament, but candidates standing in Westminster also had the benefit (or otherwise) of the proximity and resources of the administration and the Crown, the full weight of the London press and a host of ravening hack writers, caricaturists and engravers. Anything that went on in Westminster that was even vaguely newsworthy or saleable was quickly published and then disseminated across the country. As a result, there was no better borough in the country for a politician to contest if he wanted to take a symbolic stand against the administration or the King, as John Wilkes had demonstrated in the 1760s.

Following, as it did, the downfall of the Fox–North Coalition after George III engineered the defeat of Fox's East India bill, the 1784 general election was one of the few truly national and ideological elections of the eighteenth century. As it became clear that the opposition Foxites were being routed across the country by the Pittites, Fox's contest for a seat in Westminster became the focus of national attention. According to Sir Nathaniel Wraxall: 'All minor election interests were swallowed up in this struggle, which held not only the capital, but the nation in suspense'.[37] Neither side spared any energy or expense in its attempt to secure a victory. Even the King was eager to see Fox defeated.[38]

The electorate was canvassed daily, and, as was not unusual during hard-fought elections, the canvassers included elite women. Indeed, the streets of Westminster must have swarmed with groups of elite female canvassers, as at least twenty-five women can be identified as having canvassed. The Foxite women ranged from duchesses down to a demi-rep: the duchesses of Devonshire and Portland; the ladies Duncannon, Willoughby, Archer, Grosvenor, Dornhoff, Worsley, Beauchamp, Carlisle and Derby, and the Ladies Waldegrave; the Misses Keppel, Mrs Crewe, Mrs Bouverie and Mrs Sheridan; and Mary 'Perdita' Robinson. Fewer Pittite women are identifiable and they were less socially diverse, but, once again, the group extended from duchesses downwards: the duchesses of Rutland, Argyll and Ancaster; the ladies Salisbury, Buckinghamshire and Talbot; and Mrs Hobart.[39] The canvassers included famous beauties, such as the duchesses of Rutland and Argyll; leaders of fashion and society, such as the Duchess of Devonshire, ladies Duncannon and Archer and Mrs Crewe; and noted members of the artistic community in Mrs Sheridan and Perdita Robinson. With the exception of the Waldegraves and Keppels, most of the canvassers were young married women in their twenties and thirties, often with small children at home. Many, but not all, were remarkable for their beauty and grace: Mrs Hobart, in particular, was obese and awkward. She was a caricaturist's delight, but a dedicated canvasser none the less.[40]

Of all the women who canvassed, it was the Duchess of Devonshire who attracted the most attention, from both the public and the press. Young, pretty and charming – a woman who would be remembered long after her death for her 'irresistible manners and the seduction of her society'[41] – she was the foremost political hostess of the day, a leader of the *ton* and the wife of one of England's richest Whig peers. Her free-and-easy manners, her liking for outrageous fashions, her reputation for gambling and her suspiciously close friendships with rakish ne'er-do-wells such as Fox had long earned her celebrity status and a degree of notoriety which made her the target of criticism and moralizing publications.[42] Moreover, her enthusiasm and common touch made her an excellent canvasser. If any of Fox's female supporters were going to be targeted by the press, she was by far the most obvious choice.

The duchess's open electioneering began in mid-March. At the time Fox was trailing behind Sir Cecil Wray, the second of the two administration candidates. The polls opened on 1 April, and by the beginning of May he had not only closed the gap of 100 votes that had separated him from Wray, but had overtaken him – a feat that contemporaries attributed solely to the efforts of Fox's female canvassers, and particularly the duchess.[43] As one publication remarked: 'All advertisements relative to the Westminster Election should be in the Duchess of Devonshire's name. She is the candidate to all intents and purposes. Mr. Fox has not of himself polled a man this fortnight'.[44] By the time the polls closed on 17 May, Fox had widened his lead to 200 votes.[45] When it became obvious at the end of March that Fox's female canvassers were turning the election in his favour, the press began to generate a torrent of 'Newspaper abuse'.[46] A slurry was concocted from contemporary concerns about sexuality, gender and class and was sprayed unremittingly at the duchess as the most visible, high-ranking and effective of the canvassers in an attempt to sully her reputation and embarrass her so badly that she would leave off canvassing. Unfortunately, her style of canvassing, while effective, lent itself to the attack. The disdain that she showed for keeping a 'proper', ladylike social distance between herself and the voters, by canvassing on foot and entering even the lower sort of freeholders' shops and homes, and by taking some voters into her carriage (an erotically charged space in the eighteenth century),[47] made her vulnerable to charges of common and/or lewd behaviour.[48]

The Pittite response was not unique; other forceful and effective elite female canvassers had been criticised in the past for overstepping the constraints of class – for instance, Lady Susan Keck in Oxfordshire in 1754 and the Duchess of Northumberland in Westminster itself in 1774.[49] Nor was sexual slander uncommon. It too tended to be gendered and embedded in wider societal concerns: for women, accusations tended to centre on illicit sexual activity, thus casting aspersions on their virtue and reputation, whereas for men, accusations tended to take the shape of charges of impotence and/ or effeminacy – of not being 'man' enough to father children or not being 'up' to being chosen as a worthy 'member'.[50] *Double entendre* abounded. The press campaign against the duchess, therefore, had its precedents, but its viciousness was more sustained and more widely distributed than that of other eighteenth-century contests. This reflected the importance of the election, its location and the entrepreneurial commercialism of the powerful London press (which, over and above any ideological considerations, seems to have been fully aware that smut involving celebrity women sells papers). It also found its roots in genuine concerns about the impact of women's involvement in politics on the political order. Consequently, the more effective the duchess's canvassing was, and the more she took on political importance in her own right, the more her activities were depicted as sexually and politically corrupt and corrupting.

The notorious kisses-for-votes incident was a gift to the Pittites. This incident, which supposedly took place in late March, allegedly involved the duchess in exchanging kisses for votes, particularly the vote of a butcher (a trade that was symbolically important in that it represented the lower and cruder sort of freeholder):

> *Anecdote.* – The Duchess of D—asked a butcher for his vote, 'I will give your Grace a *plumper*,' says the tradesman, 'and procure you *five* more, on a certain condition.' 'What is that?' 'That your Grace will give me a kiss.' 'Why then,' says the charming Duchess, '*take one*'.[51]

This story, which was to appear in a variety of forms, broke in the *Morning Post* on 31 March: 'We hear that the D—ss of D—grants *favours* to those who promise their votes and interest to Mr. Fox'.[52] This reference to the granting of 'favours' for votes was oft repeated – and gloriously nebulous. The favours referred to could have legitimately been little more than the ordinary cockades and ribbons distributed by canvassers, or the medallions of Fox which had been specially struck for the occasion and which the duchess and her sister had been handing out to supporters.[53] Similarly, the expression also carried with it connotations of patronage, that is, promises granted for political support. It was, however, the word's association with sexual 'favours', be they kisses or other forms of intimate physical contact, that was generally implied. Notions of illicit sexuality and illegitimate female political influence were thus neatly packaged together and disseminated widely.

Whether the kisses-for-votes incident actually occurred, or, if it did, whether it happened in the way in which the newspapers and graphic satires presented it, is highly questionable. Certainly, the duchess protested her innocence sulkily to her mother when defending herself against accusations of over-enthusiastic and immodest canvassing behaviour: 'It is very hard they shd single me out when all the women of my side do as much . . . Dr Mama, I repent, as I often do, the part I have taken, tho' I don't see how I cd have done otherways. My Sr [Sister] and Lady H[?] were both kiss'd, so it's very hard I who was not shd have the reputation of it.'[54] Indeed, given the nature of the contest in Westminster and the extent of social inversion that her male counterparts were enduring in order to try and win votes, it would not have

been unusual if the freeholders had demanded kisses from canvassing aristocratic ladies in return for their support. After all, the election saw peers and
MPs swallow their pride and go so far as to act as waiters at a dinner for the
voters,[55] and Lord Palmerston recorded an electioneering anecdote in mid-
April which could have come straight out of Trusler: a butcher required Fox
to kiss his wife and daughters before telling him that he could 'kiss his arse'
but Fox still would not get his vote.[56] Furthermore, as the duchess had pointed
out to her mother, 'all the women of my side do as much': she was by no
means alone in what she was doing or how she was doing it.

What is most important for the purpose of this chapter is that while the
story was popularised in such a way as to portray the duchess as purposefully
kissing for votes – as taking the active part and using her sexuality to wrest
away the political independence of gullible freeholders – she made a point of
referring to her sister and companion as *having been kissed* and not as *kissing*.
Whether or not this was the case, it was an astute piece of positioning given
her mother's conventional views on women's political involvement. By representing the situation in this way and casting the two women as the passive
recipients of kisses, she carefully desexualised their actions and portrayed
their involvement as dutiful endurance for a political end (albeit an ideological rather than a familial end). As such, she placed them – and the electoral
kiss – within the remit of women's accepted subordinate and supportive
political roles, and in doing so distanced them from possible accusations of
corruption.

She was not to be so lucky herself. As the pivotal figure in the election
campaign, she was unrelentingly presented by the Pittite press as taking the
active part – of securing freeholders' votes through a seductively corrupting
combination of kisses, cash and more direct sexual commerce. In the six
weeks when the polls were open, the Pittite newspapers, especially the *Morning Post*, ensured that she was criticised and her actions satirised or sexualised
on an almost daily basis.[57] Scores of pamphleteers, poets and cartoonists also
joined in the fray. Even in their least offensive manifestation, these publications cast her activities, particularly her kissing, in the light of traditional
forms of political corruption – as bribery and undue influence: 'Who would
not purchase the *kiss of a favourite one* at any price? Does not the *Duchess*
who gives a *kiss* for a *vote*, pay for it a *valuable consideration*? Have a care,
fair D—n; bribery is by common law either imprisonment or the pillory.'[58]
Or: 'It certainly was an oversight in those friends to the constitution who
framed the different laws against bribery at elections, that a penalty was not
laid on handsome women, who went about kissing men out of their votes,
which ought to be considered as undue influence, especially where the women
are married ladies, and the favours they grant are not for the immediate
service of their husbands.'[59]

It was the perceived inability of male politicians to counter female canvassers' kissing voters that was especially galling. As the stereotypical old-fashioned country gentleman who was the narrator in *The Countryman's Frolick; or, Humours of an Election* commented in a poem published three days before the polls closed, there was nothing that a man could do to compete:

> What does it avail now of promising votes,
> For a Devonshire kiss in an instant turns coats,
> Besides lay a wager of five guineas to boot,
> You surely win, kiss again, bring him in.[60]

The fact that her activities were deemed, if possible, yet more dangerous and more corrupt because she was not operating from within the recognised paradigm of familial politics is in itself telling. What these writers did not know at the time was how firmly her political participation remained embedded in familial politics, despite canvassing for Fox, and how close their campaign against the duchess came to succeeding. After fleeing to her mother's in St Albans to escape the press in early April, she was forced back to London in the middle of the month to continue canvassing only by the exasperation of her sister-in-law, the Duchess of Portland, the concerted efforts of her husband's uncle and, finally, the barely veiled commands of the leader of the Whigs in the Lords, her brother-in-law, the Duke of Portland. As she was to explain to her brother later, the 'letters from the D & Dss & Ld John brought me back'.[61]

The most vicious charges against her were those that interpreted undue influence in sexual terms and sought to sully her reputation by representing her canvassing as a form of prostitution, openly sexual and commercial: 'The *Duchess of Devonshire* transacts business in a very *expeditious* manner, and therefore deserves much praise from her *favourite member*, as in her canvassing for voters she avoids being loquacious – but *kisses* and comes at once to *the point*.'[62] And the '*point*' was unquestionably sexual as well as political.

This approach was especially noticeable in the more graphic prints. In William Dent's 'The Dutchess Canvassing for her Favourite Member', for instance, published two weeks into the poll on 13 April, the duchess is presented as embracing a bovine-looking butcher prior to kissing him and simultaneously lifting his apron to caress what appears to be an erect penis (Figure 5). The message of sexual corruption is also reinforced visually and textually: the duchess's skirt is tucked up with erect fox's tails, the street sign in the corner of the print indicates that the encounter is taking place on 'Cockspur Street', and the duchess is pointedly made to say, 'I'll leave no Stone unturned to

5  William Dent, 'The Dutchess Canvassing for her Favourite Member' (13 April 1784).

serve the Cause'.[63] Then, to reinforce the commercial element of the trans-
action (and its connection to bribery and corruption), the duchess's female
companion stands behind her extending a purse full of coins – just in case
the duchess's sexual appeal is not sufficient, or as a means of sealing the
compact.

What comes across forcibly in the prints criticising the duchess is that she
had become the foremost political figure in the contest. She is frequently the
tallest, as well as the central, figure. She canvasses on her own or with a
female companion – often her sister Harriet, Lady Duncannon, or her sister-
in-law, the Duchess of Portland. When men are included in the prints as
canvassing companions, they are often subordinated, by being either placed
on the margins of the prints or in the background, or both. A commanding
presence with her high heels, bouffant hairstyles, and hats bedecked with
waving plumes or foxes' tails, the duchess forces freeholders to look up to
her, sometimes even to stretch up on to their tiptoes, as Dent's butcher is
forced to do, as she leans down to kiss them. In Thomas Rowlandson's 'The

Two Patriotic Duchess's on their Canvass' (Figure 6), published on 3 April, she embraces a slim, young, handsome butcher, who is close to her height, but this is unusual; most of the butchers are more along the lines of the short, podgy butcher of Rowlandson's 'The Devonshire, or Most Approved Method of Securing Votes' (Figure 7), published on 12 April, or of the similarly short and physically unappealing 'Old Swelter-in-Grease' of '*A Certain Dutchess Kissing Old* Swelter-in-Grease *the Butcher for his Vote*' (Figure 8).[64]

While the prints focus on the duchess because of her centrality to the election and her overall political importance, they also reflect wider concerns about gender and politics. The prints which develop the kisses-for-votes theme repeatedly show the duchess as the active party, as doing the kissing, not being kissed. She, and by extension political women as a group, are thus portrayed as 'women on top' – dominant – corrupting and upsetting the

6  Thomas Rowlandson, 'The Two Patriotic Duchess's on their Canvass' (3 April 1784).

7  Thomas Rowlandson, 'The Devonshire, or Most Approved Method of Securing Votes' (12 April 1784).

'natural' political order, threatening the social order and also, more fundamentally, challenging the 'natural' hierarchy of the sexes. The fact that
neither the critics of the duchess nor her supporters were able to find a way
to reconcile independent female political activity with contemporary notions
of male and female sexuality reflects the power of the belief which saw women
as naturally excluded from the polity because of their sexuality. Even those
publications and prints which were published in favour of the duchess and
her political activities were ambivalent. Although there were some tentative claims to female political rights or appeals to history to justify female
political involvement on the basis of pure female public virtue – for instance,
Rowlandson's depiction of the duchess as 'Female Patriotism' in his print
'Liberty and Fame Introducing Female Patriotism to Britannia'[65] – even
those Foxite supporters of the duchess who also espoused women's rights to
political involvement during the election tended not to be able to separate
women's political influence from their sexuality. They just happened to see it
in a more positive light:[66]

> The mean attempts made to injure the reputation of those virtuous female char-
> acters who have patriotically espoused the cause of the defenders of the liberties of
> their country, are surely as ridiculous as they are unmanly and unbecoming.

Ancient states and governments, remarkable for their wisdom, fortitude, integrity, and success, very judiciously encouraged a spirit of public virtue among their women. As then illustrious Princesses and distinguished patriots have not been wanting in England as much as in other nations, as they have shown abilities equal to the task of policy and government, and as they are or ought to be like the men, the most free in the world, what man that loves the sex, or respects liberty, can object to being canvassed by a British beauty?[67]

For most eighteenth-century contemporaries, however, the idea of women turning their powers to political ends, of becoming political actors in their own rights, was threatening in a variety of ways, not least because politically powerful and independent women would, Delilah-like, leave men powerless,

8 'A Certain Dutchess kissing Old Swelter-in-Grease the Butcher for his Vote' (April 1784).

sexually and politically passive and unresisting. The assumption that one thing would inevitably lead to another, with the final outcome being the enfranchisement of women and the destruction of the polity and a corresponding loss of the Englishman's ever-precious liberty and freedom, was clearly voiced in 'The Influence of Beauty':

> A sober, plain Englishman can really have no opinion of his own, if his understanding is to be attacked by the argument of eyes. He can have no chance for his liberty, if weapons so irresistible as smiles and glances are used against him. The influence of beauty therefore must be more dangerous in a free country than the Secret Influence of the Crown.
>
> If it should be admitted that Ladies have a right to canvass for their favourite candidate, and to exercise the arts of never-failing beauty against the unsuspecting hearts of Englishmen, their next step will be to vote for them; and they will maintain their franchises by arguments which we cannot refute. Having gained this, they will next get into Parliament themselves, and then farewell to our liberties as a free people![68]

Although the giving of kisses was a well-established eighteenth-century electioneering strategy, used by men and women alike, it came to be permanently associated with corruption at least where elite female canvassers were concerned in the aftermath of the 1784 Westminster election. A highly personal and intimate interchange between a man and a woman, the election kiss could not ever be completely dissociated from the culture from which it came. As such, it serves as a distinct reminder of the need to see politics as coloured and shaped by, not distinct from, the wider belief systems, ideals and concerns of a particular society at a particular point in time. By the last quarter of the eighteenth-century, therefore, the electoral kiss, especially when used by elite women who were becoming more openly politically active and independent, awoke current fears about gender and class, as well as sexual and political corruption. Thus, women who were portrayed as kissing rather than being kissed were presented as dominant, even predatory, corrupting the political system by robbing honest English freeholders of their independence.

Finally, it is also worth examining the kiss and its connections with corruption for the light that it throws on women's relation to the English polity at a point when the possibility of women being political figures in their own rights was only beginning to emerge from the realms of satire. As Carole Pateman has argued, women were 'incorporated into the political order and not merely excluded (or left in "the state of nature"), but their manner of incorporation was different from that of men, and involved exclusion from major rights of citizenship and, hence, lesser standing.'[69] In order to gain a clearer understanding of why this is so, it is important to understand the power of the 'fiction' which served as the foundation of the polity and defined it as male. Consequently, women's political involvement – and their electoral kissing – was unproblematic if it posed no challenge to the political order: if it was familial, supportive and subordinate. It was, however, when women's political involvement could no longer be easily categorised in this way and became, or appeared to become, personal (individual rather than collective), independent and, what is more, highly successful, as it did in the case of the Duchess of Devonshire in 1784, that it raised questions about the 'naturalness' of women's exclusion from citizenship and the nature of the polity itself.

### NOTES

I should like to thank the Trustees of the Chatsworth Settlement for generously allowing me to consult the Devonshire Papers at Chatsworth House.

1   *A New Geographical and Historical Grammar* (London, 1758) [unpaginated], cited in C. C. Bombaugh, *The Literature of Kissing, Gleaned from History, Poetry, Fiction and Anecdote* (Philadelphia, 1876), pp. 73–4.

2   See, for instance, Sir Roger Newdigate's notes on the Oxfordshire election of 1754: Warwick Record Office, CR136 B 2524 B/1–B.2529, Parliamentary Notes on the Oxfordshire Election of 1754 by Sir Roger Newdigate.

3   See Sarah Richardson, 'Introduction: The Petticoat in Politics: Women and Authority', in Kathryn Gleadle and Sarah Richardson (eds), *Women in British Politics, 1760–1860: The Power of the Petticoat* (Basingstoke, 2000), pp. 1–18.

4   In the borough of Maldon, for instance, where freemen's daughters had the electoral privilege of making their husbands voters, one of the successful candidates, John Huske, appealed directly to the women. See *Chelmsford Chronicle* (10 December 1773).

5   John Trusler, *The Country Election* (London, 1768, 1788).

6   *Ibid.*, p. 28.

7   *Ibid.*, pp. 17–18.

8   Justin McCarthy, 'The Petticoat in the Politics of England', *Lady's Own Paper* (9 July 1870), 20. Matthew Cragoe draws attention to McCarthy's comments, revealing that Victorian candidates and canvassers continued to see securing the influence of voters' wives as important and employed much the same techniques as their Hanoverian grandfathers and great-grandfathers. See Matthew Cragoe, '"Jenny Rules the Roost": Women and Electoral Politics, 1832–68', in Gleadle and Richardson (eds), *Women in British Politics*, pp. 153–68, at p. 157.

9   Charles Dickens, the *Pickwick Papers*, quoted in W. H. D. Rouse (ed.), *Election Scenes in Fiction* (London, 1929), p. 56. In 'Birds of a Feather all Flock Together', a poem from the Durham election of 1813, one of the candidates remarks upon George Baker's method of canvassing. He not only gives the Ladies a separate election treat – plenty 'Of Meat, Drink, and Fruit, and every thing dainty' – but also provides them with 'Dresses alike' of 'Lincoln Green', and secures their support. See 'Birds of a Feather all Flock Together', in *The Addresses Together with the Speeches, Hand Bills, and other Particulars, Relative to the Election of One Citizen to Serve in Parliament for the City of Durham, December 1813* ([Durham?], [1813?]), p. 42.

10  *Ibid.*, pp. 70–1.

11  Sean Wilentz, 'Introduction: Teufelsdröckh's Dilemma: On Symbolism, Politics, and History', in Sean Wilentz (ed.), *Rites of Power: Symbolism, Ritual, and Politics since the Middle Ages* (Philadelphia, 1985), p. 3.

12 *Ibid.*, p. 4.

13 Susan Kingsley Kent, *Gender and Power in Britain, 1640–1990* (London, 1999), p. 117.

14 As quoted in J. Hartley *et al.*, *History of the Westminster Election, Containing Every Material Occurrence, from its Commencement on the First of April, to the Final Close of the Poll, on the 17th of May* (London, 1784), p. 230.

15 For the Wilkite radicals' desire to purify and masculinise the polity, see also Kent, *Gender and Power in Britain*, p. 118.

16 *Ibid.*, pp. 120–4.

17 Bombaugh, *Literature of Kissing*, p. 74.

18 Teofilo F. Ruiz, 'Unsacred Monarchy: The Kings of Castile in the Late Middle Ages', in Wilentz (ed.), *Rites of Power*, pp. 125–6.

19 Frank O'Gorman, *Voters, Patrons and Parties: The Unreformed Electoral System of Hanoverian England, 1734–1832* (Oxford, 1991), pp. 107–12.

20 See Frank O'Gorman, 'Campaign Rituals and Ceremonies: The Social Meaning of Elections in England, 1780–1860', *Past & Present*, 135 (1992), 443–59.

21 This practice continued at least into the early years of Victoria's reign. Mrs Gwynne Holford's canvassing techniques in Breconshire in 1837 were entirely 'unreformed' in their tone, canvassing visits being followed by special gifts of luxuries such as grapes, pineapples or trout. See Cragoe, '"Jenny Rules the Roost"', p. 156.

22 'The Struggle', in *Addresses Together with the Speeches, Hand Bills, and Other Particulars*, p. 23.

23 Bodleian Library, Oxford, MS North d.10, fol. 171$^{\text{v}}$, Dartmouth to Guilford, Sandwell, 22 August 1766.

24 *The Humours of a Country Election* (London, 1734), pp. 15–20.

25 William Godwin, *Instructions to a Statesman* (1784), in *Four Early Pamphlets by William Godwin* (Gainesville, 1966), pp. 130–1. See also Paul Langford, *Public Life and the Propertied Englishman, 1689–1798* (Oxford, 1991), pp. 273–4, where he suggests that this is indicative of the political elite's rising disgust with the 'personal and social humiliation' (p. 273) inherent in the social inversion of eighteenth-century elections.

26 Robert Burns, 'Election Ballad: At Close of the Contest for Representing the Dumfries Burghs, 1790', at www.worldburnsclub.com/poems/translations/election ballad.htm. 'Bunters' were specifically those women who went around the streets collecting rags, or, more generally and contemptuously, any vulgar women of the lower sort. For the full definition of 'bunter', see the *Oxford English Dictionary*.

27 'Mr. Bower to Mrs. Montagu, Oakampton, 16 April 1754', in Emily J. Climenson (ed.), *Elizabeth Montagu the Queen of the Blue-Stockings*, 2 vols (London, 1906), p. 50.

28 See, for example, Elizabeth Montagu's tongue-in-cheek comments about behaving 'very prettily' when carrying out her duties as a political wife during the 1760 election: British Library, London, Add. MS 59,486, Dropmore Papers, fol. 92$^{\text{v}}$, Elizabeth Montagu to Anne Pitt [Newcastle?], December [1760].

29 S. Shore Jr refuses the offer of a seat in Parliament in 1788 on the dual grounds of not wanting to have to leave the country and his domestic enjoyments, and because his wife refuses to canvass for him. See Buckinghamshire Record Office, Aylesbury, D/SB/ PFE2/2, S. Shore Jr to Scrope Bernard, Norton Hall, 28 November 1788. Similarly, Lord Spencer expresses his regret to his mother that his wife, Lavinia, does not have 'spirits enough' to canvass for him in 1784. This explanation is highly unlikely, as Lavinia was a well-known termagant; her arrogance and unwillingness to mix with those even slightly lower in status was much more likely to have been the cause. See British Library, London, MSS Coll. Althorp, F.14 [unfoliated], Spencer to Countess Dowager Lady Spencer, Althorp, 1 April 1784.

30  As quoted in Donald McAdams, 'Politicians and the Electorate in the Late Eighteenth Century', PhD dissertation, Duke University, 1967, p. 2.

31  George Colman and Bonnell Thornton (eds), *The Connoisseur*, 20 (13 June 1754), 116–17.

32  George Colman and David Garrick, *The Clandestine Marriage*, in Dougald MacMillan and Howard Mumford Jones (eds), *Plays of the Restoration and Eighteenth Century* (London, 1931), p. 696. My thanks to Susan Skedd for reminding me of this.

33  See, for instance, Isabella Howard (Countess Dowager of Carlisle), *Thoughts in the Form of Maxims Addressed to Young Ladies on their First Establishment in the World* (London, 1789), pp. 1–10.

34  'ODE to the D—ss of D—e', in Hartley *et al.*, *History of the Westminster Election*, p. 434; for the newspaper excerpt, see p. 231.

35  The most detailed examination of the duchess and her political activities, including the Westminster election, can be found in Amanda Foreman, *Georgiana: Duchess of Devonshire* (London, 1998). The most recent considerations of her involvement in the election can be found in Renata Lana, 'Women and Foxite Strategy in the Westminster Election of 1784', *Eighteenth-Century Life*, 26:1 (2002), 46–69; Judith S. Lewis, '1784 and All That: Aristocratic Women and Electoral Politics', in Amanda Vickery (ed.), *Women, Privilege and Power: British Politics, 1750 to the Present* (Stanford, 2001), pp. 89–122; Kingsley Kent, *Gender and Power in Britain*, pp. 120–4; Elaine Chalus, 'Women's Involvement in English Political Life, 1754–90', DPhil dissertation, University of Oxford, 1998; Phyllis Deutsch, 'Moral Trespass in Georgian London: Gaming, Gender and Electoral Politics in the Age of George III', *Historical Journal*, 39:3 (1996), 637–56; P. J. Jupp, 'The Roles of Royal and Aristocratic Women in British Politics, *c.*1782–1832', in Mary O'Dowd and Sabine Wichert (eds), *Chattel, Servant or Citizen: Women's Status in Church State and Society* (Belfast, 1995), pp. 103–13; Anne Stott, '"Female Patriotism": Georgiana, Duchess of Devonshire, and the Westminster Election of 1784', *Eighteenth-Century Life*, 17 (November 1993), 60–84; Linda Colley, *Britons: Forging the Nation, 1701–1837* (London, 1992), pp. 242–9.

36  The size of the electorate is given as 18,000 by Foreman, but both John Brooke and Frank O'Gorman place it as 12,000 in this period: see John Brooke, *The House of Commons, 1754–1790: Introductory Survey* (Oxford, 1964), p. 31; Frank O'Gorman, *Voters, Patrons and Parties*, p. 55.

37  Sir Nathaniel Wraxall, *Posthumous Memoirs of his Own Time*, ed. Henry B. Wheatley, 5 vols (London, 1884), iii, pp. 340–1.

38  Foreman, *Georgiana*, p. 141.

39  See, Hartley *et al.*, *History of the Westminster Election*; J. Grego, *History of Parliamentary Elections and Electioneering in the Old Days* (London, 1886), pp. 269–93.

40  Little is yet known about the efforts of most of the other women who canvassed on either side. See Lewis, '1784 and All That', and Foreman, *Georgiana*, for additional information on, among others, the Duchess of Rutland, Lady Salisbury and Mrs Bouverie, Mrs Crewe and Mrs Hobart.

41  Wraxall, *Posthumous Memoirs*, iii, p. 342.

42  See, for example, William Combe, *The First of April: or, The Triumphs of Folly: A Poem* (London, 1777); *A Letter to her Grace the Duchess of Devonshire* (London, 1777).

43  Wraxall, *Posthumous Memoirs*, iii, p. 346; see also Foreman, *Georgiana*, pp. 141–3.

44  Hartley *et al.*, *History of the Westminster Election*, p. 254.

45  Foreman, *Georgiana*, p. 153.

46  British Library, London, MS Coll. Althorp, G.287, Duchess of Devonshire to Spencer [London, 23 April 1784]. For the most comprehensive contemporary collection of

press clippings and other published material relating to the election see, Hartley *et al.*, *History of the Westminster Election*.

47 Karen Harvey, 'Gender, Space and Modernity in Eighteenth-Century England: A Place Called Sex', *History Workshop Journal*, 51 (2001), 158–79.

48 The duchess's mother, Lady Spencer, tried valiantly and unsuccessfully to ensure that the duchess canvassed from her carriage, where she would remain safely elevated and separated from the masses. For more information on this and other methods of canvassing used by elite women, see Elaine Chalus, '"That epidemical Madness": Women and Electoral Politics in the Late Eighteenth Century', in Hannah Barker and Elaine Chalus (eds), *Gender in Eighteenth-Century England: Roles, Representations and Responsibilities* (Harlow, 1997), pp. 151–78.

49 Both adopted a 'hail fellow, well met' approach to canvassing which transgressed class boundaries but proved to be effective – and thus provoked criticism: Lady Susan in printed essays and election poems which criticised her for, among other things, huzza-ing and drinking bumpers with butchers; and the Duchess of Northumberland in private correspondence between disapproving male contemporaries for going 'most condescendingly out of her sphere, shakes every basketwoman by the hand'. See, for example, *Jackson's Oxford Journal* (1 June 1753); 'A Copy of Verses in Praise of Adversity', in *The Oxfordshire Contest* (London, 1753), p. 42; 'Horace Walpole to Henry Seymour Conway, Strawberry Hill, 16 Oct. 1774', in Horace Walpole, *The Yale Edition of Horace Walpole's Correspondence*, ed. W. S. Lewis, 48 vols (London, 1937–83), xxxix, p. 196; and 'William Whitehead to Nuneham, London, 1774', in *The Harcourt Papers*, ed. Edward William Harcourt, 14 vols (Oxford, 1876–1905), vii, p. 315.

50 The childlessness of young Lord Parker, who stood for Oxfordshire in 1754, laid him open to just these sorts of accusations; thus the birth of an heir in 1755 was of political as well as familial importance: see *Jackson's Oxford Journal* (1 March 1755). Given current interest in eighteenth-century masculinity, little work has been done on the gendered dimension of election rhetoric where men are concerned: see Lewis, '1784 and All That', pp. 116–20, who begins to address this topic.

51 Hartley *et al.*, *History of the Westminster Election*, p. 228.

52 *Ibid.*, p. 218; Foreman, *Georgiana*, p. 144.

53 *Ibid.*, p. 142.

54 Devonshire Papers, Chatsworth House (Chatsworth MSS), 610.1, 'Duchess of Devon-shire to Lady Spencer' [London, late March–early April 1784].

55 O'Gorman, *Voters, Patrons and Parties*, p. 92.

56 'Palmerston to Lady Palmerston, 15 April 1784', in Brian Connell, *Portrait of a Whig Peer* (London, 1957), p. 155.

57 Foreman, *Georgiana*, p. 144.

58 Hartley *et al.*, *History of the Westminster Election*, p. 232.

59 *Ibid.*, pp. 242–3.

60 *The Countryman's Frolick; or, Humours of an Election* (14 May 1784).

61 For a more detailed examination of this situation and her mother's desire to prevent her from returning to London to canvass, see Chalus, 'Women's Involvement in English Political Life', pp. 236–7; British Library, London, MS Coll. Althorp, G.287, Duchess of Devonshire to Spencer [London, 23 April 1784].

62 Hartley *et al.*, *History of the Westminster Election*, p. 248.

63 British Museum Cat. 6527, William Dent, 'The Dutchess Canvassing for her Favourite Member' (13 April 1784).

64 British Museum Cat. 6494, Thomas Rowlandson, 'The Two Patriotic Duchess's on their Canvass' (3 April 1784); British Museum Cat. 6520, Thomas Rowlandson, 'The

Devonshire, or Most Approved Method of Securing Votes' (12 April 1784); and British Museum Cat. 6533, 'A Certain Dutchess Kissing Old Swelter-in-Grease the Butcher for his Vote' (April 1784).

65 Thomas Rowlandson, 'Liberty and Fame Introducing Female Patriotism to Britannia', frontispiece in Hartley et al., History of the Westminster Election.

66 Lewis, '1784 and All That', p. 114.

67 Hartley et al., History of the Westminster Election, p. 356.

68 'The Influence of Beauty', ibid., p. 313.

69 Carole Pateman, 'Women's Writing, Women's Standing: Theory and Politics in the Early Modern Period', in Hilda L. Smith (ed.), Women Writers and the Early Modern British Political Tradition (Cambridge, 1998), p. 370.

# 7

# *Illness and impact: the mistress of the house and the governess*

<>

Carole Williams

O N 6 APRIL 1887, writing of her governess Miss Freestone, Lady Frederica Loraine noted in her diary that 'Fr came for a kiss'. She repeated this entry on 7 April 1887 and on 8 April 1887. No similar record had been made within the previous five years of her surviving married diaries and no similar references followed these three single entries within those surviving for the next six years.[1] Thus these three solitary kisses were striking, unexpected and, at the level of the diary information alone, seemingly out of context. More-over, these kisses grab the attention because of the particular relationship between these two women. This was evidence that the married, upper-class and very traditional mistress of the household and mother of four children was kissing her young, and it would seem impressionable, governess at bedtime.

In the Victorian period, the most common unifying characteristic of the kiss was the deliberate external demonstration of emotional intensity or intimacy between the participants. Nevertheless, it represented a range of human interaction across a diverse spectrum. Its powerful connotations ranged from, for example, the licentious eroticism of the brothel to the idealistic purity of the kiss between doting mother and innocent child. The private kiss could have sexual connotations when, for example, it occurred between lovers, and it was regularly used to denote the intense romance between courting couples. The engagement correspondence between Frederica St John Rouse-Boughton and Richard Orlebar is indicative in including Frederica asking Richard to 'fancy me giving you one very long endless kiss'.[2] So, too, is that of Sir Lambton and Lady Frederica (Freda) Loraine in which Lambton, separated from his love, writes to her: 'overcome with a sense of cold desolation . . . (don't think me a fool Freda) I kissed the chairs and sofa that you had occupied out of the very fervency of my love'.[3]

Kissing was, however, just as commonly recognised as the outward expression of non-sexual emotional regard. For example, in 1866, Frederica Orlebar illustrated the importance that she attributed to the kiss and its deliberate use, not in a straightforward demonstration of mutual affection between herself and her beloved son, but rather as a device to soften the effect of maternal discipline: 'If he was in a rage, I threatened very decidedly to punish him if he were not good in a few minutes and then I set him with his back towards the room to recover, always taking the precaution of kissing him first. It was strange to see how his voice and face changed when I kissed him. In a few minutes he would be quite right, the bad fit having altogether passed away.'[4] *The Spectators* understood the diverse symbolism of the kiss and the manner in which it could be consciously and effectively used to denote a wide range of relationships.

Victorians would have recognised and participated in both the public and the private kiss. The acceptable face of public kissing included that between family members and close personal friends. Exuberant family members hugged and kissed one another on meeting after a prolonged absence; elders kissed the newly engaged and recently married; mothers and fathers sent gentle kisses to their beloved offspring; delighted sisters kissed their brothers safely returned from the dangers of their military activities. These kisses shared one important characteristic: their purpose and the relationship between the participants should have been crystal clear; doubts concerning the ambiguity or uncertainty of the kiss – particularly regarding sexual undertones – were excised. If in doubt, it was perhaps wisest to check before bestowing a kiss even in what should have been straightforward circumstances. Exemplifying this, Richard Orlebar senior took no risks with his son's new fiancée, preferring to express his sentiments via his son's letter: 'my father says he is very sorry that he let you go. He was longing to kiss you at parting, but feared that you would be offended, should you have been?'[5] For the Victorians, the need for a lack of ambiguity helped to constrain the practice of acceptable kissing primarily to family and close friends. But kissing practices were not determined only by constraint.

During the Victorian period, the romantic idealisation of the family, and of the mother in particular, incorporated expectations of outward displays of familial and maternal love including the kiss.[6] In 1863 these expectations were demonstrated by the actions not only of Frederica, now the mother of ten-month-old Rouse, but also of his monthly nurse, Mrs Thrives. Both women encouraged Rouse to love his new baby brother through use of the kiss. Frederica recorded that 'it was very pretty to see him put his little head against the baby's frock and kiss and love him in his own little way. Mrs. Thrives had taught him to kiss his hand'.[7] Indeed, expectations of familial affection were sufficiently high as to result in consternation if a mother was perceived not to wish to kiss her child. The idealisation of the maternal relationship increased pressure on women who did not feel immediate love for their babies. Frederica Orlebar made it clear in her diary that the expectations of others and, indeed, herself, that she would adore her newborn baby led her to feel resentful, 'bitter' and 'unnatural' when she did not do so. In contrast the birth of her second baby facilitated adherence to the ideal and brought her great satisfaction: 'I had the baby . . . within kissing distance of my lips . . . what tender feelings that little pudgy mass inspired'.[8] There were clearly strictures about both when kisses should and should not be given, and the relationship between the participants was all-important to the public kiss.

Despite constraints on the public kiss, in private the romanticism and companionate marital ideals of the period encouraged couples' expectation of the mutual expression of tenderness and love for one another, albeit within the context of a requirement for outward reserve. This outward display of dignity and respect for others should not be misinterpreted as evidence of distant, prudish, private relationships, however, nor should it lead to simplistic assumptions about the nature of Victorian marital relations. Though Mason argues that 'this society had a widespread and principled belief that there should be discipline and unobtrusiveness in all sexual activity', there is ample evidence to suggest that behind closed doors the Victorians were both demonstrative and tactile.[9] Frederica Orlebar clearly illustrated this point in 1863 after a prolonged absence from her beloved husband, Richard:

> I was too happy to speak when I got out of the train and saw that very dear husband again. I knew I must look very undemonstrative to please him while I was in public, and I am sure we both acted our parts to perfection. Richard has a peculiar horror of looking interesting, almost a morbid horror, and the more he feels, the more utterly indifferent he appears . . . I felt wild with joy . . . I soon got into the drawing room . . . <u>how</u> kind Richard was. How quickly the ice froze when the spectators were gone. Oh <u>what a blessing</u> it was to have got back to him.[10]

In the case of Lady Freda and Sir Lambton Loraine there is regular, effusive and romantic correspondence from the time of their engagement in 1878 to 1910. Sentiment and affection were crucial components of their marriage, and this correspondence included the use of nicknames, codes and love symbols.[11] The main love symbol used by the couple was a circle, first suggested by Freda during their courtship and referred to as a 'Fairy Ring'.[12] Lambton was not satisfied with one ring but often drew a whole line of different-sized rings filled with numbers, presumably to represent his love for his wife and children:

> kisses and hugs to you my own own darling. I love you, love you, love you, love you and you are the dearest little girl that ever lived and I am your own Timmus.

And give such kisses to my babies [there follows a large circle for Eustace, his first son, a slightly smaller one for Percy, his second, a slightly smaller one for his daughter Ji, and one four times the size that has 'little Mummy' written inside it].[13]

Typical of the language used and the content is Lambton writing of 'smothering . . . his own little Fre with kisses', sending 'thousands of kisses' and sending 'love, love, love and kisses, kisses, kisses'.[14]

Engagement correspondence and diaries suggest that, despite the chaperoning of young girls in society, once engaged, some couples found private opportunities to indulge in loving encounters while nevertheless protecting and saving their all-important virginity for the marital bed. The diary of Mary Hall is a record of a courting couple which makes it plain that they were regularly left alone. Typical of the entries is that of 28 August 1895 in which Mary wrote the following about her fiancé, Jack: 'a little caressing after dinner put him right . . . I had him again after supper and he was so loving'.[15] Kissing was perhaps the archetypal exemplar of inner romance both in practice and in the sentimental longings of young Victorian women. It was not just in the novel that the kiss claimed its participants for one another and sealed their attachment without the seediness or dangers of penetrative sex.[16] Thus, the kiss between Victorian couples operated on several levels, for it was a crucially important constituent of romance and sentimental love rather than simply a precursor to the private world of genital sex. The kiss enabled the expression of intense mutual romance and love without any of the less attractive ramifications of reproductive sex. It occupied a unique and unchallenged place in the highly romantic emotional world of Victorian England. Both public and private kisses conveyed intimacy, affection and love – without (necessarily) intimations of genital sex.

Sentiment, romance and passionate attachment were, of course, not confined to heterosexual relationships in the Victorian period. Indeed, it has been argued that passionate same-sex relationships were not only common but were also exacerbated by the gendered nature of Victorian society.[17] Moreover, Jeffreys claims that it was not until the late nineteenth century that the open expression of these passionate relationships began to be seen as a threat by men worried about growing female independence.[18] Lanser argues, however, that same-sex kissing was under attack by the end of the eighteenth century.[19] The potentially threatening ambiguity of same-sex kissing in cultures promoting heterosexuality as normative appears to have posed problems of interpretation for contemporaries and historians alike. However, Victorian norms apparently dictated that same-sex kisses took place between participants whose relationship was perceived to be respectable and platonic.

The contention that Victorian women shared deeply emotional and supportive relationships with other women is irrefutable. The extent to which the majority of these relationships were of a physical rather than an emotional nature is, however, open to debate. Mother, sisters and long-standing family friends played a huge supporting role in the lives of most genteel women. This took place both at a practical level in times of crisis or a heavy workload (for example, with their help with pregnancy and childcare) and at an emotional level with regular visits and correspondence full of sympathy, advice and support. Indeed, not only women but many husbands, fathers, brothers and grandfathers also provided emotional and, albeit more limited, practical support.[20]

Frederica Loraine received practical and emotional support from her mother, sister, brother and friends and from her beloved husband. She thus possessed an extensive support network. In addition, she shared a general Victorian consciousness of class and social status. Neither Frederica nor Lambton were progressive or radical; on the contrary, they were Conservative members of the Primrose League who adopted a patronising and intrusive attitude towards their domestic 'serpents'.[21] This attitude is reflected in both their correspondence and the language used towards servants in Freda's diaries. For example, in March 1884 this correspondence makes clear the subordinate position and deference expected from servants: 'you know my maxims about not entering into the reasons for things with servants more than can be helped . . . if she is to remain with us . . . must be put back into her proper place or else affairs will be on an entirely wrong footing afterwards'.[22] Moreover, Freda notes servants as being 'defiant', 'tiresome' and 'disobedient' and Miss Noyes, her governess, as 'nagging, finding fault'.[23] As a governess, Miss Freestone may have been the most elevated of the domestic staff – although even here issues of length of service and age muddy the picture – but she was still most certainly a servant and employee. The role and position of the governess in Victorian society was fraught with ambiguity and tension. The tripartite nature of the interaction between mother, child and governess brought with it difficulties which were exacerbated by the idealisation of the maternal relationship and the contrary stereotype of the working 'lady'. Indeed, Kathryn Hughes stresses the difficulties and ambiguities surrounding the position of the Victorian governess, with a major theme of her book emphasising the inherent potential for loneliness and isolation.[24]

Families commonly struggled to negotiate the conflict between the need to pay the governess due respect as a 'lady' and as an authority over the children (especially boys) and her lower class status as an employee within the household. The possibilities for conflict were also heightened by the exaltation of and expectations surrounding the role of the mother and varying perceptions of what level of autonomy and emotional attachment should be deemed appropriate to cede to the governess. The acknowledged difficulties which the presence of the governess brought with it encouraged many mothers to delay the employment of a governess for as long as possible, and those who did employ one adopted a variety of strategies to fulfil the needs of all involved in this precarious balance of power.

A range of factors, such as personality, age and number of children, coalesced to produce a wide spectrum of qualitatively different relationships and experiences. These did not always encourage the development of too close a relationship, as the example of Clarissa Trant shows. Clarissa recognised her mistake in appointing her friend as her governess when their friendship undermined her authority. In dismissing her she wrote to her thus:

> it is difficult to unite with perfect comfort the relative positions in which you and I are placed with regard to each other. We have always been together as personal friends . . . but you must allow me to say . . . that a person of inferior attainments to yourself and over whom I should consequently feel justified in assuming entire authority would answer our purpose . . . we propose looking out for a young person who will . . . not have abilities or character to act independently but will merely act under my guidance and discretion.[25]

In Clarissa's case, limits to the friendship between the two women were considered necessary to promote the superior place of the mistress in her child's affection and within the household. However, this was not always the case, for at the other end of the spectrum, Hughes cites an instance of a mistress abandoning her husband to flee to Germany with her German governess.[26] Victorian governesses clearly experienced a diversity of situations, and this makes it difficult to assess the relationship between Freda and Miss Freestone as typical or atypical.

The relationship between Freda and Miss Freestone has been set within the context of loving and supportive relationships with family and friends; class-consciousness and condescension towards servants; and the role of the governess in Victorian society. However, as discussed above, the kiss was commonly a signifier of emotional attachment or intimacy. Did the relationship between these two particular women develop to such a level of intimacy and emotional attachment? The kisses between Lady Freda and Miss Freestone did not obviously fit into any of the normal categories. They were not kisses of greeting or farewell. They were not kisses between family members or long-standing friends. They may have been routine, although these three consecutive entries stand out in isolation. To understand why these two particular women were kissing at all, we need to consider the history of their relationship and in particular their health.

This case study will begin in 1878 with the marriage of Sir Lambton and Freda Loraine. Freda was twenty-three and Lambton thirty-nine. Like many of her time and class, Freda became pregnant shortly after her honeymoon and subsequently gave birth to four children in just over four years. However, in accordance with the prescribed model of Victorian femininity Freda was not only, for example, 'sweet' and 'gentle', but also 'delicate'. This perceived 'delicacy' encouraged an increased concentration on the possible and actual physical discomforts of pregnancy. This emphasis, in turn, led to the adoption of stringent precautionary measures and an acceptance by Freda of the lifestyle of a semi-invalid throughout the majority of these child-bearing years. However, Freda did not make a full recovery once her fourth and final child was born. Scarlet fever was an additional problem for the family and the trigger for Freda to begin a course of treatment in September 1885 which apparently signalled a significant decline in her health. Treatment included hot baths, douches, rubbings, bromide, 'electric belt', massage and salt baths. However, continuing health problems culminated in April 1886 in her taking the unconventional and quite drastic step of leaving Lambton in charge of the children and the household while she went to her sister Janie's home in Guernsey for six months in an unsuccessful attempt to convalesce. Indeed, diary entries suggest such a step was necessary as any attempt to get continuous rest at her own home was impossible owing to the duties of being mother of four children, local society member and mistress of the household.[27]

Freda's failure to recover and her relationship with a Dr Aikman arguably constituted the two major contributory factors which encouraged her to identify herself as a semi-invalid and subsequently to embark upon an almost obsessive preoccupation with her own health. In Guernsey, Freda saw Dr Aikman twenty-nine times and swallowed copious amounts of medicine. These extended the range previously taken and included belladonna, liniments, powders, bromide, Cooper's Pills and rhubarb mix, along with the use of an electric belt and a book 'on the eye and zoology generally'. However, far from making her anticipated recovery, Freda remained in low spirits with entries recording her feeling 'lazy and dispirited' and 'good for nothing'. Her recovery was seemingly non-existent as entries continued to record backache, heavy periods, headaches, bowel problems, indigestion and eyestrain and, after five months of treatment and twenty-one visits by Dr Aikman, 'great pain in waves'. As late as 30 September she began 'new powders', but had to be 'strapped up' and carried to the ship on a couch for the journey home on 18 October. Therefore, despite the extensive effort made on her behalf, she ended her stay in Guernsey with an extended range and greater intensity of symptoms. On 19 October, after six months of convalescence and initially high hopes for recovery, she left Southampton in an 'invalid carriage'.[28] The actual cause of Freda's ill health is not clear, nor is the extent to which her illness was real, psychosomatic or induced by medical ineptitude. Freda's symptoms were varied and seemingly unrelated, giving little clue to actual medical causation. However, as far as this discussion is concerned, the most important factor is not perhaps the actual cause of Freda's illness but the impact of its lengthy duration. It was Freda's failure to recover that left her frustrated and miserable at her inability to break free from a continuous cycle of suffering and pain and that perhaps also encouraged her to look for ever larger amounts of empathy, comfort and support.

Quite what Dr Aikman's influence was cannot be known, for Freda did not record their discussions. The aforementioned was, however, the background to her mental and physical health when she first met Miss Freestone. Dr Aikman may have remained influential following her return, for it is noteworthy that Freda subsequently remained in contact with him. Following her return, however, there was a change in her diaries.[29] She began to record details of the menstrual cycles of two members of her domestic staff whereas she had not previously done so. Indeed the diaries suggest that she began to take a sustained interest in the menstrual cycles of those female servants with whom she most closely identified: these were her nursing staff Nana, or Goodfellow, and her young, newly appointed governess: Miss Freestone. Following her visit to Guernsey, menstruation had become Freda's central focus, and her preoccupation with health issues was now such that she had begun to establish a regular pattern of monthly ill health. This pattern had menstruation at its core and was to reach its zenith over the next seven years.[30] I would suggest that this preoccupation with menstruation was critical in providing a shared basis of feminine experience through which Freda could search for answers, comfort and emotional support in relation to her own ill health from her nursery staff.

While a central focus on menstruation made every female of a certain age a potential fellow sufferer, it simultaneously excluded males, whether husbands or doctors, from shared experience and thereby set limits to male sympathy and support. Despite the close relationship between Lambton and Freda, his sympathy alone could not solve her problems, nor could he, as a man, fully empathise with her condition.[31] Janie, her sister, was also sympathetic and supportive, but had been unable to assist Freda's improvement, and she was now a considerable distance away in Guernsey. One cannot but feel that Freda increasingly sought to identify fellow sufferers with the potential to mitigate her ongoing despair, through the knowledge that she was not alone and that others too could fully empathise with her experience. The fact that she chose to concentrate on individuals over whom she had an element of control is noteworthy, and this may have compensated for the continuing lack of control which she increasingly felt over her own life. Therefore, while no definite reason can be given for why Freda chose her nursery staff as the focus of her attention (rather than, for example, friends, female relations or other members of staff) it is possible that these women were chosen as those most closely under her control and most regularly at her side. They provided her with the most potential for influencing behaviour, comparing notes and the development of mutual emotional support.

One could regard Freda as the epitome of the languishing, sofa-bound matron of so many Victorian novels. But Showalter and Ussher have argued that Victorian women could use illness as a strategy of empowerment or protest.[32] Historians have also suggested that it was 'acceptable, even fashionable, to retire to bed with "sick headaches", "nerves" and a host of other mysterious ailments'.[33] However, such arguments appear to leave little room for sympathy for the actual physical causes of illness. They also fail to explain why previously seemingly happy and well-loved women would have continued with a model of behaviour after it apparently became so disadvantageous to their physical and mental well-being and severely limited their capacity for enjoyment. If any of these elements were contributory factors to Freda's initial assumption of ill health, the strategy would appear to have backfired, as Freda was progressively disempowered and depressed by her illness.

In Freda's case, it does seem likely that there were genuine physiological complaints underlying her ill health. Freda's illness was of extremely lengthy duration. Marriage and motherhood rapidly turned a relatively healthy young girl into a woman who suffered continual and repeated ill health for over thirty-two years of marriage for which little or no successful cure seems to have been forthcoming. She received many letters in which her health was of great concern to the authors. For example, on 27 February 1889, an unknown correspondent was 'grieved . . . to hear of you as an invalid' and wondered whether she had seen Freda 'lying down in the square on a carpet'.[34] The letters also confirm that Freda's continued invalidity not only inspired the sympathy of friends but suggestions for remedies. Her correspondents discussed 'Plombieres baths', help from 'an advanced Christian Scientist' and 'a new mode of procuring absorption in internal cases by electricity . . . this new discovery . . . stops hemorrhage . . . they are not quacks'.[35] This reference to 'quacks' suggests an awareness that care needed to be exercised in attempting new remedies. Yet the failure of the medical professionals to find a cure no doubt increased Freda's interest in such remedies, and certainly led her to adopt ever more elaborate and engrossing coping strategies of her own which included this new focus on her nursery staff. Freda's diaries support this contention, as from 1887 they suggest evidence of newly created strategies, containing page after page of laborious daily entries, charts and tabulations surrounding her medical state. Unlike the diaries written before 1887, the diaries following her visit to Guernsey include copious information relating to her health and its impact on her daily existence. These tabulations include, for example, details of when and if she rose, her diet, whether or not she was able to go out, what medicines she took and more.

Freda's ill health appears to constitute a classic example of the 'medicalisation of women' arising from a vicious circle within which women were enmeshed to their physical and psychological disadvantage. Prevailing stereotypes of hysterical women, combined with limited advances in medicine, led few doctors to recognise the need to identify or cure the real physical cause of women's ills, while the quackery and misguided ministrations of many may well have exacerbated female ill health. Nevertheless, Freda's diaries are evidence of the active role she played in her own health management. Moreover, as noted above, the people chosen by Freda to monitor were those with relatively little power in her household. One of the gains for Freda was a close and affectionate friendship, as will be shown, but this simultaneously involved her own 'medicalisation' of other women.

Freda's extended ill health had practical implications, one of which was increased isolation from her own network of female friends and relations. She not only became less able to receive or visitors or make calls, but was also often away from wider society and social activities as she rented property by the sea or in the countryside to assist her health. Moreover, Freda was, by this time, spending over half of her life inside her own home and more than a quarter of her days in bed.[36] This lifestyle therefore not only reduced her participation in wider society but also reduced the range of domestic activities she could perform. At the same time it increased the potential for spending more time in the company of that person whose duties and capabilities most closely matched her own: her governess. As a servant, Miss Freestone could be required to join Freda to assist her with her work while simultaneously meeting her need for feminine company. As a female, Miss Freestone met the criterion of a potential fellow sufferer through whom Freda might find at least some of the comfort, empathy and support which she appeared to crave.

Miss Freestone first appeared in Lambton's correspondence to Freda during her absence in Guernsey.[37] Lambton was encouraging Miss Freestone to visit and assist him with the children. She was noted as popping in and out to see 'the chicks' as well as assisting him in taking them on a birthday treat and outings. Lambton approved of 'that nice little Miss Freestone', and although she initially had an afternoon position elsewhere, he invited her to visit the children often as 'she is such a ladylike, honest little thing that she is nice company for them'.[38] Moreover, he believed that Miss Freestone would be better for his daughter than her visits to a German Fräulein whom he described as 'a good little woman but next door to useless in Ji's education'.[39] With Lambton's encouragement, Miss Freestone was employed by August 1886. She had moved into the house while Freda was away and was therefore in attendance when Freda returned in October.

From this point, the diaries show the rapid impact of Freda's preoccupation with menstrual ill health, not only upon the quality of her relationships with her nursery staff but also directly upon *their* personal health and well-being. Nevertheless, despite Freda's apparent attempts to draw them into her own experience of regular ill health, the results were not uniform. While the extent to which Freda had control over an individual was not an insignificant factor in determining the extent to which individuals were willing to assume ill health and the depth of their accompanying relationship with her, the personality and health of the member of staff was also important. It seems likely that the younger age and inexperience of Miss Freestone, along with her inherent vulnerability as a relatively new governess, may have combined to make her more susceptible to Freda's influence, in contrast to the older, long-serving and perhaps more worldly Goodfellow. Indeed, Goodfellow's resistance to Freda's attempts to interfere in her personal and private health led to a difficult relationship between the mistress and her nanny.

Goodfellow's continued reluctance to follow Freda's advice for care, rest and dubious medicines led to accusations of willfulness, of disobedience and indeed of making both herself and Freda ill. On 30 April 1887, for example, Freda reported 'Goodfellow rebellious again', while on 1 May 1887 she wrote, 'Goodfellow very wicked, jumped about and made herself ill – Petry Powder'.[40] The ultimate power of the mistress was in evidence, however, for disagreements were usually followed by Goodfellow being 'penitent', which was, no doubt, a necessary capitulation to keep her job. For example, on 9 May 1887 Freda complained, 'Goodfellow got up and made herself worse'; but by the following day she reported, 'Goodfellow in bed – repentant'.[41] Indeed, Freda's influence appears pervasive for – despite no previous evidence of menstrual problems – from December 1886 spasmodic instances of Goodfellow's monthly sickness and lying in bed are reported in the diaries for the next six years.

The entries make it clear that Freda was actively enquiring into the private and personal details of her nursery staff's health and providing advice and medicines which she expected to be taken owing to her superiority within the household. Regardless of the increasing difficulties being caused in the household, and despite their continued failure in her own case, Freda did not appear to question the efficacy of the remedies she was pressing upon her staff.[42] Unfortunately, the new-found incapacity of her nursing staff worked to Freda's disadvantage in adding to her personal workload. When Freda's nursery staff were ill, her four young children still required high levels of care and attention. This often resulted in her having to increase the number of children for whom she cared or the amount of time that she spent with a particular child. Indeed, the diaries confirm that when all three women were ill at the same time, another servant, Alice, had to help with the children, as did Lambton, who assisted by taking them out.[43]

While Goodfellow's obstinacy resulted in friction between herself and Freda, the reverse appears to have been the case with Miss Freestone. As already explained, Miss Freestone's position as governess entailed a superior status for interaction not only with the family but also with Freda herself. Freda's first reference to Miss Freestone occurs on 19 October 1886 in connection with her return home, where she was met by 'all the four children with Miss Freestone and Nana' to her 'great joy'.[44] During the initial period of her return, references to Miss Freestone are rare, for Freda is in London and busy with friends and relations eager to see her after her absence. There are no references to the pair spending time together socially before the move to Sunninghill on 10 November, following which the situation changes as social entries for Miss Freestone begin to appear. Removed from London society and her extended family and increasingly isolated and confined within the home, Freda began to spend more and more time with Miss Freestone. However, not only Miss Freestone's duties but also her ill health began to mirror Freda's.

The diaries and correspondence note no previous references to delicacy or ill health on the part of Miss Freestone. By 15 December, however, Freda noted Miss Freestone as suffering from severe pain for which she began her on mixture thrice daily. Indeed, the pair were apparently suffering from such similar difficulties that on 20 December they were able to share a pill. What exact medicines were being provided and taken by Freda and her staff is not made clear. It seems likely, however, that among these various remedies was a potion which effectively reduced an individual's menstrual cycle while causing associated flooding and increased pain. For example, ergot, which Freda makes note of, was suspected to have been used to induce abortion and may have led to anaemia and associated weakness in susceptible individuals. Miss Freestone, having taken medicines provided by Freda, shortened her cycle to three weeks and two days and had to remain in bed on 27 and 28 December, gradually returning to work over the next three days.[45]

The year 1886 ended with Miss Freestone and Freda experiencing their first occurrence of shared menstrual discomfort, of shared symptoms, of shared medicines and of shared acknowledgement of mutual pain. One result of this seems to have been the steady re-orientation of Miss Freestone towards the role of companion to Freda rather than that of dedicated children's governess. Within less than two months, the pair had established a pattern of regular lunching and dining together and had substantially increased the amount of time spent in one another's company. The foundations for the development of a close, affectionate and mutually sympathetic relationship had been laid.

Of all Freda's nursery staff, Miss Freestone exhibited by far the highest incidence of ill health, and this was accompanied by the development of a uniquely special and intimate relationship between the mistress and her governess. The interaction of the pair resulted in a high and increasing incidence of supposed illness in Miss Freestone. Moreover it seems that this mutual perception of repeated pain, suffering and illness was a major contributory element in the development of unprecedented and unrepeated levels of intimacy and affection. Throughout January, February and March 1887, the continued ill health of the pair created an environment in which shared ill health not only set the parameters for physical and emotional interaction, but also facilitated increasing levels of this. However, while Miss Freestone's participation in so high a level of ill health encouraged the development of her uniquely affectionate relationship with Freda, it also ultimately separated the pair, by fundamentally undermining Miss Freestone's ability to do her job.

Detailed entries exemplify the extent of Miss Freestone's ill health. For example, there are eight references to illness in just twenty days during January 1887.[46] The diary is not explicit about whether or not all these occasions prevented Miss Freestone from fulfilling her duties, but she was definitely in bed all day for at least three days.[47] The entries for February indicate an even worse month for Miss Freestone, who was by then showing her own pattern of semi-invalidity. During February, for example, she was in pain on the 2nd; in bed with poultice on the 3rd; better and in Freda's room on the 4th; lying out with Freda in the conservatory on the 6th and taking a 'pill'; being 'seen' by Mr Simonds on the 8th; suffering period pain on the 9th; suffering pain and poultice on the 10th; remaining in bed on the 11th, 12th, 13th and 14th; and finally getting up but not coming downstairs during the 15th until she joined Freda for dinner. This was hardly a suitable state of health for a governess to four young and energetic children. Indeed, this long stretch of illness appears to have caused Freda to act, for she wrote to Mrs Freestone on the 12th and Dr Aikman on the 14th, and on the 16th had a talk with Miss Freestone concerning 'duty and offer'.[48] The content of these letters and of the talk between the mistress and her governess remains opaque, but the couple had a further 'talk' on the 17th. On 21 February, further efforts may have been being made in respect of Miss Freestone, for Dr Thornton came to dine and sleep and saw Miss Freestone during his visit. Miss Freestone did not significantly improve after this visit but spent the remainder of the month lying around with Freda, suffering from aches and pains, sharing similar symptoms and medicines and being described as tired and 'cranky'.[49] Freda appears to have attempted a range of strategies to assist Miss Freestone, from entertaining her by 'playing' to her after tea to dosing her with tannin, cocaine, pills and powders.[50] However, these strategies seem to have achieved little. The entries for March remain very similar, with Miss Freestone exhibiting virtually the same symptoms and complaints as those noted by Freda about herself.

At the end of March, the family were packing for their holiday at Livermere and it seems to have been decided that Miss Freestone would not accompany them, presumably owing to her continued ill health. Freda's entry of 1 April noted Miss Freestone as suffering from 'pain at heart' – presumably a worrying development.[51] On the 2nd Freda was in bed all day but was joined by Miss Freestone for dinner in her room, as she was once again on the 4th, when Lambton was away in London for two days.

Thus the entries in Freda's diary for the first three months of 1887 confirm that Freda and Miss Freestone were spending an increased and considerable amount of time together and sharing similar experiences of ill health and medicines. Moreover, a level of intimacy is further implied by, for example, their lying around together and, in particular, sleeping upon one another's beds.[52] There were spare rooms and other beds available for the women's use, but both appear to have felt comfortable appropriating one another's despite the differences which existed in class and status. Such entries support the contention that a particularly familiar relationship had by now developed between these two women. This is indicated by the presence of the words 'Fr came for a kiss', noted in Freda's diary on 6, 7 and 8 April.

Why Miss Freestone should have come for a kiss on just three occasions is not explained. However, the last such entry was accompanied by a note that Miss Freestone had 'pain under left B. shooting up to arm pit burning'.[53] In view of the close nature of the relationship, it is not surprising that Freda would showed affection when her companion was apparently in considerable pain. That there may have been a rare and fleeting moment of rebellion after Miss Freestone knew that she would not be remaining with the family is possible, for Freda noted that, on the 10th, Miss Freestone had her period but 'wouldn't take cure'.[54] But Freda's concern for her governess continued, as shown by her waking up in a fright on the 13th worrying that Miss Freestone was in a faint and being 'very done up'.[55] Miss Freestone remained ill and upon the spare room bed when the family were packing to leave, and although she attended breakfast and luncheon on the day the family left, she did not accompany them to Livermere but was replaced by a Miss Noyes in May.

Freda and the boys wrote to Miss Freestone during April and May, but she did not join them again until 27 June. Two days later she was again fractious and in pain, causing Freda to be 'distressed' about her.[56] Four days later she left; the later diaries record her returning for short holidays, to cover for absent nannies or governesses, for lunch or for Sunday visits with Freda. However, she never again returned to the family's employment for any length of time. Nevertheless, the special relationship between the mistress and her governess seems to have continued, with the pair remaining in contact throughout the diaries, even following Miss Freestone's marriage to Hugh Clark in 1891.[57] Nana attended the wedding, but not Freda, who continued to refer to her as Miss Freestone when she came to help, for example, with packing and possibly emotional support when the boys departed for school in 1892 and to participate in family activities such as playing tennis with

Lambton and the girls in September 1893.[58] Appropriately, Miss Freestone accompanied the family to church on 31 December 1893 – the close of the diaries – illustrating that she remained a family friend and occasional visitor and helper to Freda seven years after her brief period of employment.

While these relationships were always remained severely circumscribed, Hughes suggests that later in the century, 'employers began to develop relationships with their governess which went beyond the strictly limited obligations of the 1840's'. Hughes also suggests that it came to be seen as the 'mark of a genteel family that they were able to stay friends with their governess long after she left their employment' and that 'the governess could provide a useful extra pair of hands at times of particular strain'.[59] The continuing interaction of Freda and Miss Freestone appears to fit this pattern. However, given that Miss Freestone's ill health made her a potentially less able spare pair of hands than, for example, Miss Noyes, it is not immediately clear why it was Miss Freestone in particular who remained in contact. Examining the relationship through the kiss, however, enables us to explain the long-lasting and intimate relationship these women shared.

Many details surrounding these kisses remain opaque, but they are suggestive of a number of aspects of this particular relationship. First, the presence of the kiss indicates that the relationship had reached an intense level of intimacy and affection. This was far greater than might be expected between two individuals whose interaction was likely to have been distanced by their employer–employee relationship and the strict adherence to class boundaries to which Freda and Lambton both normally adhered. Second, while the kisses signified the intimate relationship between the mistress and her governess, they also signified the power of Freda's class position. As the mistress, she had power not only over the daily lives of her closest servants, but also over their physical and emotional well-being. Lady Loraine felt perfectly able to interfere in the most private and personal aspects of her servants' lives; not only the seemingly willing Miss Freestone but also the reluctant Goodfellow were subjected to her will regarding rest, medicine and the disclosure of personal information. Third, however, despite the power of Freda's class these kisses simultaneously suggest female impotence. The strength of this relationship indicates intensely high levels of female emotional interdependence, stimulated by sustained failure and frustration in finding a cure to problems which were unique to women. One might also ask whether the unprecedented levels of intimacy and affection which the kiss signalled were perhaps a by-product of the sustained failure of a predominantly male medical profession to understand or cure the 'alien' experience of the female reproductive and menstrual cycle. It was perhaps no coincidence that Freda turned to the female world in seeking hope and support which was perhaps

unattainable from men enmeshed in negative gendered stereotypes surrounding the female mind and body. This negativity aggravated feminine complaints and thereby exacerbated the sustained weakness and, arguably,
disempowerment of an unquantifiable number of women.

## NOTES

1 Suffolk Record Office, Ipswich (hereafter SRO), HA61:436/448/7, Lady Frederica Loraine,
  diary, 6, 7 and 8 April 1887. Lady Frederica (or Freda) Loraine's diaries range from 1878
  to 1893; however, there are no diaries available for 1879, 1880 or 1881. The SRO collection includes thirteen diaries under HA61:436/448/1–13 together with associated correspondence. The diary entries are largely non-attitudinal. There are daily entries which
  appear to have been written as notes for the author, and individual entries are very
  brief. However, analysis is enhanced by the diaries spanning a fifteen-year period and
  being supported by an extensive family archive which includes much correspondence.
  Nevertheless, there are still valuable details – such as the age and social background of
  Miss Freestone – that remain obscure.
2 Bedfordshire Record Office, Luton (hereafter BRO), OR2246/9, engagement correspondence between Richard Orlebar and Frederica St John Rouse-Boughton, 13 June
  1861.
3 SRO, HA61:436/31/15, engagement correspondence between Sir Lambton Loraine and
  Frederica Acton-Broke, 28 June 1878.
4 BRO, X646/199/1/2, manuscript by Frederica Orlebar, 'Frederica Orlebar's Children',
  1866.
5 BRO, OR2246/7, letter from Richard Orlebar to Frederica, 12 June 1861.
6 See Linda Pollock, *Forgotten Children: Parent Child Relations from 1500–1900* (Cambridge, 1983) for a discussion of contrasting historiography surrounding the family.
  See also *idem, A Lasting Relationship: Parents and Children over Three Centuries* (London, 1987) for further discussion and primary examples. See John Tosh, *A Man's Place:
  Masculinity and the Middle Class Home in Victorian England* (London, 1999) for a
  discussion of levels of familial affection and the 'Angel Mother'.
7 BRO, OR2244/6, diary by Frederica Orlebar, 7 May 1863.
8 *Ibid.*
9 Michael Mason, *The Making of Victorian Sexuality: Sexual Behaviour and its Understanding* (Oxford, 1994), p. 7.
10 BRO, OR2244/7, diary by Frederica Orlebar, 28 September 1863.
11 Letters between husband and wife are unfailingly affectionate and include the following bundles, all in SRO: HA61:436/31, 1878; HA61:436/36, 1879–82; HA61:436/23, 1883;
   HA61:436/28, 1884; HA61:436/27, 1886; HA61:436/1252, 1910. For reference to a suitable
   nickname for Lambton see SRO, HA61:436/31/16, letter from Lambton to Freda, 1 July
   1878.
12 SRO, HA61/436/31/16, letter from Sir Lambton to Frederica Acton-Broke, 1 July 1878.
13 *Ibid.*, letter from Sir Lambton to Lady Freda Loraine, 2 June 1883.
14 SRO, HA61:436/36/1, January 1879, HA61:436/36/15, 8 March 1879, and HA61:436/36/16,
   9 March 1879, letters from Sir Lambton to Lady Freda Loraine.
15 Diary by Mary Elizabeth Hall, 1891–95, 28 August 1895, reproduced in microfilm in
   Amanda Vickery (ed.), *Women's Language and Experience 1500–1940: Women's Diaries
   and Related Sources* (Adam Matthew Publications), part 2, reel 20, MS 596/1.

16  Women recognised these dangers and the dreadful adverse ramifications that pregnancy outside marriage could entail, as exemplified in this letter from Lillian Hamilton to Lady Freda Loraine in which she seeks her help for an unmarried but pregnant girl: 'it is all very sad. I cannot help thinking sometimes of the hopeless misery she must be suffering. A grief that must go on for ever. No other sin brings its own punishment as that one does.' SRO, HA61:436/10/4, letter from Lillian Hamilton to Lady Freda Loraine, 22 October 1888.

17  See Carroll Smith-Rosenberg, '"The Female World of Love and Ritual": Relations between Women in Nineteenth Century America', in Nancy F. Cott and Elizabeth H. Pleck (eds), *A Heritage of her Own* (New York, 1979) for a discussion of the manner in which separate homosocial worlds encouraged same-sex relationships. See also Sheila Jeffreys, *The Spinster and her Enemies: Feminism and Sexuality, 1880–1930* (London, 1985) for a discussion of why attitudes towards passionate expression between women became unacceptable.

18  *Ibid.*, pp. 102–28.

19  Susan Lanser, 'Befriending the Body: Female Intimacies as Class Acts', *Eighteenth-Century Studies*, 32:2 (1998–99), 179–98.

20  See for example correspondence of Sir Lambton and Freda Loraine as detailed in n. 11 above. See also Essex Record Office, Chelmsford (hereafter ERO), D/DLu 14/1–18 and D/DLu 15/1–6, diaries and journals by Clarissa Trant, 1800–32, for evidence of the support provided by her beloved brother and father.

21  SRO, HA61:436/29, letter from Sir Lambton to Lady Freda Loraine, 3 April 1879.

22  SRO, HA61:436/28, letter from Sir Lambton to Lady Freda Loraine, dated only March 1884.

23  SRO, HA61:436/448/8, diary by Lady Freda Loraine, entries dated 2 June 1888, 10 June 1888, 17 April 1888 and 27 May 1888.

24  Kathryn Hughes, *The Victorian Governess* (London, 1993).

25  ERO, D/DLu 14/15, diary by Clarissa Trant, November 1841.

26  Hughes, *Victorian Governess*, p. 132.

27  See SRO, HA61:436/448/5 and 6, diaries by Lady Freda Loraine, 1885 and 1886, for details.

28  SRO, HA61:436/448/6, diary by Lady Freda Loraine, 1886. See entry dated 25 August 1886 for reference to the 'book', entries dated 19 and 23 July 1886 for references to her spirits, and also entries dated 30 September and 18 and 19 October 1886.

29  See in particular the contrast between SRO, HA61:436/448/1–5, diaries by Lady Freda Loraine, 1878, 1882, 1883, 1884, 1885 and SRO, HA61:436/448/6–8, diaries by Lady Freda Loraine, 1886, 1887 and 1888.

30  For a discussion of important stereotypes and conventions during the period and the weight given to the impact and effect of menstruation see Pat Jalland and John Hooper (eds), *Women from Birth to Death: The Female Life Cycle in Britain 1830–1914* (Brighton, 1986).

31  Typical of the sympathy but impotence of Lambton's support is the following letter from Lambton to Freda: 'my sweet little girl. How I pity my own love for all the sufferings she so patiently endures. May God amply reward you, my love for these.' SRO, HA61:436/27, scrap within the bundle of letters from Sir Lambton to Freda Loraine, 1886.

32  See Elaine Showalter, *The Female Malady Woman, Madness and English Culture 1830–1980* (London, 1987) and Jane Ussher, *Women's Madness: Misogyny or Mental Illness?* (London, 1991).

33 Barbara Ehrenreich and Deirdre English, *For her Own Good: 150 Years of the Experts' Advice to Women* (New York, 1978), p. 125. See Ussher, *Women's Madness*, p. 90, for a discussion of historiography surrounding this claim.

34 SRO, HA61:436/38. This bundle of correspondence was sent to Lady Freda by various correspondents between 1882 and 1889.

35 *Ibid.* includes parts of letters referring to 'Plombieres baths'. See SRO, HA61:436/11, letter from Marion Hamilton to Lady Freda Loraine, 20 August 1888, for the reference to a Christian Scientist, and SRO, HA61:436/38, an unsigned letter from Sunningdale, dated 17 May (no year), for the new electrical discovery.

36 SRO, HA61:436/448/6, diary by Lady Freda Loraine, 1886.

37 SRO, HA61:436/27, letter from Sir Lambton to Lady Freda Loraine, 22 June 1886.

38 *Ibid.*, letter from Sir Lambton to Lady Freda Loraine, dated only July 1886.

39 *Ibid.*, letter from Sir Lambton to Lady Freda Loraine, 3 August 1886.

40 SRO, HA61:436/448/7, diary by Lady Freda Loraine, 1887.

41 *Ibid.*, 9 May and 10 May 1887.

42 As suggested above, medicines being taken continued to be numerous and various. For full details see SRO, HA61/436/448/6–7, diaries by Lady Freda Loraine, 1886 and 1887. Hot baths, electric machines and belts, belladonna, quinine, arsenic, tannin, cocaine, iodine, zinc injections, bromide, ergot, poultices and various powders and pills were just some of the range of remedies being experimented with by Freda. However, there appears to be little discernible pattern in their dosage.

43 See for example an entry in SRO, HA61:436/448/7, diary by Lady Freda Loraine, 1887: 'Freestone and Goodfellow ... brought on pain ... very worried with the chicks all morning ... broke down evening ... talk to Fr and Gd.' For assistance given by Alice and Lambton see entries for 12 and 14 February 1887.

44 SRO, HA61/436/448/6, diary by Lady Freda Loraine, 19 October 1886.

45 *Ibid.*, diary by Lady Freda Loraine, December 1886.

46 SRO, HA61:436/448/7, diary by Lady Freda Loraine, 1887; see entries for 10, 12, 15, 17, 18, 20, 21 and 30 January 1887.

47 *Ibid.*, 17, 18 and 20 January 1887.

48 *Ibid.*, 12, 14 and 16 February 1887. Unfortunately, these letters are not in the archive.

49 *Ibid.* See for example entries for 15 and 22 February 1887.

50 *Ibid.*, 23 and 24 February 1887.

51 *Ibid.*, 1 April 1887.

52 *Ibid.*, for example, 6 March 1887: Miss Freestone 'went to sleep on my [i.e. Freda's] bed'.

53 *Ibid.*, 8 April 1887.

54 *Ibid.*, 10 April 1887.

55 *Ibid.*, 13 April 1887.

56 *Ibid.*, 4 June 1887.

57 SRO, HA61/436/448/11, diary by Lady Freda Loraine, 1891.

58 SRO, HA61/436/448/12–13, diaries by Lady Freda Loraine, 1892 and 1893.

59 Hughes, *Victorian Governess*, p. 173.

# 8

# 'Kiss me, Hardy': the dying kiss in the First World War trenches

<>

Santanu Das

12 JANUARY 1916 saw a very peculiar drama enacted in the trenches – two men, who had left their girlfriends back in England, were exchanging a ritual of kisses:

> As we arrived at the barn-door he said, 'Just a moment, Frank, before we go in I've something else to give you, – put that light out.' I put the lamp out and into my pocket, wondering what was coming. Then I felt an arm round my neck, and the dear lad kissed me once – 'that's from Evelyn' [Cocker's fiancée] he said; then he kissed me again and said, 'that's from your Mother.' I returned his tender salute and said, 'that's from me.' There we were, two men, like a couple of girls, – but then, there was no one about, and the matter was a sacred one between us, – and you.[1]

This is Lieutenant Frank Cocker's letter to his girlfriend, Evelyn, written from the trenches. The exchange of this 'tender salute' is an almost climactic episode in the charged friendship between Cocker and his 'dear Charlie,' a relationship that can be pieced together from the letters he wrote to Evelyn and to his sister, Minnie. What is astonishing is not so much the nascent homoeroticism but how this kiss between two men is snugly contained within a heterosexual framework through the trope of the girlfriend and the mother. With its detailed stage management, the narrative transmits some of the excitement of the actual moment, as does Cocker's ready reciprocity with the frank acknowledgment, 'that's from me'. Physical demonstrations of such ardour could perhaps just be contained within the parameters of the 'romantic friendship' that characterised late Victorian culture and intensified during wartime.[2] Anxieties about sexuality – or at least awareness of the surreptitious nature of the act ('there was no one about') – are filtered through a mock violation of gender categories and their tactile norms with the slightly pejorative simile ('two men, like a couple of girls') intended to point up silliness rather than deviance. Yet the moment cannot so easily be dismissed. If, following the logic of the sentence, 'sacred' is taken to be a Freudian slip for 'secret' the moment hovers curiously between the sacrosanct and the furtive. On the other hand, if 'sacred' is a deliberately chosen word, it may betray an understandably over-zealous attempt to ward off 'profanity', while at the same time, maybe unconsciously, echoing the marriage vow. Situated between a radical innocence and a transgressive thrill, the exchange mirrors a moment of epistemological crisis in the interlocked histories of sexuality, gender and gesture at a crucial moment in modernist history and culture. The kiss had just started to be theorised in the realm of sexology, which in turn was beginning to be conceptualised by men such as Havelock Ellis and Sigmund Freud. Both would write pioneering essays on homosexuality, re-sulting in the epoch-making conclusion that 'the sexual object and the sexual aim are merely soldered together.'[3] It was also the time of what Alan Sinfield calls 'the consolidation of the queer image' through a nexus of effeminacy, aestheticism and decadence.[4] The war hero and wartime bonding, informed by manly sentiments and noble ends, were honorably exempt from such base charges and yet, as Cocker's letter demonstrates, not without a trace of anxiety. Insofar as historical constructions shape desire, this epistemological uncertainty might well have engendered a greater emotional fluidity: mater-nal empathy, heterosexual romance and homoerotic frisson merge in the kiss, defying the strict categories of gender and sexuality.[5]

In the trenches of the First World War, the norms of tactile contact be-tween men changed profoundly. Mutilation and mortality, loneliness and boredom, the strain of constant bombardment, the breakdown of language and the sense of alienation from home led to a new level of intimacy and intensity under which the carefully constructed mores of civilian society broke down. As the historian Joanna Bourke has documented in her exciting work on the First World War and masculinity, men nursed and fed their friends when ill, held each other as they danced and wrapped blankets around each other.[6] W. A. Quinton recalls how one night, as he lay shivering, 'old Petch put his overcoat in addition to my own over me, taking care to tuck me in as a mother would a child.'[7] A. F. B. notes, in *the Third Battalion Magazine*, that Smalley was the great favourite of the Third Battalion for 'his heart was as big as his body – his strength like a lion's – his touch to the wounded as a woman's.'[8] Another soldier, Jack, must close his letter to Miss Williams as 'my <u>wife</u> is in bed & wants me to keep her warm but it is only a Palestine wife. another Sussex boy . . . it is very chilly at night right now. & it is nice to have someone to keep each other warm.'[9] A new world of largely non-genital tactile tenderness was opening up in which pity, thrill, affection and erotic-ism were fused and confused depending on the circumstances, degrees of knowledge, normative practices and sexual orientations, as well as the available models of male–male relationships. Erich Maria Remarque, in *All Quiet on the Western Front*, would distill all the poignancy of *Freundschaft* into this silent gesture: 'Kat's hands are warm, I pass my hand under his shoulders in order to rub his temples with some tea. I feel my fingers becoming moist.'[10] Robert Cedric Sherriff's *Journey's End*, perhaps the most popular war play, culminates in a similarly intense scene of tactile tenderness: '*Stanhope . . . lightly runs his fingers over Raleigh's tousled hair.*'[11] Similarly, the sense of touch haunts war lyrics, from Rupert Brooke's 'linked beauty of bodies' to the 'full-nerved, still-warm' limbs of Wilfred Owen's dying boy and from Siegfried Sassoon's 'my fingers touch his face' to Robert Nichols's more sentimental 'My comrade, that you could rest / Your tired body on mine.'[12] If shell shock had been the body language of masculine complaint, the poetic efflorescence of the 1920s was the celebration of what D. H. Lawrence's hero Mellors famously describes as the 'courage of physical tenderness' forged among men in the trenches: 'I knew it with the men. I had to be in touch with them, physically and not go back on it. I had to be bodily aware of them and a bit tender to them.'[13] Bodily intimacy in times of physical extremity led to a state of nakedness – in the sense of vulnerability, exposure and dependence – that continued to haunt the returned soldier: 'I clasp his hand', 'he dies in your arms', 'I have held strong arms that palter' and 'I shake you by the shoulder' are recurring phrases in war literature. Whether or not there is any conscious or unconscious erotic investment in these moments, they indicate a new level of intensity and intimacy in male–male relationships. I focus on these moments of charged physical contact because they raise questions about the relation between the experiential reality of the body under physical extremity and the social constructions of gender and sexuality. They highlight the continuity and overlap between different emotions and impulses in the responses of men to other men during wartime, and show how history – an indistinguishable blend of the social and the personal – radically informs and shapes desire. Above all, these moments of physical bonding and tactile tenderness during trench warfare require us to reconceptualise masculinity, conventional gender roles and notions of same-sex intimacy in postwar England in more nuanced ways than have been acknowledged in the criticism of war culture, studies of gender and sexuality or the more general histories of the body, intimacy and gesture.[14]

### EMOTION, EXTREMITY, EROTICISM

Magnus Hirschfeld in *The Sexual History of the First World War* (1946) alerts us to that ambiguous zone between male bonding, war camaraderie and eroticism:

The comradeship which developed between the soldiers who shared all the trials and dangers of war . . . must have been especially pleasing to the homosexuals for obvious reasons . . . Very frequently, even among normal people, it penetrated beyond the outer limits of the homoerotic and was thus, to speak the language of psychoanalysis, characterised by libidinous components.[15]

Discussion of First World War homoeroticism largely centres on the latter category of 'normal', or rather straight-identified, men who formed intense and intimate bonds, often with a romantic slant – relationships that Hirschfeld regards as 'unconsciously erotic'. By the time of the Great War, Ellis and Freud had already written their essays on homosexuality, John Addington Symonds and Hirschfeld were advocating reforms, and Walt Whitman and Edward Carpenter had introduced a language of masculine desire into English poetry. But older cultural models prevailed over the scientific and literary discourses: people had yet to recover from the Oscar Wilde trials, and in the public's perception homosexuality was associated with the effeminate dandy. In a culture that demonised homosexuality, wartime relationships were often honourably exempt, as in the following loud disclaimer by Richard Aldington: 'Let me at once disabuse the eager-eyed Sodomites among my readers by stating emphatically once and for all that there was nothing sodomitical in these friendships.'[16] But other men were more sensitive to the finer shades of eroticism. Thus, J. R. Ackerley reminiscences that '[m]y personal runners and servants were usually chosen for their looks',[17] while a character in Robert Graves's play asks, 'Do you know how a platoon of men will absolutely worship a good-looking gallant officer? Of course, they don't realise exactly what's happening, neither does he; but it's a very, very strong romantic link.'[18] Discussion of wartime homoeroticism must consider such 'very, very strong romantic' links, although they often were as 'sentimental' and 'chaste' as Graves's Charterhouse friendships.[19]

In so far as the First World War has become a literary-historical phenomenon, it is perhaps possible to 'queer' it. Its three major poets, Brooke, Owen and Sassoon, had homoerotic encounters, inclinations or relationships.[20] Three of its major prose works, Goodbye to All That, The Middle Parts of Fortune and Seven Pillars of Wisdom, were written by men who had similar experiences. And three of its major plays, Journey's End, Prisoners of War and But It Still Goes On, have homoerotic themes. But any hasty claim for conscious and explicit sexual dissidence will encounter problems, both circumstantial and epistemological.[21] Central to the construction of sexuality is the idea of the male-as-subject-of-desire, a tenet that led Michel Foucault to reformulate his enquiry in The History of Sexuality: 'In order to understand how the modern individual could experience himself as the subject of a "sexuality", it was essential first to determine how, for centuries, Western man had been brought to recognise himself as a subject of desire.'[22] The application of this model, enormously influential in the discussion of same-sex eroticism from classical Greece to nineteenth-century England, is problematic in relation to the war scenario, for the male body in the trenches becomes an instrument of pain rather than of desire. The First World War lasted over four years and claimed nine million lives; an average of 6,046 men were killed every day. From the British army alone, 41,000 servicemen had their limbs amputated and 65,000 were invalided by shell shock.[23] Given this context, homoeroticism has to be understood within new conceptual parameters and a different economy of emotions. In the military, bodily contact is often the primary means of fostering loyalty, trust and unity within an army unit. In the trenches of the western front, where life expectancy could be as short as a couple of weeks, same-sex ardour, bodily contact and (in some cases) eroticism should not be understood solely in contrast to heterosexuality, nor viewed only through the lenses of gender and sexuality. Such intimacy must also be understood in opposition to and as a triumph over death: it must be seen as a celebration of life, of young men huddled against long winter nights, rotting corpses and falling shells. Physical contact was a transmission of the wonderful assurance of being alive, and more sex-specific eroticism, though concomitant, was subsidiary. In a world of visual squalor, little gestures – closing a dead comrade's eyes, wiping his brow or holding him in one's arms – were felt as acts of supreme beauty that made life worth living. Although these acts may overlap with eroticism, such experiences must not be conflated with it – nor, for that matter, with the repression or sublimation of sexual drives.

While discussing homosexual writers such as Sassoon, Ackerley or Manning, it is important to remember that they were a sexual minority writing within a masculinist, heterosexual field. Their conception of same-sex 'love' and its relation to sexual identity was distinct, verging precariously between the Victorian cult of 'manly love' and the 'unspeakable bestiality' of the Greeks.[24] Moreover, they were mostly young men in extreme circumstances whose sexuality was not yet strongly formed, in relation to either erotic experiences or an intellectual tradition of sexual dissidence, as was the case for Wilde, Symonds or Carpenter. Above all, sexual orientation should not be highlighted at the cost of other nuances of feeling. Sassoon, coming across a dead German soldier, lifts him up from the ditch: 'his blond face was undisfigured, except by mud which I wiped from his eyes and mouth with my coat sleeve'.[25] It is reductive to interpret this gesture solely, as Fussell does, in terms of Sassoon's fascination with young blond Germans:[26] the moment of tactile tenderness is equally informed by a recognition of human dignity and waste, a deep feeling of caritas that overcomes political hostility. Even when there are more consciously erotic experiences, they have to be aligned with a whole range of emotional needs such as those for succour, sympathy, assurance and security as well as states of bodily extremity.

Consequently, to discuss intense same-sex relations during war, we must introduce a different and less distinctly sexualised array of emotional intensities and bodily sensations, a continuum of non-genital tactile tenderness that goes beyond strict gender divisions and sexual binaries.[27] We will explore this terrain through the representation of the dying kiss.

### THE DYING KISS

A notoriously unstable signifier, often slipping from a sign to a sensation, the kiss was increasingly discussed in *fin de siècle* culture: 'The Curiosities of Kissing' in *Galaxy*, 16 (July–December 1873), 'The History of Kissing' in *Belgravia: An Illustrated London Magazine*, 47 (July–Oct. 1882), 'An Epidemic of Kisses in America' in *Pall Mall Magazine*, 18 (May–August 1899), 'The Kiss Poetical' in *The Fortnightly Review*, 82 (August 1904), 'Kiss' in *Catholic Encyclopaedia* (1910) and finally Ellis's 'The Origins of the Kiss' in the fourth volume of his monumental *Studies in the Psychology of Sex* (1905; 1923).[28] But how would the specifically same-sex kiss be perceived at a moment when English culture was precariously poised between the Victorian cult of 'manly love' and the 'sodomical' deeds of Oscar Wilde? In *The Kiss and its History* (1901), Christopher Nyrop remembers 'former times' when 'the friendly kiss was very common with us between man and man', but notes that in recent times 'the friendly kiss usually occurs only between ladies'.[29] But wartime extremity suspends normal tactile codes, and the male-to-male kiss had been doing its rounds in the trenches, mostly in close proximity to danger and death. 'Kissing was never out of favour' in the trenches, Evelyn muses in Lawrence's *England, my England*, while a world-weary Stanhope in Sherriff's *Journey's End* (1929) pleads with Osborne: 'Kiss me, Uncle'; in Ernest Hemingway's *A Farewell to Arms* (1929), Rinaldi's interactions with Frederic largely revolve around Frederic agreeing to a kiss which is denied throughout the novel.[30] But the dying kiss had very different connotations. The most obvious association would perhaps have been with the kiss by which grace is bestowed, varying from the New Testament kiss of peace and brotherhood (1 Corinthiais 16:20, 2 Corinthiais 13:12) to the transmission of the Holy Spirit. However, in 1924, when most of the war lyrics were appearing in print, Stephen Gaselee in an article, 'The Soul in the Kiss', traced the classical concept of a mingling and migration of souls through the kiss after death.[31] For an Englishman the religious and classical connotations would perhaps be overshadowed by a more flesh-and-blood incident from national history: Admiral Nelson's dying words: 'Kiss me, Hardy', an image of heroic martyrdom and camaraderie.[32] But what do the trench letters tell us?

The Revd Okeden writes to his wife: 'I've got a little secret . . . One dear lad very badly wounded . . . said, "Hello Padre old sport" and then "Come

and kiss me Padre" and he put his arms round me and kissed me.'[33] The Revd
Connor writes on 22 December 1914: 'I prayed to God for the dear lad – I
said, "I'll give your our mother's kiss" – "Let me do it to you," & the dear lad
kissed me.'[34] Similarly, when his close friend Jim dies, a grief-stricken Lance-
Corporal D. H. Fenton writes to his mother, Mrs Noone:

> I suddenly saw Jim reel to the left and fall with a choking sob. I did what I could
> for him, but his stout heart had already almost ceased to beat and death must
> have been mercifully instantaneous. I held him in my arms to the end, and when
> his soul had departed I kissed him twice where I knew you would have kissed him
> – on the brow – once for his mother and once for myself.[35]

The recurring, almost ritualistic phrase 'mother's kiss' suggests a powerful
reconceptualisation of both masculinity and male–male bonds through an
assumed maternal impulse of security and tenderness, a moment of 'perilous
intimacy' to borrow a phrase from Lawrence. Strangely, the dying kiss
is seldom associated with the father: though there is often a paternalistic
discourse in the discussion of the officer's relationship to his men, physical
intimacy and support even when extended by the padre (as with the Revd
Connor) remain anchored to the trope of the mother. In Fenton's letter to
Mrs Noone, the phrase 'I held him in my arms', with the subsequent connection to maternity, is almost an unconscious reworking of the *Pietà*, showing
how deeply Christian imagery makes up the repertoire of experiential reality
in shared Western culture. If a grieving Saint Veronica had wiped Christ's
brows, Fenton would go a step further, planting the kiss of life. And yet
there is a fleeting hesitancy to specify the bodily part, as if deflecting it to a
maternal prerogative were a subconscious avoidance of the merest hint of
misinterpretation. Yet it is anachronistic to mark in the kiss an actively transgressive eros: it is a response based on the perception of the male body as a
seat of pain and transience rather than of desire. Sublimated eroticism, if
present, does not exist at the level of deliberate personal intention, but results
from a deep structural overlap with sentimentalism, tenderness and aestheticism that centres on the death of a youth, as in the various representations of
the deposition of Christ. But how does literature describe such moments?
Can imaginative reconstructions by soldier-writers help us to understand the
emotional history of the Great War? I shall examine the motif of the dying
kiss in fiction, poetry and the short story in order to show the interaction
between gender, genre and psychosexual complexities.

## WAR CAMARADERIE AND THE PUBLIC-SCHOOL ROMANCE

The dying kiss appears in war literature perhaps for the first time in *Wooden
Crosses* (1920) by Roland Dorgelès.[36] This kiss was followed by one in Herman

Hesse's *Demian* (1930). But few war novels dwell on the dying kiss as length-ily or as passionately as Arthur Newberry Choyce's *Lips at the Brim* (1920). Choyce was commissioned in December 1916 as a second lieutenant in the Ninth Battalion, Leicestershire Regiment, and served in France in, 1917–18. He produced many books of war poetry such as *Crimson Stains* (1918), *Memory* (1920) and *Not until Gilboa* (1931), often marked by a lush romantic vocabu-lary. In *Lips at the Brim*, Peter Greshwin and Raymond Dronkel, close friends at school, enlist in the war as officer and soldier respectively, and Choyce shows school friendship as flowering and fusing into officer–soldier romance in the battlefields at the moment of death:

> 'Lift me higher, Peter – higher up' . . . Dumbly Peter raised his head higher, hold-ing him against his rough tunic, and wiping his lips with his own numbed fingers.
> Raymond looked into his eyes, and though Peter was half-dazed with the tra-gedy of these last hours, his heart was stirred by the adoration of friendship that he saw. It was the reallest thing he had known in his life. 'Passing the love of women.' . . .
> Afterwards he drew a deep sobbing breath and bent lower and lower, pressing his fevered mouth against the damp hair, and the cold, hard forehead, and the pitiful blood-flecked lips.[37]

The maternal empathy that one notes in the letters of Fenton or the Revd Connor is here supplanted by a language of desire – fevered mouth, half-closed eyes, blood-flecked lips – that breaks through the rhetoric of Chris-tianity, patriotism or war camaraderie. The theatricality of the scene is permeated with sentimentalism and sensationalism but the driving force is a physical frisson that extends well beyond the limits of school friendship or official duty. The blood-smeared kiss is the climactic episode in a narrative where plot and character developments are structured around a series of abortive heterosexual kisses. While sexual innocence on the part of Peter and Raymond, both straight-identified males, does not prevent the kiss from being distinctly homoerotic, eroticism is understood in terms of idealisation, affection and ardour rather than as a straightforward case of repression or sublimation of the sexual drives.

Parker, speaking of the Victorian creed of romantic friendship, notes that 'the lush unfolding of a chaste romance between two boys was clearly con-sidered charming', having 'all the agreeable elements of a clandestine yet carefree affair without the complication of sex'.[38] Contemporary forms of knowledge, types of normativity and ideological pressures not only play a part in the interpretation of sexual experience, but often underlie the structure of desire.[39] Phrases such as 'self-appointed task of devotion', 'ad-oration of friendship', 'a straight young god with a clean young body' or the biblical echo 'Passing the love of women' show that, instead of being a simple conflict between physical passion and homophobic structures, eroticism is paradoxically a function of ideological investments in contemporary discourses: the Victorian cult of manly love, the Christian rhetoric of service, the wartime duty of an officer. Love, respect, grief for a friend, a soldier, a martyr: all contribute to that mood of extravagant emotionalism. The dominant Victorian ideology of religiosity, purity and manliness, which interlocks with each of these discourses and claims a moral high ground over heterosexual conjugality, fosters the classic 'homosocial bond' that Eve Kosofsky Sedgwick speaks of in her analysis of nineteenth-century male friendships.[40]

Yet the 'blood-flecked' kiss may also characterise the genre of public-school romance that Choyce draws on. The public-school novels are marked by a tortured dialectic between earnest homoeroticism and homophobic paranoia. Friendship is celebrated through a language of high romance in novels such as J. E. C. Welldon's *Gerald Eversley's Friendship* (1896), H. A. Vachell's *The Hill* (1905) or E. F. Benson's *David Blaize* (1916). A typical example is the following passage from Sturgis's *Tim* (1891): '[Tim] felt his love for his friend almost a religion to him ... "What woman could ever love him as I do?" thought Tim ... as Tim's hungry eyes rested on the face of his friend, he turned towards him and smiled.'[41] When asked about such fraught relationships, G. H. Rendall, Headmaster of Charterhouse from 1897 to 1911, said, 'My boys are amorous but seldom erotic'.[42] In many of the novels, such as Welldon's *Gerald Eversley's Friendship* or Raymond's *Tell England* (1922), there is either an episode of 'attempted beastliness' or a figure of the 'degenerate', as if the sanctity of the central relationship could be defined only in relationship to such tropes.[43] Even more important was a strict policing of the ambiguous world of tactile contact; in the pre-Wildean England of Farrar's *Eric* (1857–58), a scene in which Eric 'stooping down kissed fondly the pale white forehead of his friend', drew a negative critical response.[44] The *Saturday Review* complained, 'to the infinite indignation of all English readers, [the boys] occasionally kiss each other, exchanging moreover such endearments as "dear fellow" and the like.'[45] In Hughes's *Tom Brown at Oxford* (1889), after Tom gives up the barmaid and is reconciled with Hardy, 'Tom rushed across to his friend, dearer to him now, and threw his arm round his neck; and if the un-English truth must out, had three parts of a mind to kiss the rough face.'[46] The male-to-male kiss is 'un-English' but, in 1889, just four years after the Labouchère Amendment, the source of anxiety is not difficult to guess. Tacked onto the Criminal Law Amendment Act (1885), this amendment criminalised homosexuality – or, as it termed it, gross indecency between males – with a penalty of up to three years' imprisonment. The climactic kiss in Choyce's narrative needs to be considered in this context of paranoia. Choyce would exploit the contemporary, tragic history not merely to relegitimise the kiss but to translate it into a narrative of sacrifice and comradeship. Given the physicality and sentimentalism inherent in the theatre of death, the kiss in Choyce's novel serves as a faultline in the contemporary construction of both masculinity and male bonding. The dying kiss between Peter and Raymond represents the fine point where homosociability and homoeroticism, occupying very different places in the Victorian ideological spectrum of male relationships, touch and blend at the levels of both experiential reality and hermeneutic interpretation.

## TRENCH POETRY AND THE LANGUAGE OF SENSATIONS

Amorousness was perhaps permissible among boys but not between men in Victorian England. The love and grief that Alfred, Lord Tennyson, felt at the death of Arthur Henry Hallam (A. H. H.) would find statement in the image of a dying kiss at the centre of 'In memoriam' (1850).[47] Whitman, in the first edition of *Leaves of Grass* (1855), would employ a more overtly erotic vocabulary to describe same-sex affection – 'comrade's long dwelling kiss' – but would carefully harness it in a working-class identity, or a rhetoric of sacrifice, as in 'The Wound Dresser': 'Many a soldier's kiss dwells on these bearded lips.'[48] Herbert Read turns to this literary tradition in 'My Company', first published in *Naked Warriors* (1919). In Read's poem, the dying kiss is set exactly in the central section: 'It is not thus I would have him kiss'd / but with the warm passionate lips / of his comrade here.'[49] In Read's modernist poetics, Whitman is invoked for both sexual and political reasons: erotic charge is made the basis of political bonding. Military relationships are here reconceptualised as personal romance: 'O beautiful men, O men I loved / O whither are you gone, my company?':

> I cannot tell
> what time your life became mine:
> perhaps when one summer night
> we halted on the roadside
> in the starlight only
> and you sang your sad home-songs
> dirges which I standing outside you
> coldly condemned.
> Perhaps, one night, descending cold
> when rum was mighty acceptable,
> and my doling gave birth to sensual gratitude.
> And then our fights: we've fought together
> compact, unanimous
> and I have felt the pride of leadership.[50]

This is the language of the amorous subject, but it draws on the rhetorics of heterosexual romance, laddish indulgences and officer–soldier camaraderie.

The shifts in register suggest that these realms, kept separate in ordinary life through varying discourses of desire, friendship and duty, have come together. Here the catalyst is clearly not physical charge but rather constant companionship, growth, mutual dependence and support. What the eroticisation of the kiss suggests is not an actively transgressive politics of sexual difference as often in Whitman, but rather two different, although related concepts. First, eroticism is primarily on the side of life, meaning and beauty; it stands in opposition to the Baudelairian grotesquery of rotting lips, and subsequent categories of homosexual and heterosexual are strictly secondary. Secondly, Read's poem asks, for a sensitive heterosexual male, can emotional intensity accommodate the physical? Or, conversely, is heterosexual desire the necessary structuring principle of social units?

If a questioning of heterosexual norms is implicit in Read's model, Nichols openly employs the motif of the dying kiss to challenge civilian domestic structures. His *Ardours and Endurances* (1917) was extremely popular, rapturously reviewed in the *Times Literary Supplement* (12 July 1917). 'The Secret', appearing in his second anthology, *Aurelia* (1920), sums up the main thrust of *Ardours*: before the war the poet was in both 'love' and 'passion,' but in a postwar life he could find solace in romantically mourning two friends: Richard Pinsent, killed at Loos (1915), and Harold Stuart Gough, killed at Ypres (1916). Initially, 'The Secret' seems to reproduce the age-old asymmetrical opposition between male camaraderie and heterosexual romance, but in the last stanza a subtle shift occurs: the difference between male–male and male–female relationship is predicated not on an absence/presence of the body but on a distinction between processes of touching. Different kinds of physicalities and masculinities vie for attention in the poem:

> I, that have held strong hands which palter,
> Borne the full weight of limbs that falter,
> Bound live flesh on the surgeon's altar,
> What need have I of woman's hand?
> I, that have felt the dead's embrace;
> I, whose arms were his resting-place;
> I, that have kissed a dead man's face;
> Ah, but how should you understand
> *Now I can only turn away.*[51]

Heterosexual investment is contrasted with noble, altruistic love of comrades, but most astonishing is the process of remembrance and representation. The gruesome memories of bandaging wounds are cherished, nightmarish experiences are transformed through language into a fantasy of romance. The overarching Christian framework of suffering and service comes up against an almost desirable relish heard in the wording, sound-pattern, rhythm and rhyme. This effect is produced not merely through the labials and sibilants ('live flesh', 'limbs', 'strong hands'), but in the way in which the falling cadence of the feminine rhyme ('palter' / 'falter' / 'altar') is gathered up by a strong masculine subjectivity grounded in the anophoric 'I' and the alliterative beat of the stressed syllables of the trochee and the spondee: 'Bound' and 'Borne'. In this romance of language between two kinds of masculinity, sympathy flows into empathy, and the 'woman's hand', receiving the trochaic stress at the wrong end of the line, grates harshly. The kiss is the climactic point in the poem: if the rhetorical dismissal of the 'woman's hand' is a repudiation of marriage, is kissing the comrade meant to show that the symbol of heterosexual romance has also lost its meaning in a postwar England?

The aestheticisation of the male body and eroticisation of male experience might result from the effort to find a suitable poetic language to articulate the specificity of war experiences. In journals, diaries and letters that are not self-consciously literary or written by public-school officers, one finds a slightly different statement of experience, as in the unpublished memoirs of W. A. Quinton:

> Sharing everything, down to the last cigarette end, the last army biscuit, the last bit of cover under an enemy bombardment, can you wonder when I say we almost loved each other. Facing hardships & death together day after day, brings out that something in a man that lies dormant in the monotonous round of everyday civilian life. I well remember on one occasion when I was sickly, how old Petch tried to nurse me. . . . taking care to tuck me in as a mother would a child.[52]

Tactile tenderness, figured through the maternal embrace, defines the final moment in Quinton's reconceptualisation of male–male bonds premised on a language of mutual dependence under extreme circumstances. The physical immediacy ('tuck me in') he suggests is of a different order from desire. The physical continuum – touching, nursing, reassuring – was central to these relationships, which did not fit either the classical or the Christian model of 'manly love', both of which largely ignored the body. Without a language to describe this physicality, most poets fell back on a model of Whitmanesque passion or Georgian aestheticism, while at the same time developing a troubled relationship to these modes as they tried to evoke a different order of experience. This is evident in the conflict that lies at the heart of Read's and Nichols's poems: the central disjunction between an experiential reality and ideology of 'greater love' and an inherited poetic language of exquisite sensations.

Perhaps retreat into older poetic modes was the inevitable result of a conjunction of class politics, literary history and the culture of mourning. Jon Silkin's enormously popular *The Penguin Book of First World War Poetry* – particularly the original edition of 1979 (this was revised with new material in 1996) – shows that what has come to be regarded as the First World War literary canon was largely built on the works of public-school officer-poets. Many of them had 'sentimental and chaste' but distinctly 'homosexual' crushes, as Graves says, at school; for many of them, the army, with its network of male relationships, was basically an extension of the public school.[53] Moreover, from the aestheticism of Walter Pater to the pastoral poignancy of A. E. Housman's *A Shropshire Lad* to the Uranian poetry of William Johnson Cory, English poetry was suffused with what Fussell calls a tradition of 'warm homoeroticism' through which the youthful male body was endlessly aestheticised, idealised and eulogised.[54] If in 1869 a slightly perturbed father of Arthur Hallam, after reading Shakespeare's sonnets, had detected 'weakness and folly in all excessive and mis-placed affection', in the case of war poetry these defects were 'redeemed by the touches of nobler sentiments'.[55] Moreover, at a time when a whole generation had been destroyed by unimaginable forms of violence, homophobia was checked through the sheer intensity of grief. The threat of homoeroticism was arrested by the absence of the desired object and the conception of the body as a seat of pain. This explains the appeal of the dying kiss: while the strength and sweetness of a whole tradition of 'warm homoeroticism' could be gathered into the 'warm, passionate' kiss, any direct homoerotic threat would be halted by the image of a dead body. It would always be a one-sided narrative, the life–death boundary overpowering transgressive eros, such that it could be written into a language of greater love.

And yet for many homosexuals, it was the source of much anxiety. Sassoon, tormented by his homosexuality (though perhaps not active at the time), mentions the dying kiss only once, but it has a painful history. By August 1915, Sassoon was deeply in love with David Cuthbert Thomas, the young Sandhurst subaltern whom he calls 'Dick Tiltwood' in *Memoirs of a Fox Hunting Man*.[56] By 18 March 1916, David was dead, and the following day Sassoon wrote in his diary:

> my little Tommy had been hit by a stray bullet and died last night . . . Had I but known! – the old, human-weak cry. Now he comes back to me in memories, like an angel, with the light in his yellow hair, and I think of him at Cambridge late August when we lived together four weeks in Pembroke College in rooms where the previous occupant's name, Paradise, was written above the door.[57]

In May 1916 Sassoon wrote 'The Last Meeting', a pastoral elegy mourning David's death. In a poem where the male body is consistently woven into a fantasy of space, purity and disembodiedness, Sassoon concludes with a surprisingly intimate gesture: 'And lips that touched me once in Paradise.'[58] By framing the kiss, happy with warmly personal details, at the climactic point of the pastoral elegy, the poet places his love on a continuum of intense male love and loss. If the Church, the state and modern sexology had reduced homosexuality to a sin, a crime or an aberration, he falls back on an 'honourable' genre that not only has the weight of classical antiquity but is incorporated within the tradition of 'Englishness' from Milton to Shelley to Arnold. But in a stunning example of how gay history is erased through homosexual panic, either personal or institutional, these lines are found only in the original draft sent to Edward Dent. The 1919 collection of *War Poems* (and all subsequent editions) changes the paradisal kiss into a dying one: 'And youth, that dying, touched my lips to song.'[59]

The kiss – or rather its absence – in the mature war poetry of Wilfred Owen is perhaps more fascinating. Male beauty, often with an erotic charge, is one of the mainsprings of his poetry.[60] But there are essential differences between Owen's deep homoerotic inclination and the more conscious homosexuality of Sassoon. First, unlike in the case of Sassoon, there is no documented evidence of any homosexual relationship or encounter on the part of Owen. For him, in contrast to Sassoon and Read, amorous investment impedes rather than facilitates political bonding. Still, he is obsessed by lips; in his writings a rigorous Protestant ethic mingled with feelings of guilty eroticism and a hatred of warfare produce tortured and violent images: 'Red lips are not so red / As the stained stones kissed by the English dead', or 'I saw his round mouth's crimson deepen as it fell.'[61] The lips that cannot be touched, morally or legally, can only be mutilated in Owen's poetry, at times producing a diatribe against innocent heterosexual kissing:

> For love is not the binding of fair lips
> With the soft silk of eyes that look and long,
> By Joy, whose ribbon slips, –
> But wound with war's hard wire whose stakes are strong;
> Bound with the bandage of the arm that drips;
> Knit in the webbing of the rifle-thong.[62]

The concluding images are at once realistic and symbolic. Regarding eroticism as 'a thorn in the flesh', he treats (male) hands as a perpetual site of intense pleasure and anxiety. Looking back on what Hibberd calls his 'love affair' with Vivian Rampton, he agonises, 'Be better if I had not touched his hand'.[63] These contradictions are gathered up into a moment of terrible guilt in the rough draft of the 'Perseus' fragment: 'Unhand me / For I have touched the goddess, touch me not.'[64] Consequently, as he sets out to sing the hymn of sacrificial love, the beautiful hands of Rampton and the de la Touch boys, the 'groping hand' and 'beautiful fingers' of 'To Eros' or 'Impromptu' are savagely mutilated. Homoerotic anxieties are thus deflected and displaced, painful sacrifice is lauded above pleasurable self-statement. Owen redefines love through a morbid image of mutilation, just as the innocuous 'ribbon', a seemingly casual reminder of heterosexuality, resurfaces with a macabre twist in the image of reddened, bruised flesh. Greater love is redefined not through the dying kiss but as a bond made by mutilated hands.

## CONTEMPORARY SEXOLOGY AND TÜGEL'S 'OVER THE TOP'

But are gender and sexual anxieties that seem to hover around the dying kiss ever directly addressed by First World War writers? A unique example is Ludwig Tügel's short story 'Over the Top', originally written in German and translated in the popular anthology *Great Short Stories of the War* (1930), introduced by Edmund Blunden. The story is set in a tiny dugout on the eve of a fatal offensive. The first-person narrator reads a letter written by his close friend Paul to his girlfriend, while Paul lies asleep. When a barrage starts outside the dugout Paul wakes up in absolute terror:

> 'You've have been reading it, haven't you? You've been reading it?'
> 'Yes,' I managed to gasp, and I saw him pull the trigger. The bullet flew past my ear; we struggled and rolled over together. Chest to chest, head to head, we were lying locked against each other.
> I don't know what happened. We were trying to bite each other's throats like savage beasts, and our lips met harshly, then relaxed and remained together. We murmured brokenly, incomprehensibly, as we wept and kissed and clung. Outside in the front of the dugout they were shouting: 'Take cover! Take cover!'[65]

The scene begins as one of male hysteria: the hour of need involves homosocial rivalry, self-loathing, and sado-masochistic fury. A moment of silence marks the slide into eroticism in the otherwise detailed narrative: 'I don't know what happened', as Tügel shows aggression flowering into desire without a break or mediating pause.

The kiss is the pivot on which the story turns, the site of complex psycho-sexual mediation. In Tügel's narrative, the kiss is situated between two other kisses. The first is the romantic kiss of Paul's girlfriend, his 'dearest memory'. But for the first-person narrator, the kiss takes him back to the 'earliest memory' of his mother: 'I threw myself on the bed and kissed you, under-standing nothing, but perhaps realising unconsciously that life gives love and only love can give life.'[66] In *The Three Essays on the Theory of Sexuality* (1905), Freud says that for the child, 'sucking at his mother's breast has become the prototype of every relation of love'; initially, 'the satisfaction of the erotogenic zone is associated . . . with the satisfaction of the need for nourishment', but with the growth of the child, his 'oral education' is connected with an emerging capacity for genital sexuality.[67] In a sentence added in 1915, Freud suggests that the instinct of self-preservation lingers on, and that sexual activity 'does not become independent of them until later'.[68] The kiss in Tügel's narrative, exchanged before imminent death, is almost a regression to the childhood world of 'love' and 'life' contained in the infantile *Lutscherli*. If, as Adam Philips does, we take Freud's ideas to their extreme, interpreting the kiss to harbour a 'narcissistic intent' (the child unsatisfactorily substituting the 'corresponding part of another's body'),[69] then the dying kiss suggests an important link between narcissism and homoeroticism. 'It's a pity I can't kiss myself,' Freud's child parenthetically exclaims.[70] If this disappointment is the grudge at the root of sexuality, making the kiss the mouth's elegy to itself, Tügel presents us with a grim literalisation as the two men go over the top, the kiss being their last – and lasting – memory: 'Paul pressed closely against me, and I sheltered him in my arms as once I might have sheltered a woman whom I loved. "All right, old man. All right." We said no more.'[71] Self-preservation, romance, camaraderie, eroticism: different emotions and instincts slip through 'lips at the brim' in Tügel's narrative universe.

The revolutionary potential of Tügel's story can be fully appreciated when placed in the context of contemporary debates about homosexuality, especially in Germany. The earliest theories of sexual inversion came from German sexologists – Karl Heinrich Ulrichs and Richard von Krafft-Ebing – who were seeking a medical explanation, thus starting the debate about congenital versus acquired sexuality. Ulrichs advanced the theory of *anima muliebris virile corpore inclusa*, a female soul in a male body, while Krafft-Ebing, in the twelfth edition of *Psychopathia sexualis* (1892), attributed same-sex desire to neurasthenia.[72] Ellis's *Sexual Inversion* (1897), though far more enlightened and sympathetic, describes sexual difference as 'a congenital abnormality, to be classed with the other congenital abnormalities which have psychic concomitants'.[73] Freud broke new ground in 1903 by separating the sexual object and the sexual aim, thus separating gender from sexuality and claiming the polymorphous perversity of human desire. By placing the kiss in the overtly masculine atmosphere evoked by wrestling and death on the battlefield, Tügel subtly discredits both Ulrichs's model of a female soul in a male body and the social construction of the effeminate dandy associated with Wilde; his story is more suggestive of Freud's argument that the sexual object and sexual aim are merely soldered together. More importantly, Tügel places sexuality in a continuum of emotions such as vulnerability, helplessness, fear and the universal need to be loved and cared for: in the meeting of 'lips', the erotics of greed are overwhelmed by the reassurances of affection. The kiss – or as Freud defined it, 'the particular contact . . . between the mucous membrane of the lips of the two people concerned', held in 'high sexual esteem' – becomes a language of support, succour and solace.[74]

Of modern subjectivity, Roland Barthes writes: 'where there is a wound, there is a subject: die Wunde! die Wunde! says Parsifal, thereby becoming "himself"; and the deeper the wound, at the body's center (at the "heart"), the more the subject becomes a subject: for the subject is intimacy ("The

wound . . . is of a frightful intimacy").'[75] Subjectivity and intimacy return to
the body as a seat of pain rather than of pleasure. At stake is the issue of
nakedness that also underlies the relations between gender, gesture and intimacy in the First World War. I use the word 'nakedness' to combine the sense
of vulnerability, exposure and service often connected with physical danger,
leading to a bodily intimacy and immediacy that is perhaps inimical to linguistic representation. In the letter to his girlfriend in Tügel's story, Paul
mentions a curious episode: 'Yesterday Frohlich the bombardier had an attack
of madness, and my friend had to tie him down in the dugout. He called me
up to show me . . . and said, quite calmly: "I'm just telling you in case you've
to do it to me".'[76] What challenged heterosexuality in postwar England was
not sexual dissidence but a memory house of such bonds. These were of
neither romantic love nor 'blokish' bonding nor homoerotic frisson: with
each of these elements there is a distinct overlap, and yet always a distinct
difference. Eroticism may or may not have played a part, but it was certainly
not the founding impulse. Sexuality had not yet hijacked an intimate history
of human emotions. 'Frightful intimacy' is perhaps as far as language can go:
the dying kiss was perhaps its true sign, the mouth filling the gap left by
language.

## NOTES

I should like to acknowledge Professor Gillian Beer for her warm support and advice, and
the staff at the Imperial War Museum, London, particularly the Department of Documents, for their help and efficiency.

1  Imperial War Museum, London (hereafter IWM), 82/11/1, Lieutenant Frank Cocker to
   Evelyn, 16 January 1916.
2  For a literary-historical elucidation of the Victorian cult of 'romantic friendship' between
   young men, see Peter Parker, *The Old Lie: The Great War and the Public School Ethos*
   (London, 1987): 'The model for the Romantic Friendship was not that of Achilles and
   Patroclus or Alexis and Corydon, but that love passing the love of women enjoyed by
   David and Jonathan' (p. 107). However, Jeffrey Richards in '"Passing the Love of
   Women": Manly Love and Victorian Society', in J. A. Mangan and James Walvin
   (eds), *Manliness and Morality: Middle-Class Masculinity in Britain and America, 1800–
   1940* (Manchester, 1987), pp. 108–24, argues for the influence of classical Greek thought
   and medieval chivalric ethic. At the same time, because of the specificity of public-
   school bonding that often lay at the heart of such 'romantic love' between young men,
   and the classical and Christian models of 'manly love' on which it frequently drew,
   these male–male relationships were quite different from the 'romantic friendships'
   between women which Lillian Faderman in *Surpassing the Love of Men: Romantic
   Friendship and Love between Women from the Renaissance to the Present* (London, 1981)
   describes as 'love relationships in every sense except the genital' (p. 16).
3  Sigmund Freud, 'Three Essays on the Theory of Sexuality', in *The Complete Psychological Works*, ed. and trans. James Strachey (London, 1953), vii, p. 148.
4  Alan Sinfield, *The Wilde Century: Effeminacy, Oscar Wilde and the Queer Moment* (London, 1994), pp. 84–108. See also Jeffrey Weeks, *Sex, Politics and Society: The Regulation*

*of Sexuality since 1800* (London, 1989), pp. 96–121. Michel Foucault's claim that 'the psychological, psychiatric, medical category of homosexuality was constituted from the moment it was categorised – Westphal's famous article of 1870 on "contrary sexual sensations" can stand as its date of birth' (*The History of Sexuality*, i: *Introduction*, trans. Robert Hurley (New York, 1980), p. 43) has been seriously challenged more recently. The works of scholars such as Stephen Orgel, Jonathan Goldberg, Alan Bray, David Halperin and Randolph Trumbach have alerted us to alternative and earlier histories of homosexuality/queerness. But for a widespread familiarisation with and codification of homosexuality through the intersection of different discourses, the late Victorian period was particularly momentous. The trials of Stella and Fanny in 1871 were widely publicised, and the notorious Oscar Wilde trial following the Labouchere Amendment (1885) led to the crystallisation of a definite and widespread image of the 'sexually invert' centring on the notions of aestheticism, effeminacy, leisure and luxury. Another unique feature of this period was the contemporary development of sexology and the appeal to medical knowledge among activists such as Magnus Hirschfeld, Karl Heinrich Ulrichs, Havelock Ellis and John Addington Symonds for homosexual rights. For Victorian discourses on homosexuality, please refer to n. 72.

5 One might place Cocker's kiss on a 'bisexual continuum'. However, the kiss in Cocker's narrative wavers not merely between sexual categories but also between nuanced emotional registers that are historically contingent. See Clare Hemmings, 'Resituating the Bisexual Body: From Identity to Difference', in Joseph Bristow and Angelia R. Wilson (eds), *Activating Theory: Lesbian, Gay and Bisexual Politics* (London, 1993), p. 118; Jonathan Dollimore, 'Bisexuality, Heterosexuality, and Wishful Theory,' *Textual Practice*, 10:3 (1996), 523–39.

6 Joanna Bourke, *Dismembering the Male: Men's Bodies, Britain and the Great War* (London, 1996), pp. 133–6. Her valuable work has pointed me to important archival material.

7 IWM, 75/32/1, W. A. Quinton, Unpublished memoirs.

8 A. F. B., 'Smalley,' *Third Battalion Magazine* (August 1918), 8.

9 IWM, 85/4/1, Jack to Miss D. Williams.

10 Erich Maria Remarque, *All Quiet on the Western Front*, trans. A. W. Wheen (Oxford, 1970), p. 245.

11 R. C. Sherriff, *Journey's End: A Play* (London, 1929), pp. 82–3.

12 Rupert Brooke, 'Fragment', in *The Collected Poems* (London, 1987), p. 318; Wilfred Owen, 'Futility', in *The Poems of Wilfred Owen*, ed. Jon Stallworthy (London, 1990), p. 135; Siegfried Sassoon, 'The Last Meeting', typescript, Cambridge University Library, Add 7973, S51–end; Robert Nichols, 'Casualty', in *Aurelia and Other Poems* (London, 1920), p. 75.

13 D. H. Lawrence, *Lady Chatterley's Lover* (Harmondsworth, 1961), p. 290. Also see Elaine Showalter, 'River and Sassoon', in Margaret Higonnet (ed.), *Behind the Lines: Gender and the Two World Wars* (New Haven, CT, 1987), p. 64.

14 While most studies on gender and the First World War tend to focus on the relation between the sexes, as in Sandra Gilbert and Susan Gubar, *No Man's Land: The War of Words*, ii (New Haven, CT, 1989), or on the response and condition of women, as in Higonnet's *Behind the Lines*, my analysis emphasises the relation between the experiential reality of the male body in times of physical extremity and constructions of gender and gesture.

15 Magnus Hirschfeld, 'Homosexuality and Transvestism in the Trenches', in *The Sexual History of the World War* (New York, 1946), pp. 116–17. Also see Paul Fussell, *The Great War and Modern Memory* (New York, 1975), pp. 270–309; Martin Taylor, *Lads: Love*

*Poetry of the Trenches* (London, 1998), pp. 1–58; and Jeffrey Weeks, in *Between the Acts: Lives of Homosexual Men, 1885–1967* (London, 1991), who interviews a First World War soldier who met his partner in the trenches (p. 7). Hirschfeld documents similar cases, but agrees that such examples are few (*Sexual History*, p. 115). Taylor notes, 'Given the physical conditions of the front line, the filth, the lice and the lack of privacy, and the probable sexual orientation of most soldiers, it is unlikely that any sexual contact was possible or even desirable' (*Lads*, p. 27). The only reference to a court martial related to homosexuality I have found appears in a letter written by Raymond Asquith to Lady Diana Manners in September 1916: 'I had two terribly strenuous days – 10 hours each before a court martial defending a fellow officer upon 5 charges of "homosexualism" – unsuccessfully.' See Raymond Asquith, *Life and Letters*, ed. John Jolliffe (London, 1980), p. 292.

16  Richard Aldington, *Death of a Hero* (London, 1929), p. 26.

17  J. R. Ackerley, *My Father and Myself* (London, 1968), p. 119.

18  Robert Graves, *But It Still Goes On* (London, 1930), p. 245.

19  Robert Graves, *Goodbye to All That* (London, 1929), pp. 40–1.

20  While in Brooke's case there is documented evidence of at least one encounter, Sassoon was a self-confessed homosexual. Owen's letters and poems evince a strong homoerotic impulse but provide no evidence of any actual encounter or relationship, in spite of a strong attachment with some very young boys. See John Lehmann, *Rupert Brooke: His Life and his Legend* (London, 1981); Jean Moorcroft Wilson, *Siegfried Sassoon: The Making of a War Poet: A Biography, 1886–1918* (London, 1998); Jon Stallworthy, *Wilfred Owen* (New York, 1974); and Dominic Hibberd, *Owen the Poet* (New York, 1986).

21  A good example of the dialogue between past and present is David M. Halperin's *One Hundred Years of Homosexuality and Other Essays on Greek Love* (New York, 1990). See Paul Hammond, *Love between Men in English Literature* (London, 1996) and George E. Haggerty, *Men in Love: Masculinity and Sexuality in the Eighteenth Century* (New York, 1999). Sinfield notes in *The Wilde Century*, ' "Same-sex passion" is the best term I have been able to find for the period up to 1900' (p. 11). 'Passion' is intended to include both an emotional and a physical charge, while avoiding the fraught term 'desire'.

22  Michel Foucault, *The History of Sexuality*, ii: *The Use of Pleasure*, trans. Robert Hurley (Harmondsworth, 1992), pp. 5–6.

23  Niall Ferguson, *The Pity of War* (Harmondsworth, 1998), pp. 436–7.

24  Richards, ' "Passing the love of women" ', pp. 108–24. See also Taylor, *Lads* and Parker, *The Old Lie*.

25  Siegfried Sassoon, *Memoirs of an Infantry Officer* (1930; London, 1997), p. 57.

26  Fussell, *Great War*, p. 276.

27  Owing to the peculiarity of war circumstances, the continuum of non-genital tactile tenderness seems to combine Sedgwick's 'homosocial desire' with certain features of Rich's paradigm of the lesbian continuum of 'resignation, despair, effacement, self-denial'. See Adrienne Rich, 'Compulsory Heterosexuality and Lesbian Existence', in *Blood, Bread and Poetry: Selected Prose, 1979–1985* (London, 1986), pp. 53–4. The bonds I examine are not based on triangulated desire, are more physical than in Sedgwick, and need not be consciously erotic, nor associated with power. See Eve Kosofsky Sedgwick, *Between Men: English Literature and Male Homosocial Desire* (New York, 1985), and Richard Dellamora, *Masculine Desire: The Sexual Politics of Victorian Aestheticism* (Chapel Hill, 1990).

28  For a detailed study of the kiss, see Nicolas James Perella, *The Kiss Sacred and Profane: An Interpretive History of Kiss Symbolism and Related Religio-Erotic Themes* (Berkeley,

1969); Willem Frijhoft, 'The Kiss Sacred and Profane: Reflections on a Cross-Cultural Confrontation', in Jan Bremmer and Herman Roodenburg (eds), *A Cultural History of Gesture: From Antiquity to the Present Day* (Malden, MA, 1991), pp. 210–36.

29 Christopher Nyrop, *The Kiss and its History*, trans. William Frederick Harvey (London, 1901), pp. 141–2.

30 D. H. Lawrence, *England, my England* (1915 version), in *England, My England and Other Stories*, ed. Bruce Steele (New York, 1990), p. 227; R. C. Sherriff, *Journey's End* (London, 1929), p. 25; Ernest Hemingway, *A Farewell to Arms* (London, 1999), p. 151.

31 Stephen Gaselee, 'The Soul in the Kiss', *Criterion*, 2 (April 1924), 349–59.

32 Christopher Hibbert, *Nelson: A Personal History* (New York, 1994), p. 376. Hardy kissed Nelson not once but twice, the first time on Nelson's bidding, 'Then, as though he thought Nelson might think he had kissed him only because he had been asked to do so, he knelt down again and kissed his forehead.'

33 IWM, 90/7/1, Revd Parry Okeden to May Okeden.

34 IWM, 87/10/1, Revd Connor, diary entry.

35 IWM, 87/13/1, Lance-Corporal D. H. Fenton to Mrs Noone.

36 Raymond Dorgeles, *Wooden Crosses* (London, 1920), pp. 264–6.

37 Arthur Newberry Choyce, *Lips at the Brim: A Novel* (London, 1920), pp. 165–6.

38 Parker, *The Old Lie*, p. 114.

39 As Jonathan Dollimore notes, 'What is less often conceded or, if conceded, considered – Bersani being a significant exception – is that if gender is socially constituted, *so too is desire*. Desire is informed by the same oppressive constructions of gender that we would willingly dispense with. Desire is of its "nature" saturated by the social.' See *Sexual Dissidence: Augustine to Wilde, Freud to Foucault* (Oxford, 1991), p. 325.

40 Sedgwick, *Between Men*.

41 H. O. Sturgis, *Tim* (London, 1891), pp. 158–9.

42 Parker, *The Old Lie*, p. 106.

43 Richards, 'Passing the love of women', pp. 113–17.

44 F. W. Farrar, *Eric or Little by Little* (London, 1857–58), pp. 139–40.

45 H. Montgomery Hyde, *The Other Love* (London, 1972), p. 131.

46 Thomas Hughes, *Tom Brown at Oxford* (London, 1889), pp. 193–4.

47 Alfred Tennyson, *The Poems of Alfred Tennyson*, ed. Christopher Ricks (Harlow, 1987), ii, p. 337 (section XVIII).

48 Walt Whitman, *The Portable Walt Whitman*, ed. Mark Van Doren (New York, 1977), p. 229.

49 Herbert Read, *Collected Poems, 1913–25* (London, 1926), p. 88.

50 *Ibid.*, p. 85.

51 Nichols, 'The Secret,' in *Aurelia and Other Poems*, p. 77.

52 IWM, 79/35/1, W. A. Quinton, unpublished memoirs.

53 Graves, *Goodbye to All That*, pp. 40–1.

54 Fussell, *Great War*, pp. 270–86.

55 Alan Sinfield, *Alfred Tennyson* (Malden, MA, 1986), p. 127.

56 Wilson, *Siegfried Sassoon*, pp. 237–8.

57 Siegfried Sassoon, *Diaries, 1915–16*, ed. Rupert Hart-Davies (New York, 1983), pp. 44–5.

58 Siegfried Sassoon, 'The Last Meeting', Cambridge University Library, Add 7973, S51–end.

59 Siegfried Sassoon, *The War Poems*, ed. Rupert Hart-Davis (1919; New York, 1983), p. 35.

60 Jon Stallworthy, 'Wilfred Owen', *Proceedings of the British Academy*, 56 (1970), 13.

61  Wilfred Owen, *The Poems of Wilfred Owen*, ed. Jon Stallworthy (London, 1985), pp. 143, 100.

62  *Idem*, 'Apologia pro poemate meo,' *ibid.*, p. 101.

63  Hibberd, *Owen the Poet*, p. 22.

64  Wilfred Owen, *The Complete Poems and Fragments*, ed. Jon Stallworthy (London, 1983), ii, p. 467.

65  Ludwig Tügel, 'Over the Top', in *Great First World War Stories* (London, 1994), originally published as *Great Short Stories of the War* (London, 1930). References here are to the 1994 edition.

66  *Ibid.*, pp. 298–9.

67  Freud, *Complete Psychological Works*, vii, pp. 181–2.

68  *Ibid.*, p. 182.

69  Adam Phillips, *On Kissing, Tickling and Being Bored* (New York, 1993), pp. 106–7.

70  Freud, *Complete Psychological Works*, vii, p. 182.

71  Tügel, 'Over the Top', p. 297.

72  For a detailed discussion of sexological debates at the time, see Jeffrey Weeks, *Coming Out: Homosexual Politics in Britain from the Nineteenth Century to the Present* (London, 1977); Frank Mort, *Dangerous Sexualities: Medico-Moral Politics in England since 1830* (New York, 1987); and Lesley A. Hall, *Hidden Anxieties, Male Sexuality, 1900–1950* (Malden, MA, 1991). See also J. A. Symonds, *Studies in Greek Love* (1883) and E. Carpenter, *Some Friends of Walt Whitman: A Study in Sex-Psychology* (London, 1924).

73  Havelock Ellis, *Studies in the Psychology of Sex*, i: *Sexual Inversion* (London, 1897), p. 137.

74  Freud, *Complete Psychological Works*, vii, p. 150.

75  Roland Barthes, *A Lover's Discourse*, trans. Richard Howard (Harmondsworth, 1990), p. 189.

76  Tügel, 'Over the Top', p. 294.

# *Afterword*

<>

## Keith Thomas

We have in the lips a highly sensitive frontier region between skin and mucous membrane, in many ways analogous to the vulvo-vaginal orifice, and rein-forcible, moreover, by the active movements of the still more highly sensitive tongue. (Havelock Ellis, *Studies in the Pyschology of Sex*, iv: *Sexual Selection in Man*, 1905, Philadelphia, 1923, p. 22)

Sir: I was horrified to see our Prime Minister kissing the President of Russia. Can you imagine Neville Chamberlain kissing Hitler, or Churchill kissing Stalin?

Anglo-Saxon men have never gone in for this kissing performance. Some-times they shake hands, but never the double two-handed shake or clasping of the arm. Only the Gallic race and the Arabs go in for hugging and kissing. No British general would even think of giving or accepting a kiss from another man, surely? (D. M. C. Rose, Lieutenant-Colonel, letter in *The Spectator*, 10 May 2003)

Look at these people! They suck each other! They eat each other's saliva and dirt! (The Tsonga people of southern Africa on the European practice of kiss-ing: Henri A. Junod, *The Life of a South African Tribe*, 2nd edn, London, 1927, i, p. 353)

I N WHAT must still be the longest single work ever devoted to the kiss – *Opus polyhistoricum . . . de osculis* (Frankfurt, 1680), a fat volume of 1040 closely packed pages – the German polymath Martin von Kempe (1642–83) assembled excerpts from classical, biblical, patristic, ecclesiastical, legal, medical and other learned sources to form a sort of encyclopedia of kissing. He listed more than twenty different types of kiss. They included the mystical kiss, the kiss of veneration, the kiss of peace, the kisses bestowed by Christians on images and relics, and by pagans on idols, the kisses given each other by the early Christians, the kiss of homage and subjection, the kissing of the Pope's foot, the kiss bestowed by superiors on inferiors, the kiss used in academic degree ceremonies, the lovers' kiss, the lustful and adulterous kiss, the kiss exchanged by couples sealing their marriage vows, the kiss between close friends and relations, the kiss of reconciliation, the healing kiss, the kiss carrying contagion, the valedictory kiss given to the dead and dying, the hypocritical kiss and the kiss of Judas.[1]

It would not be difficult to prolong von Kempe's list *ad infinitum*. For kisses can take so many different forms. They can be given in private or in public, by men to men, men to women, women to women, adults to children or children to each other. They can be unilateral or reciprocated. They can be on the lips, on the cheek, on both cheeks, on the hand, on the foot or on any other part of the body. They can be given to objects or to one's own hand or blown in the air. They can be bestowed with the lips open or closed or with the tongue projected or merely by a touching of the cheeks; they can be silent or they can be delivered with an audible smacking noise. They can be a solitary gesture or they may accompany an embrace or a handshake. Within the prescriptions of any particular ritual, they can be prolonged or perfunctory, solemn or satirical, deft or clumsy. Even erotic kissing can take many forms, as medieval clerical confessors were well aware.[2] There is an infinity of different ways in a which a kiss can be delivered; and its meaning, both to participants and to onlookers, will vary accordingly. It can express deference, obedience, respect, agreement, reverence, adoration, friendliness, affection, tenderness, love, superiority, inferiority, even insult. There is no such thing as a straightforward kiss.

The same is true, of course, of any other gesture. The early nineteenth-century clerical wit Sydney Smith classified handshakes:

> there is the *high official* – the body erect, and a rapid, short shake, near the chin. There is the *mortmain* – the flat hand introduced into your palm, and hardly conscious of its contiguity. The *digital* – one finger held out, much used by the high clergy. There is the *shakus rusticus* – where your hand is seized in an iron grasp, betokening rude health, warm heart, and distance from the Metropolis, but producing a strong sense of relief on your part when you find your hand released and your fingers unbroken. The next to this is the *retentive shake* – one which, beginning with vigour, pauses as it were to take breath, but without relinquishing its prey, and before you are aware begins again, till you feel anxious as to the result, and have no shake left in you. There are other varieties, but this is enough for one lesson.[3]

Nuances of gesture like this are so subtle, so evanescent and so difficult to describe that their interpretation provides a formidable challenge to the social anthropologist or participant observer. To the cultural historian, separated by hundreds of years from social practices which normally leave no evidence of any kind, the task of understanding the gestural behaviour of the past must seem particularly daunting. For the meaning of most gestures was seldom articulated by contemporaries,[4] and, if it had been, it is unlikely there would have been general agreeement as to what it was. Were an analysis ever carried out of the practice of social kissing in modern Britain, it would show wide divergences, some reflecting differences in age and social class, but others the product of personal temperament or disposition. When should such kisses be exchanged and with whom? On which cheeks, in which order and how many times? Uncertainties on such matters create abundant scope for social embarrassment today; and there is no reason to think that matters were necessarily any more straightforward in the past.

Yet, even if some of their subtleties will forever escape us, there is a great deal which can be found out about bygone gestural codes and their meaning to participants, as the chapters of this book have abundantly shown. The task of investigation, however, is a very difficult one. Like so many other central topics in social and cultural history, the kiss has been largely neglected because there is no single cache of material which the researcher can explore in a limited time in the reasonable certainty of emerging with a satisfying conclusion. Instead, the evidence is as widely scattered as it could possibly be. As Karen Harvey points out in her Introduction, there is scarcely any material which is not potentially relevant: plays, poems, court depositions, private letters, paintings, state papers, novels, medical treatises, courtesy books, autobiographies, theological writings – the list is endless. Moreover, one cannot tell in advance which play or which court deposition will prove to be the revealing one. Because the evidence is so dispersed and at the same time so ubiquitous, there is no quick route to success. Typically, progress in an area like this can be made only by the accumulation of chance references gathered over a lifetime's reading. Or so it is usually assumed.

The young scholars who have contributed to this volume have effectively overturned this pessimistic assumption by showing that much can be achieved in a relatively short time. They have not done this by attempting to construct a classification or typology of kisses, in the way that Martin von Kempe did. Rather than studying *the* kiss in all its different manifestations, they have chosen to examine the meaning and resonance of some particular form of kiss at a specific time. Their subject, as Karen Harvey explains, is less the act itself than the attitudes of contemporaries to it, and the light those attitudes throw on their values and anxieties. In this way, the kiss becomes a key with which to unlock the larger mental assumptions of an age.

In her Introduction, Karen Harvey identifies this preoccupation with meaning and context as characteristic of the anthropologically-informed history which is now so widely practised. She is, however, perhaps unduly dismissive of what she calls 'antiquarian interest in instances and types of kiss'. For historians need antiquarians. It is necessary to chart the history of changing practice in the use of the kiss, and the contexts in which it was customarily employed, before the cultural historian can begin the task of explaining the meaning of any particular kiss to participants and observers. For example, we have to know whether it was customary for Jacobean gentlemen to embrace each other before we can attempt to assess the meaning of King James I's behaviour towards his favourites, Somerset and Buckingham. Since we cannot directly observe the societies of the past in the manner of an anthropologist doing field-work, we depend upon the antiquarian collection of infinite detail before we can begin to attempt the 'thick description' which is the cultural historian's ultimate goal. We need to know the grammar and the vocabulary before we can understand the language. The ethnography has to precede the analysis.

It in no way diminishes the achievement of the contributors to this volume to say that, even after their stimulating work, the history of the kiss remains in its infancy. They have unearthed some fascinating material and sketched out some bold and stimulating hypotheses, mostly relating to the history of the kiss in Britain and Europe between 1500 and 1918. But the sheer lack of relevant antiquarian knowledge makes it difficult, if not impossible, at present for anyone to produce a historical account of kissing which can do justice to the complex nuances, subtleties, pleasures and embarrassments with which the practice must have always been associated.

The conventions governing the use of the kiss as a gesture of greeting or farewell, for example, have, for most historical periods, been established only in the most fragmentary outline, and then usually only for the upper classes of society. What sort of gestures, if any, were exchanged on meeting and parting by two twelfth-century serfs? When, if at all, did an eighteenth-century collier's wife kiss her friends? These are not questions to which it is yet possible to give a confident answer. Even when historical sources do contain material on the subject, they are often too general to be properly understood. For it is usually unclear whether a 'kiss' was given on the cheeks or the lips or whether an 'embrace' also involved a kiss. For the ancient and medieval world, it is unlikely that we shall ever manage to get beyond very broad generalities. But there are other periods, for example, the nineteenth century, for which the wealth of potential evidence is much greater; and when historians choose to study it seriously, an altogether more complex degree of understanding is likely to be achieved.

Meanwhile, there has, since the days of Martin von Kempe, been a good deal of writing on the history of the kiss, much of it anecdotal, some of it learned and illuminating. The most helpful of these earlier works are cited in the footnotes to the preceding chapters, and more has been published since they were written.[5] But this book takes the subject a whole stage further and will surely set the agenda for future inquiries.

In the first place, the contributors make it clear that the kiss *does* have a history. Psychologists and psychoanalysts tend to write as if kissing has a universal and unchanging meaning. For Freud, the erotic kiss simulates the infant's suckling; it is an attempted return to the security of the mother's breast. For others, the kiss is linked to sniffing, licking, tasting or eating. Some see its essence as lying in an exchange of breath and saliva, comparable to the exchange of blood which traditionally accompanied the sealing of a solemn pact.[6] Yet others regard it as the physical preliminary to or accompaniment of sexual intercourse. In 1982, a distinguished literary scholar asserted that kisses in Shakespeare's plays 'need little historic or symbolic gloss . . . their essential meaning does not change'. She quickly qualified this statement by conceding that 'a kiss's essential meaning may not change, but the fashion and occasion for certain kinds of embrace do vary, both from Shakespeare's time to our own, and also within the Shakespearean canon'.[7]

For, whatever its biological or psychological foundations, the kiss has its own distinctive cultural history. It is far from being a universal practice. It seems to have played a less conspicuous part in either the ritual or the erotic life of most Asiatic, Polynesian or sub-Saharan societies,[8] while in the West, the norms and conventions governing its employment have, from the beginning, been constantly evolving.

One could attempt to summarise this evolution by saying that the use of the kiss as a ceremonial means of expressing and cementing social, personal and political relationships has, during the last eight hundred years, tended to diminish, whereas its erotic significance has been increasingly emphasised. In modern times, the kiss has lost much of its ritual importance and become instead a bearer of emotional and sexual meaning. This is what Craig Koslofsky, in the first chapter of this book, calls 'the shift of the kiss from the social to the erotic, and from the communal to the private'.

Koslofsky reminds us that, since the days of the early Church, Christians had exchanged a holy kiss of peace. It was a symbol of their unity in Christ and may originally have been envisaged as a means of transmitting the Holy Spirit. Eventually it became part of the ceremony of the Eucharist.[9] But in due course the male and female members of the congregation were segregated so as to avoid kissing between the sexes and, from the thirteenth century onwards, in England and elsewhere, the members of the congregation began to kiss the *osculatorium* or pax-board rather than each other. In the sixteenth century Protestants omitted the kiss altogether. In the feudal ceremony of homage, the kiss on the lips between lord and vassal was originally a central feature, but by the sixteenth century, it had either been omitted from the ritual or replaced by a kiss on the cheek.[10]

Other forms of ceremonial kissing also disappeared, though the exact chronology and the geographical location of these changes have yet to be established.[11] The kiss of peace had, in the Middle Ages, been frequently employed as a symbol of reconciliation between former enemies; but, when, in mid-seventeenth-century England, two men who had quarrelled were urged to 'kiss and be friends', the injunction was as likely to have been metaphorical as literal.[12] For, at some point in the late medieval or early modern period, the handshake, the oath and the written document had superseded the kiss as the accepted symbols of reconciliation.[13] In France, the kiss on the mouth (*ore ad os*) ceased in the thirteenth century to be used as a way of confirming contracts.[14] In medieval English gilds it had been common for newly admitted members, male and female, to kiss all the other members of the fraternity.[15] This practice too seems to have disappeared in the early modern period, though, once again, the chronology has yet to be established.

In late medieval and Tudor England it had been customary for hostesses to kiss their male guests on the lips, even if they were total strangers, a practice which caused much pleasurable astonishment among foreign visitors. George Puttenham declared in 1589 that it was only in England that women gave their mouths to be kissed; in other countries, they offered their cheek or their hand, or waited for the ritual phrase, 'I kiss your hands.'[16] In fact, the Dutch also gave and received social kisses on the mouth.[17] This distinctive practice, 'the English salutation',[18] may have gone out of fashion at the Elizabethan court.[19] It seems to have been on the wane in seventeenth-century England and to have disappeared altogether during the following century. Several articles published in *The Spectator* in 1711–12 suggest that those years may have been the moment when the bow was replacing the kiss as the polite way of saluting ladies in fashionable company.[20] In France the kiss on the mouth had similarly given way to the kiss on the cheek or the kissing or shaking of hands.[21] Yet as late as the 1780s a German visitor commented on the survival of the custom of publicly embracing married women: 'Practice', he claimed, 'has thus rendered a fashion entirely indifferent, which, in Italy, would be regarded as a presumption which the offender could only expiate with his blood.'[22]

In England, at least, social kissing between men may never have been the general rule. It is true that, in the mid-sixteenth century, a foreign visitor to England found that all the gentlemen he met, 'taking me first by the hand, lovingly embraced and bade me right heartily welcome.'[23] There was certainly ceremonial kissing at the meeting of great personages; and at the courts of James I and Charles II it was still an important sign of favour when the monarch or some other high-ranking figure publicly kissed and embraced a subordinate.[24]

Yet kissing between males on other occasions was clearly unusual, other than within the family. Literary scholars have pointed out that, in his *Troilus and Criseyde* (late 1380s), Geoffrey Chaucer notably minimised the degree of physical contact between men which he found in the Italian source for his story.[25] When Thomas Coryat, an experienced courtier, visited Venice in

1608, he thought it 'an extraordinary custom' that, when two male acquaintances met and talked together, they would 'give a mututal kiss when they
depart from each other, by kissing one another's cheek: a custom, that I
never saw before, nor heard of, nor read of in any history.'[26] In 1633 Richard
Brathwaite's *The English Gentleman* illustrated the theme of 'acquaintance'
with an illustration of two male twins hugging each other, but in the 1641
edition it was replaced by the image of a disembodied handshake.[27] A French-
man who visited England in 1697 reported that when Englishmen met, they
saluted each other only by giving their hands and shaking them heartily.[28] In
William Congreve's *The Way of the World* (1700), it is only in the country
that 'great lubberly brothers slabber and kiss one another when they meet';
in the metropolis, ''tis not the fashion.'[29]

In the eighteenth century, English travellers found the kisses which French-
men exchanged with each other ridiculous or even abhorrent.[30] For Englishmen, the normal form of greeting was now a bow or a handshake. 'This
ceremony repeated more or less often', reported a German visitor, 'expresses
the different degrees of goodwill, friendship and esteem. People sometimes
act this pantomime in such a forcible manner, that they make each other's
hands and arms ache.'[31] In Walter Scott's novel *Waverley* (1814), the Baron of
Bradwardine, 'having first shaken Edward heartily by the hand in the English
fashion . . . embraced him *à-la-mode Françoise*, and kissed him on both sides
of the face'.[32] In Dickens's *Edwin Drood* (1870), two characters 'shook hands
with the greatest heartiness, and then went the wonderful length – for Englishmen – of laying their hands each on the other's shoulders, and looking
joyfully each into the other's face'.[33]

Meanwhile, the erotic meaning of the kiss became increasingly central. In
1649, an English observer could write that the kiss was used 'in salutation,
valediction, reconciliation . . . congratulation, approbation, adulation, subjection, confederation, but more especially and naturally in token of love.'[34]
Because its sexual connotations were now more blatant, it became increasingly difficult to employ the kiss for ritual or social purposes. The public kiss
declined or withered away altogether, leaving the kiss as an essentially personal matter, a sign of love, affection or desire, which it was more seemly to
exchange in private. As the English gentlewoman Dorothy Osborne remarked
in 1653 of a young man given to kissing his wife in public, it was 'a foolish
trick that young married men, it seems, are apt to . . . 'tis as ill a sight as one
would wish to see, and appears very rude, methinks, to the company.'[35]

According to this explanatory model, therefore, the central motor of change
was the growing eroticisation of the body, in particular, of the mouth. The
latter became more welcoming with the advent of more effective dentistry,
which did something to diminish halitosis and produce gleaming white
teeth.[36] The kiss, it is suggested, had originally been a gesture devoid of sexual

significance. But, as time went on, its sexual connotations became more apparent and its meaning more ambiguous. Eventually the ambiguity proved too much; and, for social and ritual purposes, the meeting of lips had to be replaced by other words and actions, less susceptible to misinterpretation. The non-erotic kiss might survive for a time in highly stylised contexts, but only at the risk of moral criticism or leering innuendo. The English social kiss between men and women had been on the lips and therefore disappeared, whereas the French kiss on the cheeks was less blatantly erotic and accordingly proved more enduring.

Any form of kissing between men similarly became objectionable once the idea of homosexuality had been clearly formulated. Even in Jacobean England public displays of masculine friendship could be misinterpreted.[37] In 1626 the writer William Vaughan deplored the 'unnatural kiss of man with man, a minion-kiss, such as Jupiter used to Ganymede his cup-bearer, and, which I am sorry to hear of, such as some of our Italians do practise'.[38] Under the later Stuarts, French influence on courtly manners created a temporary fashion for foppish young men to kiss each other on the cheek. In Etherege's *The Man of Mode* (1676), when the fashionable gentlemen Dorimant and Medley embrace, they are observed by Nan, the orange-woman, who exclaims, 'Lord, what a filthy trick these men have got of kissing one another!'[39] As a satirist wrote in 1691:

> The world is chang'd I know not how
> For men kiss men, not women now;
>
> . . .
>
> A most unmanly nasty trick
> One man to lick the other's cheek;
> And only what renews the shame
> Of J. the First, and Buckingham.[40]

In the eighteenth century men seen kissing were likely to be accused of sodomy.[41] The shameful anal kiss or *osculum infame*, discussed by Jonathan Durrant in Chapter 2, maintained its metaphorical value, both in everyday speech and in caricature, as a symbol of humiliatingly obsequious abasement.[42]

Affectionate kissing and touching between women friends and acquaintances lasted much longer, because the notion of lesbian love was slower to take root than was that of male homosexual desire. Even so, physical tokens of affection between women were thought more seemly if not exchanged in company or in the presence of men.[43] For the Victorians, as Carole Wlliams shows in Chapter 7, the need to avoid any ambiguity effectively confined public kissing to family and close friends. It remained acceptable – just – to kiss other people's babies, but the late twentieth- and early twenty-first-century obsession with paedophilia is doubtless putting a stop to that.

This interpretation, according to which the sexual meaning of a kiss gradually drove out all other meanings, has much to be said for it. But it is open to two obvious objections. First, it glosses over the fact that the kiss has always had an erotic connotation. The sexual charge involved in the meeting of two pairs of lips is not the invention of the modern world. It is expressed in the Bible and in classical literature, in troubadour poetry and medieval romance; and it can be found at every stage during the last two thousand years. Sometimes it was said that the kiss blended the souls of the two lovers; sometimes that it kindled their sexual appetites. In either case, the kiss was recognised as the route to intimate personal union.[44] For the Jacobean playwright John Ford, the erotic kiss was 'the first taste of love, the first certainty of hope, the first hope of obtaining, the first obtaining of favour, the first favour of grant, the first grant of assurance, the first and principallest assurance of affection, the first shadow of the substance of after-contented happinesse, happy pleasure, pleasing heauen.'[45] It is possible to argue that the lover's kiss was more prominent in literature and art during the Renaissance than it had been during the Middle Ages or in biblical times.[46] But, at most, the difference is only one of degree.

Nevertheless, some commentators claim, rather perversely, that, in medieval culture, kissing had not yet acquired late twentieth-century erotic connotations.[47] They argue accordingly that the social embrace of two men, whether in dramatic representation or in daily life, could be easily tolerated, because it had no sexual implications: 'it is today's audience . . . that insists on seeing the embrace as a form of "sexualised" communication.'[48] One historian, writing of the early modern period, even claims that 'our notion of kissing as a private, purely pleasurable activity was unthinkable at a time when sexuality was not yet conceived of as a thing in and of itself. In reality, love kisses were probably not particularly pleasurable. They were more like love bites, intended to be felt, to leave a mark, and even to draw blood.'[49]

Notwithstanding the remarkably intimate knowledge of the past implied by such assertions, a safer conclusion would be that in all ages the kiss has been a potentially ambiguous gesture. In ancient times as now, the lips were an erogenous zone, whatever cultural conventions may have implied. There were always problems about using so intimate an act for the purposes of public ritual. That was why the early Fathers, like Tertullian or Clement of Alexandria, were worried about the kiss of peace; and why men and women were expected to sit on separate sides of the church, so that they would not be required to the kiss each other during the mass. The second-century Christian apologist Athenagoras found it necessary to warn against people giving each other a second kiss of peace because they had found the first one enjoyable.[50] It was because the gesture had erotic connotations that some medieval ladies were said to have refused to kiss their feudal lord on the mouth in the homage ceremony;[51] and alternative arrangements had to be made when a monk and a lady were parties to an agreement which would normally have been concluded with a kiss.[52] There was always scepticism and distrust of the Neo-Platonic notion that kisses could unite souls without awaking a desire for the union of bodies; as Helen Berry shows in Chapter 3, most people in the late seventeenth century found it hard to believe that close friendship between men and women could lack a sexual dimension. Similarly, in Chapter 6, Elaine Chalus shows that there was real ambiguity about the nature of the kisses bestowed by female canvassers upon voters in eighteenth-century elections.

Some of the ambiguity was linguistic. The Romans had distinguished the friendly *oscula* from the loving *basia* and the passionate *suavia*; and, in modern French, *embrasser* and *faire la bise* have replaced *baiser*, which has become indecent. But the English language makes no such distinctions. The early Christian notion had been that a 'chaste' kiss was one given with the lips closed;[53] and, in the same spirit, early modern casuists attempted to differentiate 'civil' and 'honest' kisses from 'light' and 'lascivious' ones.[54] One early seventeenth-century writer observed of the 'complemental kiss, which the English allow by way of complement and friendly ceremony to salute their friends' wives withal, or any of the feminine kind, oftentimes giving it with a smack to relish the better' that this was 'a harmless kiss, justifiable both at coming and parting'.[55] Many contemporaries could have told him otherwise.

Medieval literature abounds in equivocal kisses, with lovers and lechers exploiting the social and religious conventions of the day in order to advance their own particular sexual agendas; as Burrow remarks, the public kiss between men and women always carried 'at least the possibility of erotic implication'.[56] The fine line separating social from sexual kissing, well described for early modern Britain by David Turner in Chapter 4, had always been there; it caused much social anxiety and it provided rich possibilities for drama, both comic and tragic.[57] An English traveller to Scotland in the 1770s, where French-style social kissing was practised, remarked that 'it very seldom happens that the salute is a voluntary one, and it frequently is the cause of disgust and embarrassment to the fair sex'.[58] A late eighteenth-century conduct manual explained that the practice of saluting (i.e. kissing) ladies on first acquaintance had been dropped because 'these liberties' had 'occasioned, at times, a great deal of unhappiness'.[59] As Sir Raymond Firth pointed out years ago, the peculiarity of Western societies was that they were prepared to live dangerously, by employing for ritual and social purposes a gesture which was intrinsically erotic; in requiring people to keep the different kinds of kiss entirely separate, they were skating on very thin ice.[60]

This inherent potential for misunderstanding is what distinguishes the history of the kiss from that of most other gestures. It might have been tempting to argue that historical changes in the use of the kiss have no intrinsic significance; and that it is a matter of indifference whether a hostess greets her guests by kissing them on the mouth, as in Tudor England; by shaking hands, as in mid-twentieth-century Britain; by clasping together her upraised palms, as in India; or by rubbing noses, as in Polynesia. They are all ways of making strangers welcome; and, so long as everyone concerned understands the conventions, it might seem of no greater consequence which one is employed, than whether we indicate assent to a proposition by nodding our heads or shaking them. But it would be wrong to come to such a conclusion. For what distinguishes the kiss from so many other multi-purpose gestures is that its sexual nature has always lent a potential ambiguity to its meaning.

The second objection to the notion that the ritual kiss was subverted by the erotic kiss is that its view of historical change is far too unilinear. It implies that the trend was all in the same direction. In fact, there were periods when the movement was the other way. The early Middle Ages had seen the rise of the kiss, as it came to occupy an unprecedently central position in a wide range of secular and ecclesiastical rituals. The Romans, by contrast, did not employ even the social kiss until the period of the Empire, and then only among the aristocracy.

In the early modern period, the social kiss between men seems to have fluctuated according to fashion. The habit among elegant young males at the later Stuart courts of kissing each other has already been mentioned. 'Sir, you kiss pleasingly', says one of them in an early eighteenth-century play, 'I love to kiss a man, in Paris we kiss nothing else.'[61] In the eighteenth century it continued to be common for male friends and relatives to exchange embraces. In a letter to John Wesley in 1740, one of his friends asks after his brother Charles and adds, 'Kiss him, and take a kiss yourself'; while in 1780, the poet William Cowper writes to his friend William Unwin, 'I return you kiss for kiss.'[62] In a remarkable account of relationships between soldiers in the trenches of the First World War (Chapter 8), Santanu Das shows how the imminent threat of death could lead to a suspension of normal codes of behaviour and restore the male kiss as a non-sexual symbol of intimacy.

In the late twentieth century, the social kiss between men made yet another return, at least in sophisticated circles. The diarist James Lees-Milne records in 1979 that, at a funeral, 'Tony Snowdon came up and kissed me on both cheeks'; and in 1981, after a male friend had responded to a proffered embrace by unexpectedly attempting to kiss him on the lips, he writes: 'Perhaps all the young kiss on the mouth these days without implying emotion. When I was their age it meant only one thing, that both were in love or intended to go to bed together there and then. Alas for those halcyon days.'[63] At a less exalted social level, it has become commonplace for men on the football field to exchange kisses at moments of triumph.

These developments are part of an altogether larger relaxation of bodily inhibitions which has occurred in the West since the 1960s. The social kiss and hug have returned, much to the embarrassment of middle-aged Britons, who have grown up accustomed to a far greater degree of bodily distance, even between close friends. As a recent writer remarks, 'Kissing, on greeting, all members of the opposite sex' has become 'a custom now so widespread, so mandatory, that not to do so can be construed as a deliberate snub'. 'When,' he asks, 'did this social-kissing business start?'[64]

A full historical explanation of these fluctuations in fashion over the centuries will have many different considerations to take into account. It is not just a matter of changing attitudes to sexuality. The declining importance of the kiss in public ritual may owe less to prudery than to literacy; bureaucracy and record-keeping obviated the need for such bodily gestures.[65] Important for the history of the social kiss is the element of cultural diffusion, for dominant societies have always exported their mores to their neighbours and dependants. In the seventeenth-century Netherlands, for example, it may have been the influence of French fashion which drove out the male–female social kiss on the mouth.[66] In modern times, a distinctively British bodily reserve and inhibition have been broken down by the loss of Empire and the greater influence of European codes of behaviour. For the social kiss is a gesture which implies equality betwen the two parties involved. That is why, in many periods of history, it has been only the upper classes who have confidently used the gesture. The rigidities of social hierarchy have obstructed its wider employment. Today, the decline of deference and the spread of more egalitarian attitudes have assisted its dissemination. But, even today, who would kiss the Queen?

The subject also has a medical dimension. For the attitude to kissing can change when breath and saliva are regarded as potential instruments of infection. The Roman Emperor Tiberius (14–37 AD) issued a decree banning kissing, because it was believed to be responsible for the spread of an unpleasant fungoid disease called *mentagra*, which disfigured the faces and bodies of Roman nobles and could be cured only by bone-deep cauterisation.[67] In 1439, the English House of Commons petitioned King Henry VI, asking that kissing might be temporarily omitted from the homage ceremony for knight-service, so as to avoid endangering the King's life at a time of pestilence ('an infirmity most infectious').[68] In the seventeenth century, the Dutch practice of social kissing was blamed for the spread of scurvy,[69] while, in England, a writer on venereal disease suggested that the disease could be contracted by kissing the lips of an infected person, especially when the person concerned had scabby lips or a sore mouth. He concluded that the 'custom of saluting all strangers' was therefore 'hazardous'.[70] In the eighteenth century, as Luke Davidson notes in Chapter 5, some people believed that, although 'chaste' kisses were safe, venereal diseases could be transmitted by 'lascivious' ones.

Not that the avoidance of bodily contact was always so rational. Norbert Elias famously drew attention to historical changes in the threshold of repugnance, when bodily habits which had been happily tolerated in one age became wholly unacceptable in another. Up to a point, kissing seems to have been one of them, though the chronology of disgust it evoked does not follow Elias's one-directional model. No-one has ever exceeded the Roman epigrammatist Martial (late first century AD) in evoking the nauseous experience of having to kiss lips and faces covered with dirt, snot, ulcers and scabs, and exuding a foetid smell, the aftermath of oral sex.[71] It was Martial whom Michel de Montaigne cited when, in the later sixteenth century, he became one of the first post-classical figures to suggest that kissing could be intrinsically disgusting if the person kissed was dirty and ugly.[72] Thereafter there were many such complaints. When Sir John Percival stayed at a Scottish tavern in 1701, 'being told that it was the custom to kiss our hosts to make them give us the best, we desired her to wipe her mouth, and then fell to our duty'. On leaving, 'we were forc'd to thank our Lady for our good reception with another kiss, which had certainly brought up my dinner, had not the bread been as heavy as lead in my stomach'.[73] In Chapter 5, Luke Davidson shows that the social and physical squeamishness of eighteenth-century doctors prevented them from adopting mouth-to-mouth resuscitation as a respectable medical practice, even though they were aware of its life-saving potentialities. In the same century, authorities on politeness condemned the practice of those who 'put their faces so close to yours as to offend you with their breath' as a 'horrid and disgustful habit'.[74] When aristocratic Romans of the Imperial age took up the practice of kissing friends and clients, they perfumed their breath with myrrh.[75] How far, one wonders, have modern dentistry and breath-sweeteners been a precondition of the return of the social kiss in modern times?

It is testimony to the stimulating achievement of the contributors to this book that it leads the reader to ask such large and, at present anyway, unanswerable questions. We should be grateful to them for drawing attention to the rich potentialities of a neglected subject and for reminding us that there is no aspect of human behaviour which does not have a historical dimension.

### NOTES

1 Martinus Kempius (Martin von Kempe), *Opus polyhistoricum, dissertationibus XXV de osculis . . . absolutum* (Frankfurt, 1680).

2 The French theologian Robert de Sorbon (1201–74) warned confessors against descending to questions about special kinds of 'inordinate' kissing ('Hic caveat, sibi, confessor, ne descendat ad speciales modos osculandi inordinate'): 'De confessione',

in *Maxima bibliotheca patrum et antiquorum scriptorum*, ed. Marguerin de la Bigne, xxv (Leyden, 1677), p. 355.

3 Lady Holland, *A Memoir of the Reverend Sydney Smith*, 2nd edn (London, 1855), i, pp. 353–4. I once had occasion to shake hands with Mr Yasser Arafat, President of the Palestinian National Authority. To my surprise, he did not let my hand go, but amiably walked with me, my right hand in his right hand, the full length of the quadrangle of my college. Newspaper photographs of Mr Arafat's encounters with other world leaders suggest that this may be his usual practice, an interesting cultural peculiarity, and one, no doubt, productive of occasional misunderstanding.

4 A notable exception is the work of Andrea de Jorio on gesture in early nineteenth-century Naples: *La mimica degli antichi investigata nel gestire napoletano* (Naples, 1832), trans. Adam Kendon (Bloomington and Indianapolis, 2000). For his deliciously subtle analysis of the complexities involved in simulated kisses, see pp. 106–11.

5 Notably J. A. Burrow, *Gesture and Looks in Medieval Narrative* (Cambridge, 2002).

6 Jacques Le Goff, *Time, Work, and Culture in the Middle Ages*, trans. Arthur Goldhammer (Chicago and London, 1980), p. 252.

7 Ann Pasternak Slater, *Shakespeare the Director* (Brighton and Totawa, NJ, 1982), pp. 79, 80.

8 Havelock Ellis declared that the kiss was 'not usually found among rude and uncultured peoples': *Studies in the Psychology of Sex*, iv: *Sexual Selection in Man* (1905; Philadelphia, 1923), p. 217 (and p. 23).

9 L. Edward Phillips, *The Ritual Kiss in Early Christian Worship* (Cambridge, 1996).

10 J. Russell Major, '"Bastard Feudalism" and the Kiss: Changing Social Mores in Late Medieval and Early Modern France', *Journal of Interdisciplinary History*, 17 (1987); 509–35; Yannick Carré, *Le Baiser sur la Bouche au Moyen Age: Rites, symboles, mentalités, à travers les textes et les images, XIe–XVe siècles* (Paris, 1992), pp. 198–202, 214–15.

11 For a tabular summary of the disappearance of the kiss on the mouth from public rituals in France between the fourteenth and seventeenth centuries, see Carré, *Baiser sur la bouche*, pp. 332–3.

12 Margaret M. Verney, *Memoirs of the Verney Family* (1892; London, 1971), iii, p. 301.

13 Herman Roodenburg, 'The "hand of friendship": Shaking Hands and Other Gestures in the Dutch Republic', in Jan Bremmer and Herman Roodenburg (eds), *A Cultural History of Gesture* (London, 1991); Carré, *Baiser sur la bouche*, pp. 179–86.

14 Émile Chénon, 'Le Role juridique de l'*osculum* dans l'ancien droit français', *Mémoires de la Société Nationale des Antiquaires de France*, 8th series, 6 (1919–23), 136.

15 Toulmin Smith (ed.), *English Gilds*, Early English Text Society (S.I., 1892), pp. 6, 9.

16 George Puttenham, *The Arte of English Poesie*, ed. Gladys Doidge Willcock and Alice Walker (Cambridge, 1936), pp. 285–6.

17 John Ray, *Observations . . . Made in a Journey through Part of the Low-Countries, Germany, Italy and France* (London, 1673), p. 55; William Brenchley Rye, *England as Seen by Foreigners in the Days of Elizabeth and James the First* (London, 1865), p. 90; Roodenburg, 'The "hand of friendship"', p. 187.

18 The term is used by Bulstrode Whitelocke, *A Journal of the Swedish Embassy in the Years 1653 and 1654*, ed. Charles Morton, rev. Henry Reeve (London, 1855), ii, p. 187. For the practice, see e.g. Rye, *England as Seen by Foreigners*, pp. 90, 225, 260–2; Polydore Vergil, *Beginnings and Discoveries: Polydore Vergil's De inventoribus rerum*, trans. and ed. Beno Weiss and Louis C. Pérez (Nieuwkoop, 1997), p. 311; W. D. Robson-Scott, *German Travellers in England 1400–1800* (Oxford, 1953), p. 52.

19 Cf. William Shakespeare, *As You Like It* (c.1600), Act III, Scene ii ('You told me you salute not at the court, but you kiss your hands').

20 *The Spectator*, 240 (5 December 1711) and 272 (11 January 1712); ed. Donald F. Bond, 5 vols (Oxford, 1965), ii, pp. 433–4, 561. In 1710 Jonathan Swift wrote affectionately of the daughters of the Duke of Ormonde that 'the insolent drabs came up to my very mouth to salute me': *The Journal to Stella*, ed. Harold Williams (Oxford, 1948), i, pp. 23–4. See also Robson-Scott, *German Travellers in England*, p. 130; Paul Langford, *Englishness Identified: Manners and Character, 1650–1850* (Oxford, 2000), pp. 163–4.

21 Carré, *Baiser sur la bouche*, p. 113.

22 [J. W.] D'Archenholz, *A Picture of England* (London, 1789), ii, p. 104.

23 Levine Lemnie, *The Touchstone of Complexions*, trans. Thomas Newton (London, 1581), fol. 47ᵛ.

24 Henry Cecil Wyld, *A History of Modern Colloquial English*, 3rd impression (London, 1925), pp. 377–8; Joan Wildeblood and Peter Brinson, *The Polite World: A Guide to English Manners and Deportment from the Thirteenth to the Nineteenth Century* (London, 1965), pp. 199–200; Alan Bray, 'Homosexuality and the Signs of Male Friendship in Elizabethan England', *History Workshop Journal*, 29 (1990), 1–19, at 4–5.

25 Sanford B. Meech, *Design in Chaucer's Troilus* (Syracuse, NY, 1959), p. 186; Burrow, *Gesture and Looks in Medieval Narrative*, p. 117.

26 Thomas Coryat, *Coryat's Crudities* (Glasgow, 1905), i, pp. 398–9.

27 As noted by Jeff Masten, 'My Two Dads: Collaboration and the Reproduction of Beaumont and Fletcher', in Jonathan Goldberg (ed.), *Queering the Renaissance* (Durham, NC, and London, 1994), pp. 281, 305 n. 7.

28 Cited in Rye, *England as Seen by Foreigners*, p. 262.

29 William Congreve, *The Way of the World* (1700), Act III, Scene i.

30 Jeremy Black, *The British Abroad: The Grand Tour in the Eighteenth Century* (1992; Stroud, 1997), p. 233.

31 D'Archenholz, *Picture of England*, ii, p. 103.

32 Walter Scott, *Waverley; or, 'Tis Sixty Years Since*, ed. Claire Lamont (Oxford, 1981), p. 42.

33 Charles Dickens, *The Mystery of Edwin Drood*, ch. 21; ed. Margaret Cardwell (Oxford, 1972), p. 184.

34 J[ohn] B[ulwer], *Pathomyotomia, or A Dissection of the Significative Muscles of the Affections of the Minde* (London, 1649), p. 220.

35 Dorothy Osborne, *The Letters of Dorothy Osborne to William Temple*, ed. G. C. Moore Smith (Oxford, 1928), p. 95.

36 For the early stages of this development, see Colin Jones, 'Pulling Teeth in Eighteenth-Century Paris', *Past & Present*, 166 (2000), 101–45.

37 Bray, 'Homosexuality and the Signs of Male Friendship', 15.

38 William Vaughan, *The Golden Fleece* (London, 1626), i, p. 43.

39 George Etherege, *The Man of Mode*, Act I, Scene i, in *The Dramatic Works of Sir George Etherege*, ii, ed. H. F. B. Brett-Smith (Oxford, 1927), p. 191.

40 *Mundus Foppensis: Or, The Fop Display'd* (London, 1691); Augustan Reprint Society (Los Angeles, 1988), pp. 12–13.

41 Alan Bray and Michel Ray, 'The Body of the Friend: Continuity and Change in Masculine Friendship in the Seventeenth Century', in Tim Hitchcock and Michèle Cohen (eds), *English Masculinities, 1660–1800* (London, 1999), p. 80.

42 Examples in Herbert M. Atherton, *Political Prints in the Age of Hogarth: A Study of the Ideographic Representation of Politics* (Oxford, 1974), fig. 28; and David Alexander, *Richard Newton and English Caricature in the 1790s* (Manchester, 1998), fig. 58. For 'kiss my arse', see *The Oxford English Dictionary*, 2nd edn, (ed.) J. A. Simpson and E. S. C. Weiner (Oxford, 1989), viii, p. 463 ('kiss, *v.*', 6. l).

43  C. Dallett Hemphill, *Bowing to Necessities: A History of Manners in America, 1620–1860* (New York and Oxford, 1999), p. 185; John R. Gillis, 'From Ritual to Romance: Toward an Alternative History of Love', in Carol Z. Stearns and Peter N. Stearns (eds), *Emotion and Social Change: Toward a New Psychohistory* (New York and London, 1988), p. 113.

44  There is much on this theme in Nicolas James Perella, *The Kiss Sacred and Profane: An Interpretative History of Kiss Symbolism and Related Religio-Erotic Themes* (Berkeley, 1969). See also Carré, *Baiser sur la bouche*, esp. pp. 58–91.

45  John Ford, *Honour Triumphant*, Shakespeare Society (London, 1843), pp. 14–15.

46  See, for example, Clifford Davidson, 'Gesture in Medieval British Drama', in *idem* (ed.), *Gesture in Medieval Drama and Art* ([Kalamazoo, MI], 2001), p. 76; Betty J. Bäuml and Franz H. Bäuml, *Dictionary of Worldwide Gestures*, 2nd edn (Lanham, MD, and London, 1997), p. 406.

47  The idea may have originated with Havelock Ellis, who, in accordance with his Darwinian notion that erotic kissing was a mark of more advanced civilisations, asserted that the kiss was not widely known in medieval Europe as an expression of sexual love: *Studies in the Psychology of Sex*, iv, pp. 217–18.

48  Pamela Sheingorn, 'The Bodily Embrace or Embracing the Body: Gesture and Gender in Late Medieval Culture', in Alan E. Knight (ed.), *The Stage as Mirror: Civic Theatre in Late Medieval Europe* (Cambridge, 1997), p. 88.

49  Gillis, 'From Ritual to Romance', p. 91.

50  John Bossy, 'The Mass as a Social Institution 1200–1700', *Past & Present*, 100 (1983), 29–61, at 55; Fernand Cabrol *et al.* (eds), *Dictionnaire d'archéologie chrétienne et de liturgie* (Paris, 1907–53), ii, pp. 118–19.

51  Alfred Franklin, *La Civilité, l'étiquette, la mode, le bon ton du XIIIe au XIXe siècle* (Paris, 1908), p. 132. Contrast the female vassal who announced that she was greatly looking forward to kissing her feudal lord, because he was the best-looking bishop in the land: Carré, *Baiser sur la bouche*, p. 204.

52  Chénon, 'Le Role juridique de l'*osculum*', 135.

53  Carré, *Baiser sur la bouche*, pp. 223, 355–6.

54  William Ames, *Conscience with the Power and Cases Thereof*, Eng trans. (n.p., 1639), iii, p. 214; David M. Turner, Ch. 4 above; Christopher Nyrop, *The Kiss and its History*, trans. William Frederick Harvey (London, 1901), pp. 156–7.

55  Vaughan, *Golden Fleece*, i, pp. 42–3.

56  Burrow, *Gesture and Looks in Medieval Narrative*, pp. 55, 17, 34, 125, 150–1, 184. Cf. J. Huizinga, *The Waning of the Middle Ages*, Eng. trans. (1924; Harmondsworth, 1955), p. 125; Perella, *Kiss Sacred and Profane*, p. 103; Bonaventure des Périers, *Contes et nouvelles et joyeux devis* (c. 1538; Cologne, 1711), ii, pp. 99–104 ('D'un gentilhomme, qui mit sa langue en la bouche d'une damoiselle, en la baisant').

57  David M. Turner, *Fashioning Adultery: Gender, Sex and Civility in England, 1660–1740* (Cambridge, 2002), pp. 79, 80, 100–1, 167 and *passim*. Cf. Shakespeare's *Othello* (c.1602–4), where Cassio insolently kisses Iago's wife, Emilia, on the lips, claiming ''tis my breeding / That gives me this bold show of courtesy': Act II, Scene i.

58  [Edward Topham], *Letters from Edinburgh Written in the Years 1774 to 1775* (London, 1776), p. 37.

59  John Trusler, *Principles of Politeness and of Knowing the World*, 12th edn (London, 1780), p. 11.

60  Raymond Firth, 'Verbal and Bodily Rituals of Greeting and Parting', in J. S. La Fontaine (ed.), *The Interpretation of Ritual: Essays in Honour of A. I. Richards* (London, 1972), pp. 26–7.

61 C[olley] C[ibber], *Love Makes a Man or, The Fop's Fortune* (London, 1701), p. 4 (Act I); also John Ashton, *Social Life in the Reign of Queen Anne*, new edn (London, 1897), p. 67. Cf. Philip Carter, *Men and the Emergence of Polite Society, Britain 1660–1800* (2000; Harlow, Essex, 2001), p. 145.

62 John Wesley, *The Works of John Wesley*, xxvi: *Letters*, ii, ed. Frank Baker (Oxford, 1982), p. 4; William Cowper, *The Letters and Prose Writings of William Cowper*, ed. James King and Charles Ryskamp (Oxford, 1979–86), i, p. 387.

63 James Lees-Milne, *Deep Romantic Chasm: Diaries 1979–1981* (London, 2000; paperback edn, 2003), pp. 35, 129.

64 P. J. Kavanagh, 'Bywords', *Times Literary Supplement* (1 May 1998), 16.

65 Jean-Claude Schmitt, *La Raison des gestes dans l'occident médiéval* (Paris, 1990), pp. 15, 357–8.

66 Cf. Roodenburg, 'The "hand of friendship"', p. 157.

67 Suetonius, *De vita Caesarum*, iii. xxiv; Pliny, *Naturalis historia*, xxvi.i–iii; both cited by N. M. Kay, *Martial Book XI: A Commentary* (London, 1985), pp. 265–6.

68 *Rotuli parliamentorum*, ed. John Strachey (London, 1767–77), v, p. 31.

69 Kempius, *Opus polyhistoricum . . . de osculis*, pp. 735–6.

70 E. Maynwaringe, *The History and Mystery of the Venereal Lues* (London, 1673), p. 82.

71 Martial, *Epigrams*, ed. and trans. D. R. Shackleton Bailey, Loeb Classical Library (Cambridge, MA, and London, 1993), esp. vii. 95; xi. 98; xii. 59; J. P. Sullivan, *Martial: The Unexpected Classic: a Literary and Historical Study* (Cambridge, 1991), pp. 84, 189, 203.

72 Michel de Montaigne, *Essais*, iii.5; trans. M. A. Screech (London, 1993), p. 997.

73 *The English Travels of Sir John Percival and William Byrd II: The Percival Diary of 1701*, ed. Mark R. Wenger (Columbia, MO, 1989), pp. 186, 187.

74 Trusler, *Principles of Politeness*, p. 11.

75 Martial, *Epigrams*, ii. 12.

# Index

<>